DEVIL'S
MILE

ALSO BY ALICE SPARBERG ALEXIOU

Jane Jacobs: Urban Visionary

*The Flatiron: The New York Landmark
and the Extraordinary City that Arose with It*

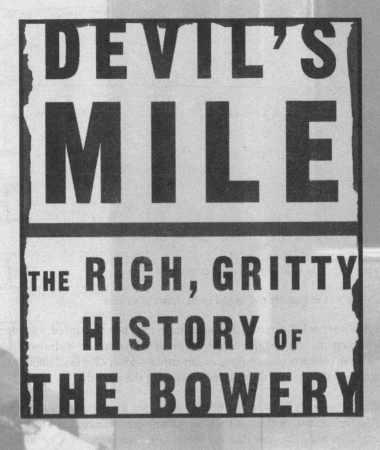

DEVIL'S MILE

THE RICH, GRITTY HISTORY OF THE BOWERY

Alice Sparberg Alexiou

Empire State Editions
An imprint of Fordham University Press   New York   2024

Fordham University Press has no responsibility for the persistence or accuracy of URLs for external or third-party Internet websites referred to in this publication and does not guarantee that any content on such websites is, or will remain, accurate or appropriate.

Fordham University Press also publishes its books in a variety of electronic formats. Some content that appears in print may not be available in electronic books.

Visit us online at www.fordhampress.com/empire-state-editions.

Library of Congress Cataloging-in-Publication Data available online at https://catalog.loc.gov.

Printed in the United States of America

26 25 24   5 4 3 2 1

First edition Fordham University Press edition, 2024

To my sons,
Alex and Joseph Alexiou

CONTENTS

Contents

FOREWORD

BY PETER QUINN

New York has more than its fair share of legendary streets and thoroughfares—Fifth Avenue, Broadway, 42nd Street, et al. None has a richer, more glorious, more notorious history than the subject of Alice Sparberg Alexiou's engrossing book *Devil's Mile: The Rich, Gritty History of the Bowery*.

Alexiou is a first-class storyteller as well as a punctilious historian. "Almost every building and lot has a good story in its history," she writes. "No matter the ups and downs, the soulful history of the place is always present and somebody will always find it." In her hands, that promise becomes a self-fulfilling prophecy.

Knowns and unknowns, the famous and the infamous, the would-be and the burnt out, all found a home here. Walt Whitman sang of the Bowery as "racy of the East River," its denizens embodying "a picturesque freedom of looks and manners, with a rude good nature and restless movement."

A century later, his spiritual descendant Allen Ginsberg celebrated those "who ate the lamb stew of the imagination and digested the crab at the muddy bottom of the rivers of Bowery."

Charles Hurstwood, ill-fated lover of Theodore Dreiser's Caroline Meeber (Sister Carrie), ended as a flophouse suicide, his last words a cri de coeur shared by generations of the down-and-out: "What's the use?"

Real-life Stephen Foster, the progenitor of American popular music, dubbed by Alexiou "the poignant bard of the Bowery," died cold and alone in the attic of a hotel, his throat slit either by accident or design.

Minstrelsy, "with its edgy and shame-inducing racial content," grew to a national rage after the Virginia Minstrels' 1843 debut at the Bowery Theater. Israel Beline (a.k.a. Irving Berlin) remembered his turn-of-the-century "musical education on the Bowery" among "real tough people."

At century's end, CBGB's, a cave-like bar on the ground floor of a flophouse, hosted punk pioneers like the Ramones and Patti Smith and became the hothouse for the re-blossoming of rock 'n' roll's rebellious soul.

Alexiou leaves no doubt that America began as much on the Bowery as at Jamestown and Plymouth Rock. Immigrants of all shades and persuasions began here. Industrious Dutch, conquering English, enslaved Africans, famished Irish, fleeing Chinese, penniless Italians, persecuted Jews.

The history that Alexiou relates in her enlightening account is overwhelming in its richness. She writes without exaggeration that "the Bowery was more than a street. It was, is, a place that transcends time."

The Bowery was the seed and stem from which the Big Apple grew. In the beginning were the Dutch who founded New Amsterdam in 1625. Governor Peter Stuyvesant established his bouwerij (farm) beside a Native American footpath that soon became a bustling lane.

Freed slaves settled in nearby swampland, which came to be called "Negros Land." Native Americans were swept away by smallpox and military force. As property values rose, the ex-slaves were displaced.

The Dutch lost control of the colony to the British. They renamed it in honor of the Duke of York, who became James II and shortly after was kicked off the throne. Before the British were tossed out by their colonial subjects, they turned Bowery Lane into "the southernmost leg of a comprehensive postal highway to link New York and Boston."

Loyalist families like the Delanceys fled and left behind nothing but a street name.

The great scheme of New York real estate, which would one day propel an odious huckster to the presidency, was hatched here. Fittingly enough, the art of the deal originated in butchery and skinning. Heinrich Ashdore came to New York from Walldorf, Germany, with Hessian mercenaries employed by George III.

After his royal boss was booted, Ashdore stayed and reinvented himself as Henry Astor, set up shop on the Bowery, and grew wealthy as a purveyor of fresh meat. His brother Johann Jakob (John Jacob) followed him to New York and made a fortune in the fur trade.

Henry and John had a fraternal relationship of the Cain-and-Abel kind. They invested heavily in real estate, competing with one another as they bought and divided Bowery lots, and squeezed larger and larger profits from tradesmen and small-business owners. When John opened a downtown theater, Henry bested him with the capacious Bowery Theater, which boasted a capacity of three thousand seats. Alexiou correctly identifies the Bowery as "the very place where American popular culture was starting to emerge."

The street itself was a theater. Young, American-born, working-class males made it their headquarters. The Bowery b'hoys, as they came to be called, featured their own haircut and outfit, as well as a trademark slang and strut. Nativist embodiments of the rude, boisterous, assertive (to some, threatening) spirit of Jacksonian democracy, they brought to life the edgy urban cool adapted by street dudes from Damon Runyon's guys and dolls to today's hip-hop artists.

The Bowery was a great American frontier, the Wild East as opposed to the Wild West. The unwashed and unfettered roamed here, those who reveled in the American Dream and those defeated by it. Here, the rules and proprieties of sober, God-fearing society ended and the country of anything goes began. Its combination of danger and diversion was an irresistible draw that, for some, didn't always end well. Cautioned one music hall ditty: "They say such things and do strange things / On the Bowery! The Bowery! / I'll never go there anymore."

The Bowery's raison d'être went beyond "the pursuit of happiness" to an open-ended hunt for the bête noir of Yankee puritanism—fun. Before Las Vegas, gambling dens were rampant. Yiddish theater prospered. Dime museums appealed to fans of the outré and offbeat. It was where gay men from across the social spectrum found a haven, and where Gotham's 1 percent went slumming among the no percent. "Sex on the Bowery," Alexiou allows, "went at bargain rates."

Reformers loathed the Bowery not only for its promiscuity but for its politics, especially the Irish variety perfected by Tammany Hall. Reverend Charles Parkhurst made an anonymous tour of the dives and brothels of the area, demanding at each stop to be shown something worse, until he emerged to lead a citywide crusade against lust, drink, and Tammany. The Reverend was convinced that if the country rid itself "of rum and the Irish, it could close three-quarters of its poorhouses and tear down half its prisons."

Presiding over Bowery politics was its undisputed king, Big Tim Sullivan. King though he was, he treated voters as equals, not subjects. Long after the Irish had ceased to be a numerical majority, Sullivan earned the loyalty of Jews and Italians. In the days before a social safety net, he provided everything from jobs and meals to children's shoes. If he profited handsomely from politics, which he most certainly did, Alexiou credits that "he gave back more than he took by looking out for his constituents."

Après Sullivan came the deluge. World War I deposited growing numbers of unemployed veterans, many physically or mentally scarred, who filled up the missions and cheap rooms. Prohibition closed the saloons, which along with alcohol offered companionship and basic amenities. "Without the saloons," Alexiou laments, "the bums were lost." Rotgut whiskey and chemical wines pushed by illegal dives left some blind or dead. New York's most historic, vibrant, freewheeling street descended into a byway of the broken and abandoned.

The Bowery bum, a synonym for a hopeless, panhandling, transient alcoholic, found a sympathetic chronicler in filmmaker Lionel Rogosin. *On the Bowery* featured two genuine Bowery denizens, Gorman Hendricks and Ray Sayler. It was shot in 1956 for $60,000 and used a skeletally scripted plot that followed their three-day interactions. An early example of cinema verité, the film captured the pathos of men whose days revolved around finding the next drink and a place to sleep. Sayler's good looks and natural style earned him a shot at an acting career, but he chose to return to points unknown.

Eventually the El that had long shackled the Bowery sky came down, but daylight only added to the desolation. It was tagged for "urban renewal" (i.e., demolition) by power broker Robert Moses, who swept aside acres of the city to erect highways and high-rises. Moses's reign ended before he got to bulldoze the Bowery, but crime and drugs and the city's economic decline left it a bleak and dangerous place.

Alexiou has it exactly right when she concludes that in New York "every story begins or ends, with real estate." The next chapter in the saga of the Bowery pits the dogged resistance of preservationists and a dwindling number of longtime residents against the mounting advance of speculators, developers, and the new urban gentry. Once more, the future of "New York's quirky and fabled street" is in play.

Alexiou's gem of a historical Baedeker is not just for everyone who cares about the Bowery but also for anyone interested in the play of change and continuity—of memory and history—that gives a city its soul. Hers is a tribute, not a lament. She records the Bowery's multiple manifestations as cultural playground, moral underground, and urban wasteland. She gives us what was and is. She never loses hope. "The Bowery! The Bowery! / They say such things and they do strange things / On the Bowery! The Bowery!"

LIST OF ILLUSTRATIONS

List of Illustrations

To see the Bowery in its glory, one must visit it at night. It is a blaze of light from one end to the other. The saloons, theatres, concert halls, and "free-and-easys" are gayly ornamented with lamps of all colors, and the lights of the street venders give to the sidewalks the appearance of a general illumination. The concert halls are filled, and sounds of music and shouts of laughter float out from them into the street. Wretched transparencies mark the entrances to the low dives, in and out of which a steady throng pours. The pavements are full of abandoned women, boldly plying their trade, regardless of the police, who are out in force along the thoroughfare. The larger German music halls have the only respectable audiences to be found in the Bowery. The shooting-galleries are a feature of the streets, and are brightly lighted and open to the sidewalk. They are ornamented with targets consisting of gaudily-painted figures, and offer innumerable inducements to passers-by to try their skill. The theatres are brilliant with transparencies and illuminated glass signs, and are well filled with pleasure-seekers. Men and women in all stages of intoxication stagger along the pavements, and here and there is a sturdy policeman with some offender in his grasp, hastening on to the station-house. Vice offers every inducement to its votaries, and the devil's work is done nightly upon a grand scale in the Bowery. The horse-cars, with their colored lights and jingling bells, and the rapidly rushing elevated trains over-head, give an air of briskness to the street. The scene is gay and animated, but must be witnessed to be properly appreciated.

—JAMES McCABE JR.,
New York by Sunlight and Gaslight, 1882

PROLOGUE

O nce upon a time, the Bowery was the street synonymous with despair.

It was where you went to drink away your sorrows. The mere mention of it invoked images of bums passed out on the sidewalk. People called it Satan's Highway, the Mile of Hell, the Devil's Work, the Street of Sorrows, the Street of Forgotten Men, the One-Way Street. Officials were always wringing their hands over the bad old Bowery. Sometimes they made half-hearted attempts to clean it up. But New York's outcasts needed a place that embraced them, and so did the city. For more than a century, the Bowery functioned as New York's dumping ground—and also its shame. So much so that the little businesses along the Bowery—stationers, dry goods sellers, jewelers, hatters—periodically asked the city to change the street's name. To have a Bowery address, they claimed, was hurting them; people did not want to venture there.

But during the 1990s, as New York was exploding into a real estate frenzy, developers discovered the Bowery. Starting around 2000, they rushed in and began tearing it down. Today, the bad old Bowery no longer exists. A Whole Foods, the übersymbol of gentrification, stands on what was once an empty lot where the bums burned old insulation over oil drums to extract metal to sell to junk dealers. Former dive bars are now hipster nightspots, and the flophouses that sheltered the down-and-out have been converted into expensive lofts. Or they have been torn down and replaced with glass-and-concrete condos and hotels that rise to heights never before seen there. The privileged young urbanites buying these apartments talk about Bowery bars, but they have never heard of the expression "Bowery bum."

The New York City government, grateful that private interests are solving the Bowery "problem" that bedeviled New York for more than a century, encourages development along this once-infamous street. At the same time, the city is destroying the Bowery's heart. The destitute who once congregated there and the many artists who existed side by side with the bums are being pushed out as the ramshackle buildings where they lived—some of them nearly 200 years old and of immense historic value—are destroyed.

By the 1930s, the Bowery was famous as the place where lost souls ended up and drank themselves to death. The Bowery bum became a permanent image in American culture. But before that, the Bowery was many things. It played a crucial part in every phase of New York's history.

The Bowery—and so, too, Broadway, New York's other legendary thoroughfare—was originally a Lenape footpath. Each corridor was part of a network of trails that the Indians* created along the shores and through the forests that then covered Manhattan. The two that became the Bowery and Broadway originated at Manhattan's southern shoreline—probably not at the same spot, but close to each other. Geographer Jack Eichenbaum, who knows every inch of Manhattan Island and the other four boroughs as well, told me they are "a classic high-road–low-road duo. Lower Broadway follows the ridge of Lower Manhattan; walking there, you'll see that the land slopes down on

---

* Throughout this book I use the term "Indians" as did the European colonists, that is, to denote the indigenous peoples of North America.

either side of the street. In contrast, what today we call the Bowery is a continuation of the road along the East River: it begins as Pearl Street, then becomes St. James Place at Madison Street and then the Bowery at Chatham Square."* At this point, Broadway and the Bowery remain briefly parallel to each other before once again angling in opposite directions and continuing north.

These two streets came to personify New York, but in opposite modes: To be "on Broadway" implied having attained the glittery apex of success. But the Bowery meant Loserville.

Something else: people often say that the Bowery is New York's oldest street, but you can make this claim equally about Broadway. When the Dutch landed in Manhattan in the 1620s, they appropriated both of the original Indian paths, widened them, and used them as their highways; which one they used first is anybody's guess. (When I asked Jack Eichenbaum his take on this, he said, "My guess would be Broadway. The Dutch were very water oriented for transportation; the lower shoreline—Pearl Street—was likely navigated rather than used as a street.") Between Broadway and the Bowery, they carved out farms; the name "Bowery" comes from *bouwerij*, the old Dutch word for "farm." During the eighteenth century, as the city began to expand beyond the original settlement at Manhattan's southern tip, wealthy merchants built country estates along the Bowery. But by the Civil War, Broadway was becoming genteel. Rich folks were moving those few blocks west to Broadway or to the still-pristine woods of northern Manhattan. They left behind the Bowery to immigrants and the working classes, and it was then that the street became defined by the characteristics we have long associated with it: noise, dirt, poverty, tawdry entertainment, homelessness, the underground arts scene, wholesale commerce, restaurant supply places. In his famous book

---

* The formal designation "Bowery" started with the English. I go into this in more detail in chapter 3.

How the Other Half Lives, the social reformer and photojournalist Jacob Riis called the Bowery "the great democratic highway of the city."

It is difficult to define the Bowery. Today, real estate brokers sell it as New York's hottest new neighborhood, but the Bowery is a two-way thoroughfare and therefore denotes motion: starting at Chatham Square and ending at Cooper Union, it runs through Chinatown, the Lower East Side, Little Italy, and Tribeca. Back in the days of New York ward politics, these neighborhoods corresponded to the Fourth, Sixth, and Tenth Wards, and the Bowery comprised a piece of all of them. But it didn't fully *belong* to any one ward. While ward bosses sometimes fought for control of the Bowery, the only one who ever succeeded was Tammany bigwig Big Tim Sullivan, whom they called King of the Bowery.

You might see the Bowery as a state of mind where all manner of human interaction was permitted to take place, right out in the open. Once upon a time, it was where people bought, sold, and pawned cheap goods during the day. At night it was where prostitutes solicited, slummers came from all over the city to the dime museums, and cutting-edge music was invented—first in the concert saloons and later at CBGB's. The Bowery was where you went for a good time, and it was dangerous. It was also New York's earliest theater district. Yiddish theater, precursor to the Broadway musical, began on the Bowery. In fact, much of American popular entertainment was invented on the Bowery: tap dancing (an amalgam of Irish and black elements), vaudeville, the songs of Stephen Foster, punk rock.

As development along the Bowery continues, it feels urgent that I tell its story now: before all its old buildings—and the memories associated with them—disappear.

CHAPTER ONE

THE DUTCH

In the early summer of 1625, three Dutch vessels—the *Paert* (Horse), the *Koe* (Cow), and the *Schaep* (Sheep)—dropped anchor off the southern tip of the island that native inhabitants called Mannahatta (the island of many hills). It was a beautiful wilderness: hilly in parts, thickly wooded, and crisscrossed with streams. The ships, all property of the Dutch West India Company, carried about forty-five passengers. Most were French-speaking Huguenots—Walloons—from what is now Belgium. There were 103 head of livestock, each housed in its own stall. Cargo included plows, other farm equipment, and many sorts of seeds. All would be used to build a settlement on the island, which was populated only by Indians—they numbered perhaps 1,500 at the most—and a few hardy souls who had arrived on an expedition the previous year. Among them were Cryn Fredericks, an engineer, and Willem Verhulst, whom the Company had appointed director of the colony. There were also about a dozen enslaved Africans who had been seized from Spanish ships and immediately put to work on Nut Island, just a gunshot away from the shore: they cut down trees, fashioned a crude sawmill, and kept hacking out more logs with which to feed it.

The settlement was to be called New Amsterdam, and it would serve as headquarters of New Netherland, which stretched from New

England to Virginia. The Dutch had claimed the vast territory—a claim the English refused to recognize—after Henry Hudson in 1609 sailed the *Half Moon* up the river that would bear his name.

Hudson and subsequent explorers described the newly discovered land as a Garden of Eden filled with all sorts of resources ready for the picking: fish and oysters; berries, grapes, and nuts; and forests dense with timber, supplies of which were by then dwindling in Europe. The Indians grew corn and squash. There was also an abundance of game for hunting as well as otters and beavers to supply fur, which Europeans especially coveted. On the Continent, fur, like trees, had been overharvested. It was the mention of fur that had most caught the attention of investors in Holland, leading to the incorporation of the Dutch West India Company. But so far there were only a handful of people—perhaps a hundred adventurous immigrants from the Netherlands—who were engaged in fur trading. They lived scattered in the wilderness along the Hudson near the Mohican tribes who sold the foreigners pelts, which were then shipped downriver, to be loaded onto ships that crossed the Atlantic to Holland. The intersection of the Hudson and the Atlantic, then, was a natural hub where business could be transacted, including privateering, the Company's biggest source of income, against Spanish ships en route to the Caribbean.

Along with the cattle and farming equipment, the Dutch West India Board had sent detailed instructions addressed specifically to Verhulst and Fredericks. The engineer was to erect a fort at the tip of the island, lay out streets, and build houses: twelve of them with sufficient land for farming and grazing. This was a priority. Five of the farms—*bouweries*—were to be leased to colonists for a period of six years; they were to draw straws for the privilege. The goal, for the time being, was to make the colony self-sufficient. The rest of the lots would go to the Company directors. The instructions specified that besides the slaves, Fredericks was to use anybody who was willing to work for labor, including Indians. They, however, would be paid only half as much as white men and not in specie but trading goods.

Fredericks placed the footprint for the fort on the spot that is now the old Custom House, just behind Bowling Green. Around it, he put the houses. But there was no room there for all those farms. So he did some exploring in the sticky summer heat (for which Manhattan remains famous) and discovered footpaths that the Indians used at the shore, right behind where he was planning the fort. (This is now the foot of Pearl Street, so named because of all those lovely oysters that once proliferated in the waters around New York.) One of the paths veered east through the woods along what is now Park Row and up to Chatham Square. It then turned north, parallel to the other branch, and continued into the wilderness. To the west of the path and surrounded by hills (where now stand the state supreme court and parts of Chinatown) was a huge freshwater pond, its surface in places covered with lily pads. Between the hills stretched flat, marshy terrain teeming with aquatic life: red-winged blackbirds, coots, herons, bullfrogs, beavers. Several streams undulated through the flat areas, flowing in and then out with the tides, and then draining into each of the great rivers on either side of Manhattan. Indians in canoes traversed the island via the streams, which provided them with shortcuts to the rivers. The rivers were in fact tidal estuaries and therefore consisted of saltwater, so the streams, too, were salty at high tide when they were running toward the pond. But by the time they flowed into it, they were running fresh. Sometimes, in spring or high tide, the marshy, wet terrain around the pond was completely flooded.

Between the western shore of the pond and the area's highest hill—it measured almost 110 feet high—Fredericks came across an Indian settlement called Werpoes. The word means "thicket"; thorn and berry bushes covered the surrounding hills. The inhabitants were the Manhates—one of the branches of the Lenape group—who lived in the southern part of the Hudson Valley. This was a wonderful spot, accessible to both rivers by canoe via streams that flowed to and from the pond (the one that emptied into the East River was later filled in and became the eponymous Canal Street). The pond provided the Manhates with drinking water and fish. In the flat area along its banks they grew the "three sisters": corn, beans, and squash. The crops

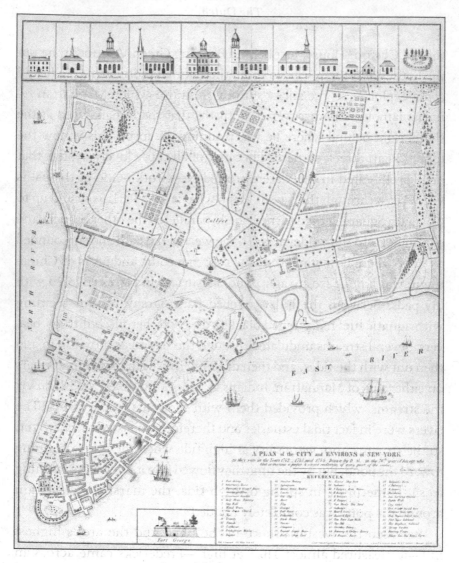

Lower Manhattan, 1742–44.

were beautifully arranged, with the squash and its abundant green leaves in between the corn, which was planted on mounds of earth, and the beans climbing up the corn stalks, feeding nitrogen to the other two crops through its roots. The Dutch were soon calling the pond Kalck Hoek—"calcium hook," that is, hook as in "corner," after the oyster shells piled up around it. The name mutated into "Collect Pond" or "Collect," after English supplanted Dutch as New York's lingua franca. (Oysters were a big part of the Lenape diet; they also used the shells to make the wampum they used for currency.)

Imagine Fredericks's awe, walking along the path in the heat of summer and taking in this unspoiled land. Except for the sounds of nature—the bullfrogs croaking, the loons moaning to each other, the leaves rustling in the breeze—there was silence. He realized that he had found the perfect location for the farms—bouweries. He would place them along the footpath, six on each side.

The bouweries varied in area from about 50 to 200 acres. Fredericks designated the northernmost one—120 acres of forest in the middle of which St. Mark's Church in-the-Bowery now stands on Second Avenue and Stuyvesant Street—for the company director. Fredericks considered the proximity of the Manhate settlement a real bonus: the native peoples, he thought, would help clear the forest and show the new farmers how to cultivate the land. Fredericks set to work. He had slaves and Indians widen the footpath to accommodate carts and animals. Trees were cut and the farms were carved out of the woods. The livestock that had been temporarily parked on Nut Island were then distributed among the farmers. As it was not the custom among the Dutch to fence their animals, cows, horses, sheep, and pigs—all animals the native people were seeing for the first time—were soon wandering into the nearby fields and eating up the crops that the Manhates had carefully planted. The white settlers were already upending the lives of the native people; and while the Manhates continued to use their old path to traverse the length of Manhattan, just as they had for thousands of years, it was no longer theirs. The Dutch used it as a public road, which they called the wagon road to Sapokanican, another Indian settlement along the Lenape path in what is now Greenwich Village. The section of the path they had widened with the Indians' sweat was being trampled with wooden carts and filled with the scat of those strange animals that were now devouring the corn and squash.

As Fredericks was overseeing the clearing of woods and the laying out of farms alongside the Lenape trail, Peter Minuit, who had succeeded Verhulst as the colony's director, bought Manhattan Island for sixty guilders' worth of goods. The year was 1626. The Dutch sources do not name the Indians who were involved in the transaction. They could have been the Manhates at Werpoes given that they were living nearby. Dutch documentation of the sale exists, although no actual deed was ever found. We don't know the Indians' version of these events, because they left no written records of it or anything else. But certainly the concept of humans owning land was alien to them. Probably the Indians saw Minuit's offering as the symbol of an agreement between the two peoples to share Manhattan, and doubtless they expected something in return.

But as far as the Dutch were concerned, the island now belonged to them. (They had also started a settlement in the northern wilds of Manhattan Island, which they called Nieuw Haarlem, after the city where its inhabitants came from.) They believed that they had conducted the purchase of Manhattan with the utmost integrity. The Company had sent specific instructions on how to acquire land in the new colony, and Minuit had followed them to the letter:

Commissary Verhulst, assisted by the surveyor, Cryn Fredericks, shall investigate the most suitable place, abandoned or unoccupied, on either river, and then settle there with all the cattle and build the necessary fortification. And finding none but those that are occupied by the Indians, they shall see whether they cannot, either in return for trading-goods or by means of some amicable agreement, induce them to give up ownership and possession to us, without however forcing them thereto in the least or taking possession by craft or fraud, lest we call down the wrath of God upon our unrighteous beginnings, the Company intending in no wise to make war or hostile attacks upon any one, except the Spanish and their allies, and others who are our declared enemies.

What an interesting bit of evidence this is about the Dutch character. In the context of seventeenth-century Europe, when it was the social norm to buy, sell, and work Africans as if they were cattle and to persecute and kill people based on their religion, the Dutch often showed themselves to be surprisingly liberal. But mixed in with their professions of respect for the Indians was pure pragmatism. The Dutch were essentially urban people, without any knowledge of the wilderness. They did not know how to hunt or trap animals. Without the Indians, they could not survive in New Netherland. The Indians supplied them with food and, most important, pelts.

The Dutch made that dependence mutual.

Before the Europeans arrived, Indians had mostly survived by hunting and fishing, but only as much as they could consume. The newcomers turned this world upside down by introducing the Indians to what was for them a novel idea: profit. This translated into the exploitation of resources. The white men cut down forests not just to clear fields but also to export the timber to Europe, where the supply was dwindling. At the same time, they were destroying the Indians' habitats, along with the ecology that had sustained them for thousands of years. The European demand for furs meant that the Indians were now killing animals for trading rather than for mere survival. In the meantime, the Indians had come to desire—and soon need—the things that Europeans offered them in exchange for pelts: metal pots, which were more durable than pottery; woolen duffel cloth, which unlike animal skins protected them from the rain; guns, which killed much more efficiently than arrows; and alcohol, to which the Indians had no tolerance.

But the Europeans had brought with them something far more dangerous than alcohol: their diseases. Smallpox epidemics were annihilating entire communities, and those few indigenous people who survived unknowingly spread the virus farther by joining kin living elsewhere.

It took several years for the Dutch settlers to complete the fort at the tip of Manhattan. As material they used sod, and it began to crumble immediately, leaving the inhabitants of New Amsterdam vulnerable to attack. They were not worried about the Indians: from where they were sitting, matters between them and the native peoples were going just fine. But they feared invasion by whites from the rival English colonies to the north and south.

The Indians no doubt saw things differently. Their numbers were dwindling. The Manhates at Werpoes were soon gone. We don't know the circumstances; perhaps they succumbed to disease or were driven off their land by settlers on the neighboring farms. (Possibly the Manhates migrated to Brooklyn and joined a Canarsee settlement there, also called Werpoes.)

In the meantime, New Amsterdam was attracting more immigrants. But very few of them came from the Netherlands, because the economy there was booming, thanks in large part to all its colonies—Angola, Brazil, and Curacao—and that meant opportunity. This was the era historians would later call the Dutch golden age. The merchant class was growing and having fun too. Therefore, it was hard to find people who wanted to leave the Netherlands either for economic reasons or religious, which is often the impetus for people to emigrate. The religious persecution then raging throughout Europe was nonexistent in the Netherlands; on the contrary, many minorities, such as the English Puritans, found refuge there. The Dutch were decidedly laid back when it came to religion, and the Dutch West India Company did not even mention it in the charter. All that mattered to them was that an immigrant would help increase their investment; his religion or nationality was irrelevant. Already, on Manhattan Island, money transcended everything.

In 1628, New Amsterdam's population totaled several hundred people, including the slaves. Most lived in the area around the fort, where slaves had constructed thirty rude shacks out of hickory wood from trees on Nut Island. The settlement also had a stone warehouse for storing the beaver pelts coming in from upriver and three windmills. One of them was located on the Bowery, near the new farms. Apparently, the farms were producing grain, because the Reverend

Jonas Michaelius wrote to the Company on August 11, 1628: "The harvest, God be praised, is in the barns, and is larger than ever before." But the good pastor—he was New Amsterdam's first, sent over by the Company—didn't find much else to feel happy about. The common people, he wrote to his bosses back home, were "rather rough and unrestrained." It was hard to find workers, because "many would have liked to make a living, and even to get rich, in idleness rather than by hard work, saying they had not come to work; that as far as working is concerned they might as well have stayed at home, and that it was all one whether they did much or little, if only in the service of the Company." As for the Indians, he found them "entirely savage and wild, strangers to all decency, yea, uncivil and stupid as garden poles, who serve nobody but the Devil."

The curmudgeonly Michaelius was right about one thing: the new inhabitants had no incentive to work hard. New Amsterdam was not a colony in the legal sense but rather a trading post that existed solely for the benefit of investors. Everybody there worked for the Company, which is where all profits went. The Dutch government had also granted a monopoly to the Company on all the fur trade and everything else they could get their hands on in New Netherland. The Company passed Michaelius's complaints on to the government in a report dated October 23, 1629: "The people conveyed by us thither have found but scanty means of livelihood up to the present time; and have not been any profit, but a drawback, to this Company." Still, the report stated, the fur trade was excellent. "But one year with another, we can at most bring home 50,000 guilders." In fact the place was turning a profit—but not large enough to satisfy investors.

Still, too much capital had been invested in New Amsterdam for the Company to just walk away. So it hung on to its grimy new venture and tried to stimulate its economy. Huge land tracts were offered for sale, to be managed and exploited as the new owners—patroons—saw fit. The Company also ended its trade monopoly; now anybody could buy and sell furs or anything else for that matter in New Netherland. The new initiatives worked: immediately immigration increased. People were coming to New Amsterdam from all over; you could hear eighteen languages spoken in the streets. Dutch speakers were in the minority; the rest were French and Belgian Huguenots (the latter known as Walloons), Irish, Swedes, Germans, and English. Among the latter were members of dissident Protestant sects from Massachusetts who were escaping the persecution of the Puritans (who, ironically, had fled religious intolerance in England only to invent a more strident variety of their own in the New World).

The refugees from Puritan New England and its dour ways found New Amsterdam a real eye-opener. It was a wild place. Its population was overwhelmingly male, and when it came to policing morality, the Dutch took a decidedly relaxed approach. After fur, alcohol was the most lucrative business. The Company produced its own beer, and thus did Brouwer Street (now Stone Street) in Lower Manhattan derive its name. One out of four structures housed a tavern; they stayed open all the time, even on Sundays. Everybody drank all the time, everywhere, and openly. Drunkenness led to frequent violence, and prostitution thrived. Policing all this vice was complicated by the fact that New Amsterdam had no real government. The director ruled by fiat, and there was no right of appeal.

New Amsterdam was also falling apart physically by the 1630s, because there weren't enough people—or slaves—willing to perform the necessary manual labor to keep it together. The fort, though rebuilt, remained flimsy. The sawmill on Nut Island that the Africans had built upon the settlers' arrival and the windmills constructed soon after had fallen into ruins. Hardly any grain or other crops were being produced. The farms along the Bowery that Fredericks had laid out were now deserted: Those lucky men to whom the lands had been allotted in the mid-1620s soon realized there was more money to be made in fur trading. Consequently they'd decamped, taking all the livestock with them, which they sold.

In 1638, the Company brought in a new director general to clean up this lawless mess. Willem Kieft was a businessman with no experience in governing. His business ventures were questionable: it was rumored that he had been hired to ransom Christians who were being held captive in Constantinople, but he kept the money without freeing the prisoners. Despite this, he had family connections with Company members, which perhaps explains why they chose him.

Kieft's predecessor, Wouter van Twiller, had improved the director's farm with a "dwelling house," a "very good barn," a boat house, and a brewery covered with tiles. But Kieft declined to live there, instead choosing to move into quarters inside the fort. During his first few years as director he heard and decided dozens of complaints, some of them criminal matters involving theft, murder, and rape. At the same time, England was trying to horn in on New Netherland, which was severely underpopulated and therefore vulnerable to attack. Despite these urgent problems to deal with, Kieft made going after Indians his first priority, not just on Manhattan Island but throughout the colony. His impulse was completely irrational: Even though the Indian population was shrinking, they still vastly outnumbered the Dutch. So it was a war he could never win. Moreover, it violated the Company policy.

Kieft started his crusade by imposing a tax on the Lenape as the price of "protecting" them from the more aggressive Mohicans and Mohawks to the north. The Lenape, incredulous at Kieft's demand, ignored it. "He must be a very mean fellow to come to live in this country without being invited, and now wish to compel us to give us our corn for nothing," a group of Tappans complained to a sympathetic patroon named David Pieterszoon de Vries, who had a farm on Staten Island. So Kieft searched for a reason to pick another fight. He saw his chance when some Company-owned pigs on De Vries's Staten Island farm were killed. It was not clear who the guilty party was, but Kieft insisted that it was a group of Raritans living nearby. He sent one hundred soldiers to the settlement to demand satisfaction from the Indians. The soldiers had orders not to attack, but things quickly spun out of control. Four European men were killed along with several Indians. One soldier tortured the brother of the chief "in his private parts, with a piece of split wood," one horrified witness reported. "Such acts of tyranny perpetrated by the servants of the Company were far from making friends with the inhabitants." To say the least: one year later, in 1641, Raritans descended on De Vries's farm, burned his house, and killed his men.

De Vries, furious, tried to get Kieft to back off before the director inflicted more damage. Up until then, the patroon had had good relations with the Indians. This sophisticated merchant was born in La Rochelle, France—home to many Huguenots—to Dutch parents, who then returned with him to the Netherlands, where he grew up and learned how to conduct trade. Curiosity and possible business opportunities took him first to Newfoundland, around the Mediterranean, and back to the Netherlands. Then, attracted by a possibility of a patroonship, he crossed the Atlantic a second time in 1632. During the following decade, he'd been sailing along the coasts of New Jersey and Staten Island, acquiring tracts of land, and turning them into farms. Along the way, he kept a journal filled with accounts of his many dealings with various Indians, some of whom he befriended. He observed them carefully and mostly with respect.

When they dance they stand in two, three and four pairs. The first pair carry a tortoise in their hands, as this nation say that they have descended from a tortoise-father, at which I laughed. They then asked me where our first father came from. I said he was called Adam, and was made of earth. They said I was a fool to say that he was made of a thing that had no life. I replied that it was full of life, for it produced all the fruits upon which they lived. They answered that the sun, which they looked upon as a God, produced it, for in summer he drew the leaves from the trees, and all the fruits from the ground.

De Vries warned Kieft that Indians were vengeful people. "Like Italians," he said. (Reading his words some 400 years later tells us just how far back this obnoxious cultural stereotype goes.) But Kieft refused to listen. "In this country," he said, "I am sovereign, the same as the Prince in the Netherlands." Tensions between the white men and the Indians increased: soon after the incident at the De Vries farm, a young Indian, carrying beaver pelts to trade, showed up at the house of an old Dutchman named Claes Smits in the wilderness along the East River. When the Indian saw an ax leaning against the wall, he grabbed it and cut off the old man's head.

The Indian had not gone to Smits's house with the intention to murder him. But when he saw the ax, something in him snapped. The sight of it brought him back to something terrible that had happened when he was a small boy: He had gone with his father and uncle down to the fort at the tip of the island to trade pelts with some Dutch settlers. One of the men had killed his uncle, and the others had stolen the pelts. Since then, the Indian had sought vengeance. Now, with Claes Smits's ax, he had gotten it.

Claes Smits's murder gave Kieft the ammunition he was looking for to escalate his gratuitous war. A few months later, in February 1643, a group of Mohawks or Mohicans from the area around Albany—then a fur station that the Dutch called Fort Orange—attacked and killed some Lenape near Manhattan. Five hundred survivors fled south through the snow to one of De Vries's farms in New Jersey. They begged the patroon for protection. De Vries, feeling overwhelmed by the sudden influx of unexpected guests, left his house and rowed down the ice-choked river by canoe to Fort Amsterdam. There, he asked Kieft to lend him some soldiers, because, in his words, "I was not the master of my own house, because it was so full of savages, although I was not afraid that they would do me any harm; but it was proper that I should be master of my own house." Kieft said that he had no soldiers, but he told De Vries to come back the following evening if he still needed help. But the next morning, the Indians left De Vries's farm. Some travelled all the way into Manhattan to take shelter in Corelaer's bouwerie (the Lower East Side). But most went to Pavonia (now Jersey City), a fortified Dutch settlement just across the river from Fort Amsterdam.

The following day, as De Vries was dining at Kieft's house, the director general suddenly burst into a tirade. "I will put a bit into the mouths of these savages," he yelled. He told De Vries that he had given his soldiers orders to cross the river to Pavonia that night to kill the Indians encamped there. De Vries was aghast. "You cannot kill all the Indians," he told the director, adding that surely the survivors would retaliate. In effect Kieft would also be murdering all the settlers who were living, unprotected, in the open country. De Vries also reminded Kieft that because of the director's unprovoked attack on the Raritans, two years earlier—in 1641—they had burned down the patroon's farm on Staten Island. But Kieft blew him off and went to bed. De Vries spent that night in the director's house, sitting by the kitchen fire. He was too worried to sleep. Around midnight, he heard screams from across the river. He ran to the ramparts of the fort and looked toward Pavonia, but it was too dark to see anything. The next morning, the soldiers returned and told him that they had killed eighty Indians the previous night as they lay sleeping. Kieft's men hacked off limbs, slashed bellies, and pulled out entrails. Children were torn from their mothers' arms and chopped to pieces or thrown, still alive, into the freezing river. When their parents jumped in to try to save their precious ones, the soldiers prevented them from coming on land.

De Vries was beside himself. Kieft, after congratulating his soldiers for a job well done, kept up the bloody momentum he had started. He committed one atrocity after another against Indians, regardless of whether they had been on friendly terms with the Dutch up to then. Then came a tipping point: the trauma being inflicted on all the tribes caused them to put aside their differences and unite against the Dutch—Sewannekens, they called them, which means "bitter" or "salty people."

The Indians began attacking settlers everywhere. They set fire to everything in their path: "houses, farms, barns, grain, haystacks," De Vries later wrote. "They also burned my farm, cattle, corn, barn, tobacco-house, and all the tobacco." Unable to bear life under Kieft any longer, De Vries decided it was time to cut his losses. He left New Netherland in the fall of 1643, first for the English colony in Virginia, where he had purchased some tobacco plantations, and then on to

Europe. He never returned. Other colonists were also leaving; most, like De Vries, returned to Europe. Those who remained abandoned their lands and fled to the fort at the tip of New Amsterdam. The area under attack, which stretched ten miles east and west and seven miles south and north of New Amsterdam, was now devoid of white people; there was nothing to stop the Indians from heading straight into the settlement at the tip of the island. It was only a matter of time.

Kieft knew that he had to do something to protect what remained of the colony. So he decided to create a buffer zone by offering anyone brave enough to live there title to any of the empty farms that flanked the Bowery. This was a tough sell to the traumatized survivors of the war he had brought on. So Kieft came up with a novel idea: he would offer the land to slaves. In fact, he would free some slaves himself expressly for this purpose. He reasoned that they would prove especially conscientious at keeping the Indians at bay.

By then, slaves made up nearly one-quarter of New Netherland's population. The Dutch were no different from the rest of the Europeans in their assumptions about race: blacks, they believed, were inherently inferior. But slavery had no legal basis in New Amsterdam. There, in theory at least, slaves had the same rights as anybody else and sometimes fared rather well, considering the times. In New Amsterdam, slaves deemed to have served long and faithfully were often freed, and those who remained in bondage were permitted to moonlight for wages. As for the color line, it proved at times to be flexible. At the request of the colony's minister, Everardus Bogardus—he had replaced Michaelius in 1633—the Dutch church in Amsterdam sent over a schoolmaster to "teach and train the youth of both Dutch and blacks, in the knowledge of Jesus Christ." Rotund, beer-loving Bogardus, who had served as a minister in Ghana, invited slaves into the Dutch Reformed Church. He married them, baptized their children, and had them serve as witnesses to Dutch baptisms. Occasionally, blacks and whites married each other. Slaves drank alongside whites in Dutch taverns, testified against them in court, and even on occasion sued them—sometimes successfully.

In 1643, Kieft distributed the first land grants to slaves whom he had sent to do battle with the Indians. During the next several years, he distributed more land along the Bowery to freed slaves and the occasional white settler. The tract came to be called the Negros land, and it consisted of 130 acres of swampy land along the Bowery. There's an irony here: Kieft's attempt to address the mess he'd created in New Amsterdam with his unprovoked attacks on the Indians led him to create the first free black community in North America. In the meantime, New Amsterdam's inhabitants had become so fed up with him that in 1644 they drafted a letter documenting his incompetence and sent it to the Dutch West India Company. The Company had already received plenty of complaints about him, but so far they'd been sitting on their hands. However, after receiving this latest missive, they realized the governor was bad for business and decided it was time to do something about him.

CHAPTER TWO

THE GOVERNOR WITH
THE SILVER LEG

In 1647, a replacement for Kieft arrived from the Netherlands. Peter Stuyvesant was in his thirties and as the son of a Calvinist minister, a man who took his religion seriously. He hated sectarian Protestants (especially Lutherans), Quakers, Jews, and, naturally, Catholics. With a large, misshapen nose and small eyes set too close together, he was, frankly, quite ugly. He hobbled about on the wooden peg that would be forever associated with him. His lower right leg had been amputated three years earlier after having been mangled by a cannonball in a sea battle that he—then governor of Curacao—had instigated in an attempt to capture the island of Saint Martin from the Spanish. The attack failed. The leg—fashioned in Holland—was of exceptional craftsmanship with a tip made of silver.

Stuyvesant was a complicated person. His hard-assed righteousness made him the antithesis of New Amsterdam's freewheeling zeitgeist and ran counter to the Dutch West India Company's relaxed policy about religion and race. Their priority was business, period. So when a handful of Dutch Jews arrived in New Amsterdam in 1654 from Brazil—the Portuguese had just wrested the colony from the Dutch and were now importing the Inquisition there from Europe—and Stuyvesant didn't want them to stay, the Company was furious. They ordered him to let the refugees remain "because of the large amount of capital, which Jews have invested in shares of this company." Stuyvesant had to comply but he then tried to deny the Jews the right to trade or buy real estate. Once again, the Company slapped his hand, declaring: "The Jews may quietly and peacefully carry on their business as before and exercise in all quietness their religion within their houses." Stuyvesant next went after Lutherans, followed by an out-and-out persecution of Quakers. Again, the Company made him back off: "It has always been our intention to treat the Lutherans quietly and leniently."

But in other ways he exhibited exactly the qualities needed for his new job. Stuyvesant had been working for the Company since he was young, and they liked him. In fact, they liked him so much that when they offered him Kieft's post, they insisted he also continue as director general of Curacao. This was quite a workload for one man. But his stint in Curacao had proven that he was up to it. The New Amsterdam colonists' demands for more representative government needed to be slapped down, hard, and Stuyvesant was the man to do it.

From the minute he stepped off the ship in New Amsterdam, Stuyvesant antagonized people. He behaved "like a peacock, with great state and pomp." He told the crowd who greeted him at the shore—among them were a few former slaves—that he would remain in their midst for three years but no longer, as if they should consider themselves lucky to have a man of his stature governing their miserable, underpopulated colony. This display of high-handedness, carried out at the beginning of his tenure, showed a serious lack of political judgment on Stuyvesant's part. He, as an outsider, was at an obvious disadvantage: he didn't know anybody in New Amsterdam or anything about the place's ins and outs. How could he have thought he wouldn't need some modicum of goodwill from the people who already lived there? Especially since the colony he was to manage was a festering mess. Whatever progress had been made there prior to Kieft's tenure had been reversed by the Indian wars. The Bowery was the only navigable road out of the main settlement at the tip of the island, and it was still mostly deserted, except for the small plots that Kieft had granted to the freed slaves. Inside the settlement—it extended as far as where Wall Street stands now—mayhem ruled. The beer shops never closed and alcoholism was rampant; for the few who did prefer to pray rather than drink on Sundays, there was no church. Kieft had started building a church inside the fort, but it was only half-finished. People put up structures—wooden shacks mostly—anywhere they pleased, unhampered by any building regulations. As for the fort built twenty years prior, it still had not been properly enforced; its crumbling earth walls could easily be breached. This presented a serious security matter: the threat of invasion was omnipresent, not only by Indians but also by the English, who continued to deny the Dutch claim to New Netherland, which they badly wanted. Because if not for the Dutch, the English would have control of the entire Eastern Seaboard.

Immediately after his arrival, Stuyvesant, his wife, Judith Bayard, and their infant son, Balthazar, moved into the director's quarters inside the fort. The new director then dived head-on into the business at hand. Within days, he was issuing proclamations, which were then obediently rubber-stamped by a group of Company-appointed men who had accompanied him from Holland. The first issue Stuyvesant tackled was alcohol: he forbade its consumption on the Sabbath, and he forbade the sale of it to Indians. At the same time, he also imposed an excise tax to secure money to fix the settlement infrastructure.

People reacted to the director's new tax with outrage, and Stuyvesant realized that he would have a rebellion on his hands unless he threw the colonists some sort of bone. So he grudgingly appointed a "Board of Nine" in September 1647 to give the impression that he was not governing unilaterally. The Board's role, however, was to be strictly advisory. Among the members were a Bohemian named Augustine Hermann and a very savvy young man named Adriaen van der Donck, whom Stuyvesant had recently taken into his confidence. The Board chose Van der Donck as its president.

Among New Netherland's raunchy, motley population, Van der Donck stood out: He was Dutch, highly educated—the only lawyer in the colony—and from a wealthy family. He had studied law at the University of Leiden, a hotbed of liberal ideas. Upon finishing his studies, Van der Donck sailed to New Netherland in 1641 to serve as the *schout*—a kind of all-around administrator—of the Amsterdam diamond merchant Killaen van Rensselaer's vast patroonship near Troy, New York. Leaving Holland for the wilds of the New World seemed an unlikely move for a young man from such a privileged background. But Van der Donck was a free spirit. Once he had arrived at Rensselaerswyck, he mostly ignored the job that Van Rensselaer had hired him to do. Instead, he spent most of his time travelling around the upper Hudson, going native among the Mohawks and Mohicans. He learned their languages and customs, taking voluminous notes that he turned into a long narrative. In it, he sometimes referred to the Indians as "Americans"—the first known use of the term.

Van Rensselaer, understandably angry at Van der Donck, did not renew his contract when it expired. The young man then headed down to New Amsterdam, while it was still in a state of chaos under Kieft. This translated into an opportunity for Van der Donck. The New World, with no kings and no popes, provided a perfect laboratory for testing out some of the ideas—for example, the then-revolutionary notion that a leader should rule not by divine fiat but by consent of the governed—which he had soaked up as a student in Leiden. Van der Donck soon discovered that he was a natural-born leader. Drawing on his legal training, he had been instrumental in composing the document for the Dutch West India Company in 1644 that catalogued Kieft's incompetence and finally forced the Company to act. Simultaneously, he was helping Kieft write a peace treaty to end the Indian war. Kieft, unaware that Van der Donck was playing both sides, felt so grateful to the young man for his help that he rewarded him with a huge tract of land along both sides of the Hudson River. Van der Donck as a result acquired a moniker: Jonker, which in seventeenth-century Dutch meant a young man with a country estate. Today Van der

Donck's gift from Kieft comprises part of the Bronx and the city of Yonkers.

In 1645, Van der Donck married an Englishwoman, thereby learning English. So when Stuyvesant arrived on the scene in 1647, Van der Donck, once again sensing opportunity, offered the new director his help in negotiating with the English colonies to the north. Stuyvesant accepted. Soon a relationship developed between the two men, and the director general appointed Van der Donck to the Board of Nine.

The first thing the new Board did was to immediately demand that Stuyvesant help implement a formal investigation against Kieft, who was still in New Amsterdam.* They assumed that Stuyvesant would support them in this, but they were wrong: Stuyvesant became so furious that "the foam hung from his beard." He told the Board: "It is treason to petition against one's magistrates, whether there be cause or not." He believed that only the Company had any legal right to question a director general's actions. Allowing anybody else to do so would, he feared, set a dangerous precedent. Then, as if this request did not cause him enough agita, letters kept arriving from the Company that not only contradicted previous directives but also criticized just about everything he was doing. The Company agreed that the church needed to be completed to get the place on the straight and narrow, but they refused to provide Stuyvesant with the funds, saying: "We notice also that it has been very expensive; the Colony cannot yet bear such expenses." In another reversal they first told him that he must contain the settlement's "very wild and loose morals" but followed by telling him to go easy: "A tree grown too high and too luxuriantly must be trimmed carefully and bent by a tender hand, giving it good shape. The native inhabitants of our conquests have shown the necessity to govern them with mildness." They warned him to push

---

* Kieft voluntarily left in 1647 for Amsterdam to plead his case to the Company, but his ship was wrecked off the coast of Wales. He was among the eighty-six aboard who died; twenty-one survived. See Russell Shorto, *The Island in the Center of the World* (New York: Vintage, 2004), p. 339.

back hard at settlers who demanded that their voices be heard, because there were many English living in Dutch villages who had "the assurance to elect Magistrates on their authority. We consider this rather a dangerous precedent." They then retreated from that position, writing: "We suppose that only mild measures can induce them to give up this plan of self-government, for it seems, these people living there will not endure a harsh government."

Stuyvesant, assailed on all sides, reacted by kicking Van der Donck off the Board of Nine in March 1649, and then jailing him on the charge of treason. But this only made the young lawyer more popular, so Stuyvesant was forced to release him. Van der Donck then spent the next several months seeking out anybody willing to go on the record with their complaints about New Amsterdam's governance, both past and current. He found plenty of people who were happy to talk to him and carefully recorded what they said. He then used his notes to compose a detailed account with the Board of Nine, outlining the ways in which the Company was mismanaging its colony. The resultant document, the elegantly written *Remonstrance of New Netherland*, was completed in the summer of 1649 and signed by Van der Donck and eleven other men, including the remaining members of the Board of Nine. In mid-August, with *Remonstrance* in hand, Van der Donck, accompanied by two of its cosigners, boarded a ship for Holland. When the men arrived two months later, they handed the precious document directly to the States General—the legislature of the Netherlands—not the Company. This was nervy of them, because the Company was chartered by and so answerable to the government. In effect Van der Donck and his associates were going over their bosses' heads, never a good idea. Officials in the Hague were surely going to be annoyed to receive yet another complaint about New Amsterdam.

The *Remonstrance* began with a long and rapturous description of New Netherland, which then suddenly turned into a self-effacing encomium: "We cannot Sufficiently thank the Fountain of all Goodness for having conducted us to so good, so fertile and so wholesome a land which we, however, did not deserve, on account of our manifold sins exceedingly increased by us every day in this country." "Us," of course, meant the Company, which the document then bluntly stated had reduced New Netherland to its current ruinous condition because of "bad government." It cared only for short-term profit and nothing about its inhabitants. As for the directors the Company had chosen, they were corrupt or at the very least completely inept. The current one, Peter Stuyvesant, was an imperious ass ("whom he opposes has both sun and moon against him"). The *Remonstrance* then proposed a bold remedy for this mess: the States General should take over the colony from the Company and install there a

suitable municipal government . . . that those interested in the country may also attend to its government and keep a watchful eye over it, without its being entrusted to a set of hair brained people, such as the Company flings thither, but to such as obtained in New England . . . [we should take an example from them] where each town, no matter how small, hath its own court and jurisdiction, also a voice in the Capital, and elects its own officers.

The States General immediately convened a special committee to study the contents of the *Remonstrance*. In the meantime, Van der Donck and his two colleagues found a printer to publish the *Remonstrance* in the form of a cheap pamphlet, which quickly circulated around Amsterdam. The description of the colony as a Shangri-La— but with all its fabulous potential unrealized because of the Company's abysmal management—caused a sensation. Suddenly, of all the Dutch colonies, New Amsterdam became *the* place to go. Immigrants once again began arriving from across the ocean, reversing the population decline brought about by Kieft's war during the previous decade. In a letter to Stuyvesant dated February 16, 1650, two Company officials wrote: "Formerly New Netherland was never spoken of and now heaven and earth seem to be stirred up by it and every one tries to be first in selecting the best pieces there."

The tropical colonies offered spices, coffee, sugar, and, yes, the slave trade. But Manhattan, with its freezing winters and rough ways, had land that, thanks to Van der Donck's eloquent arguments, was now being perceived as an undervalued commodity to be snatched up before somebody else got to it first.

This, arguably, was the point at which Manhattan's obsession with real estate began. It has continued ever since.

Shortly after Van der Donck had sailed to Holland with the *Remonstrance* in 1649, Stuyvesant went to have a look at the director's farm at the northernmost reaches of the Bowery. The place was just empty acreage—the barn, house, and tile-covered brewery Van Twiller, Kieft's predecessor, had built there had all been destroyed in the latter's war—and it seemed to Stuyvesant like a perfect place to build a country home. He constructed a large stone house and a barn on the land, which abutted two small properties that belonged to freed slaves. The proximity of the farms belonging to Anthony Congo and Bastiaem d'Angola, both recipients of Kieft's grants several years earlier, made the location of the director's farm especially desirable. It offered peace and quiet—something he badly needed amid the turmoil of New Amsterdam's politics—but with the presence of the former slaves it was not completely vulnerable.

Stuyvesant was struggling politically. After Van der Donck handed the *Remonstrance* to the States General, the director received an angry letter from the Dutch West India Company, rebuking him for not sufficiently standing up to the young lawyer. Moreover, in the midst of this, Stuyvesant had to travel north to the English colonies of Connecticut and New Haven to conclude a border treaty with the governor, Edward Hopkins. The treaty conceded just about everything to the English, but there was nothing Stuyvesant could do about it: the Dutch did not have nearly enough colonists to defend all of New Netherland. The Company was angry at what they considered Stuyvesant's capitulation, so it refused to recognize the treaty.*

---

* Not that it mattered: the Crown didn't recognize it either, since it had never

28

Even as blows were coming at Stuyvesant from all sides, he knew he wasn't going anywhere. No matter how difficult everybody was making it for him, he kept his eye on the prize: land. Especially along the Bowery, one of the settlement's two main roads—the other was *De Heere Straat*, which the English would later call Broadway—land had to be a good investment.

So he decided to buy the director's property outright. He sent an agent to the Netherlands to negotiate with the Company. The deal, which included the adjoining farm and additional land along his property's northern border, was closed March 12, 1651. (Today, this area extends from Fifth Street to Seventeenth Street, in some places all the way to the river on the east side and to Broadway on the west.) Included in his purchase were two slaves ("young Negros"), six cows, and two horses—all for 6,400 guilders (the equivalent of $2,560), which represented quite a bargain.

Stuyvesant immediately began adding barns, gardens, and orchards to his new farm. But he had to halt his improvements the following year when the Company ordered him to begin preparing for an invasion by the English from their colonies to the north. Company slaves built a wooden barricade at the northern boundary of New Amsterdam proper (this border later would be called Wall Street). The Company also told Stuyvesant that it was time New Amsterdam had a municipal government. This would de facto give the place recognition and, the Dutch government hoped, assuage its inhabitants' perennial dissatisfaction with Stuyvesant and the Company. Otherwise, there would be no hope that they would defend the colony if the English attacked.

Stuyvesant did as the Company asked. He appointed a committee to draw up a charter for New Amsterdam, which he unveiled in 1653. This meant that it was now an actual *place* with a separate identity and no longer just the Dutch West India Company's candy store. At least this was true in principal.

---

accepted the Dutch claim to New Netherland.

But the charter did not change anything in the day-to-day affairs. It established a municipal board, which de facto acted as Peter Stuyvesant's rubber stamp. The fact was there was nobody to challenge Stuyvesant. His main rival, Van der Donck, had so incurred the wrath of the Company when he'd presented the *Remonstrance* directly to the Hague rather than to them in 1649 that they had prevented the young lawyer from returning to New Netherland for two years—and then only on the condition that he stay out of politics there permanently. So Van der Donck could not participate in the writing of the charter. What a bitter pill that must have been for Van der Donck to swallow—and how sweet for Stuyvesant.

Van der Donck went back to his English wife and his farm along the Hudson and laid low. Two years later he was dead, perhaps a casualty of an Indian incursion from the north, the first disturbance since the peace treaty ending Kieft's war ten years earlier, in 1645. It happened suddenly: Indians descended in their canoes along the Hudson, burning farms and taking hostages on the way before reaching Manhattan early one morning. On the beach next to the fort, 500 armed men debarked from sixty-four canoes and immediately ran through the streets, breaking into the houses of the sleeping inhabitants. There were no Company soldiers around to protect them: ten days earlier, all the soldiers—they numbered between 600 and 700—had piled into ships and with Peter Stuyvesant sailed down to Delaware to upend Swedish settlements there. The Indians then crossed the river to Staten Island and attacked the Dutch settlement. Dutch accounts reported that 100 people were killed in nine hours, and hundreds of others were taken hostage. Those living outside the town abandoned their properties and headed for New Amsterdam, where they sought shelter inside the walls of the fort. There, the survivors huddled together, wailing over their losses.

The day after the attack, the Board sent off a letter to Stuyvesant, begging him to return to Manhattan as fast as he could. "For to lie in the fort night and day with the citizens has its difficulties as they cannot be commanded like soldiers." Some, after a few days no longer able to abide being cooped up inside the fort, ventured back to their farms in the countryside only to be captured by Indians or killed.

Stuyvesant received the letter on September 29. He left Delaware immediately, and reached Manhattan on October 12, accompanied by his troops. By then the violence had ended, but there was no question which side had prevailed in this latest disaster. The mood in New Amsterdam was grim. All over, properties had been burned down or deserted. Stuyvesant's farm survived, but only because his wife, Judith Bayard, had hired ten Frenchmen to guard it in the absence of the Company soldiers. People whose loved ones were being held hostage rushed back and forth to the Indians, trying to ransom them. Rumors began to spread, then panic. To squelch it, Stuyvesant and the Board forbade any more communication between whites and Indians.

In addition to the trauma everybody was suffering after the Indian incursions, winter was so cold that year that all the rivers surrounding New Amsterdam froze; you could cross the East River on foot over the ice from what is now Whitestone, in Queens, to Manhattan. Some members of the Board suggested that Indians be captured and held as ransom, to exchange for settlers still being held hostage. But Stuyvesant vetoed the idea. "Because," he said, "new occasion may thus be given to the savage tribes, either to murder the captives or to carry them off further inland, without leaving us hope to ransom them." This, he added, should be done "by the friendliest means, even if it were by giving them some contraband articles as presents."

Stuyvesant also made the Board pass an ordinance on January 18, 1656, mandating all the inhabitants of New Netherland to form villages "as have our neighbors in New England." Those who didn't comply would remain isolated on their farms at their peril and be fined annually 25 guilders a year. During Stuyvesant's frequent trips to the English colonies, he'd taken note that settlers there did not live isolated on farms scattered about the wilderness like their Dutch counterparts.

Instead, they formed villages—whence the template of the typical New England setting that exists to this day, clumped around a village green arose. Indeed, despite the commercial rivalry between the Dutch and the Crown, Stuyvesant admired the English and their ways.

Stuyvesant soon realized that his ordinance was unenforceable, because New Netherland quite simply did not have enough people. The area around Stuyvesant's Bowery estate was still barely populated. Anthony Congo and Bastiaem d'Angola, the former slaves who lived on the little lots abutting the director's farm, which marked the northern-most end of the Bowery, were his only neighbors. South of his property, the Bowery stretched across deserted woods and fields. A few freed slaves still lived at the edge of Werpoes—where the Manhates once lived—on the so-called Negros Land. An Englishman, Thomas Hall, had acquired one of their tracts in 1652, which was shaped like "a triangle that fitted like a key stone into the circular arch of the road." On it, Hall operated a tavern called the Plow and Harrow. But all fifty acres of the fertile, marshy land north of the Collect—that is, Werpoes—lay empty. This belonged to a Bohemian named Augustine Hermann, a signer of the *Remonstrance* and one of New Amsterdam's biggest landowners; he had purchased Werpoes at the same time Stuyvesant had bought the director's farm. Hermann left New Amsterdam for Maryland in 1655 and remained there. On the eastern side of the Collect, a Dutchman, Wolfert Webber, had a farm and a tavern that fronted the Bowery. After milestones were placed along the Bowery, everybody called this tavern the Half-Mile; it stood (at what was then Orange Street—now Baxter Street—and Chatham) just north of one of the windmills that were built right after the Dutch arrived in Manhattan. Behind the Half-Mile was a stream with the best-tasting water on the island, so Webber installed a pump there. It came to be known as the tea water pump, because vendors went there and filled wooden barrels that they then wheeled around the city, hawking the water as the best for making tea.

These few bodies constituted the entire population along the

Bowery, and it was only a matter of time before the Indians would again attack.

Stuyvesant knew that he had to do something to beef up New Amsterdam's security. So in early 1658 he followed the example of his predecessor, Kieft, by freeing a handful of slaves and giving them two-acre plots abutting his property. It was none too soon: Esopus, a settlement to the north, was then becoming the frequent target of Indian attacks. Fearing the disturbance would spread down to New Amsterdam, Stuyvesant, accompanied by fifty soldiers, boarded ships and sailed up the Hudson to Esopus. There, he advised the shaky inhabitants to defend themselves by—yes—forming a village surrounded with a stockade.

The unrest continued intermittently in Esopus over the following year and a half, but it never reached Manhattan. During this time, Stuyvesant made several trips back, trying to broker a peace treaty with the Indians. In the interim, he freed more slaves, to whom he also granted property. By 1660, the population of former slaves living around Stuyvesant along the Bowery totaled forty souls. Their presence made him feel safe. ("Let the free and the Company's negroes keep good watch on my bouwery," he wrote to the Board while sailing up the Hudson on one of his trips to Esopus.) They also provided him with labor: one of them, a woman, cleaned his home every week in return for her freedom. All the while, Stuyvesant kept improving his property. He built a schoolhouse and then a chapel. He hired the Reverend Henricus Selyns to conduct Sunday evening services there every week (for a salary of 250 guilders a year). Selyns had recently arrived from the Netherlands to serve as pastor in the village of Breuckelen, directly across the East River from Fort Amsterdam. His new job meant that every Sunday, after conducting the morning services in Breuckelen—in a barn, because as yet the village had no proper church—he rode to what is now Gravesend, got on a boat, and crossed the East River to New Amsterdam. Then he rode up the Bowery to preach in Stuyvesant's chapel. It was quite a full workday, but Selyns was in his twenties and had abundant energy. Apparently he was quite the charmer; people came from all over to hear him.

Selyns described Stuyvesant's property in idyllic terms. It was "a place of relaxation and pleasure, whither people go from the Manhattans for the evening service," he wrote to the *classis* in Amsterdam. "There are there forty negroes, from the region of the Negro Coast, beside the household families." Selyns, like Bogardus before him, welcomed blacks to his Sunday sermons. He even married black couples in Stuyvesant's chapel. But when black parents asked the reverend to baptize their children, he refused. The reason, he later explained, was "the material and perverted object which they had in view: nothing else than liberating their children from bodily slavery, without striving after godliness and Christian virtue." So the Dutch, although noticeably more relaxed regarding matters of race than other Europeans, still considered blacks viscerally inferior to whites. Moreover, the Dutch were heavily vested in the slave trade. Under Peter Stuyvesant's governorship of Curacao, the Company made handsome profits selling African slaves to the English to work to death in the sugar plantations of Barbados. During his time there more slaves—a few at a time— were brought to New Amsterdam from Curacao. As soon as Stuyvesant arrived in New Amsterdam, the Company pressed him to get the colony into the slave trade. He did as he was told, and by 1655 whole shiploads of Africans in chains were arriving directly to New Amsterdam from the continent's western coast.

As Stuyvesant was enlarging his Bowery estate, the landowners Wolfert Webber and Thomas Hall petitioned for and were granted permission also to create their own village. It was soon combined with Stuyvesant's, so now the first village along the Bowery, besides the school and the church, also included a tavern—Webber's—and the source of the sweetest water on the island. Soon the settlement had a blacksmith and a market as well. The latter attracted the area's farmers. And because it was located outside New Amsterdam's actual city limits, the produce sold there was not subject to municipal taxes. So, despite all the chaos and problems Stuyvesant was facing trying to govern New Netherland, there was one thing that was going well for him: he had put down roots on the Bowery, and he was turning his holdings into a real place.

Meanwhile, on the other side of the Atlantic, the English were busy figuring out how to wrest New Netherland from the Dutch. They were particularly determined to get Manhattan, through which all the commodities from the English colonies—tobacco from Virginia, sugar from the Caribbean—passed.

On March 12, 1664, King Charles II—his ascension to the throne four years earlier had restored the English monarchy after a decade of Puritan rule—granted his younger brother James, the Duke of York, all of New Netherland. James was eager to claim his gift. He immediately ordered the outfitting of four man-of-wars in Portsmouth, England. As the ships were being readied, a Boston merchant named Thomas Willet—he apparently had regular business dealings with the Dutch colony, which at just around this time contracted with him for "a quantity of beef and pork, payment therefor to be made in negroes"—received a letter from a friend in England. It described four frigates "each mounted with between 40 @ 50 guns, lay at Portsmouth ready to go to sea, having on board three hundred soldiers and each ship one hundred and fifty sea-men." Willet then passed this information to Stuyvesant: "Old England," he wrote to the director general, "is set to conquer New Netherlands."

The ships left Portsmouth on May 25, 1664. At the end of June, Stuyvesant received a letter from the Dutch West India Company confirming Willet's assertion. It was now summertime, people were outside, and the rumors of invasion spread. Most, frankly, did not feel unhappy about it. People were sick of Stuyvesant; perhaps, they thought, the colony would fare better under the English. In any case, everybody knew that New Amsterdam could not possibly survive an attack. The shores along both rivers lay completely open, and the fort had still not been properly reinforced; it would not withstand even three days of enemy assaults. Moreover, there were at most 250 men capable of bearing arms in a population totaling only 1,500. The Dutch colonists were ridiculously outnumbered by the British soldiers; in addition, recruits from the New England colonies were standing by to join the invasion.

In the face of such impossible odds, the Dutch colonists waited for the inevitable. The Reverend Selyns, by then at the end of the four-year contract he had signed with the Company, did not offer to extend it. "You have heard of the sad state of New Netherland," he wrote to the Company. "The English have declared, that they would take our town [New Amsterdam] and all Long-Island with flying colors." By the beginning of August, he was on a ship bound for Holland. (The former slaves living on Stuyvesant's farm, who had regularly attended Selyns's sermons, grieved over the Reverend's departure.) As for Stuyvesant, he tried to hold it together. "We keep the military force under our command as close together as possible, heighten the walls of our fort, strengthen it with gabions and make all arrangements for defense," he wrote to the Company. The truth was that the "arrangements" he referred to consisted of erecting old, rotten palisades along parts of the shoreline, against which earth was piled at most three feet high. In the same letter, Stuyvesant asked the Company to send military supplies: powder, lead, grenades, and small arms. "It is not our least anxiety, that we have so little powder and lead on hand, there being only 2500 lbs in the magazine and besides that not over 500 lbs among the militia and inhabitants here and at Fort Orange . . . You can easily judge that this supply will not last long."

Indeed.

At the end of August, 1664, the four British ships sailed into the mouth of the Hudson River and dropped anchor near Staten Island. From there, Colonel Richard Nicolls, the commander of this mission, sent a message to Stuyvesant: In the name of the King of Great Britain, English soldiers were to take possession of New Netherland.

And if this could not be done in an amicable way, the soldiers would attack and then be allowed to plunder, rob, and pillage. Stuyvesant refused to surrender. The ships then moved east, to Gravesend, where the soldiers disembarked and marched to the ferry launch, just across the river from Fort Amsterdam. From there, Nicolls and Stuyvesant began to talk back and forth via letters that they sent to each other by boat. The King, Nicolls wrote, was claiming his "'unquestionable' right and title to these parts of America." The "forraigners" were "usurpers." He demanded the surrender of "the Towne, Scituate upon the Island commonly knowne by the Name of Manhatoes with all the fforts there unto belonging." Nicolls offered generous terms along with his ultimatums. ("I do assure you that if the Manhatoes be delivered up to his Magestie, I shall not hinder, but any people from the Netherlands may freely come and plant there, or there abouts. And such Vessells of their owne Country may freely come thither and any of them may as freely returne home, in Vessells of their owne Country, and this, and much more is contained in the privledge of his Magisties English Subjects.")

Stuyvesant still refused to back down.

By then a week had passed since Nicolls first asked the Dutch to surrender, and New Amsterdam's citizens had reached the limits of their patience with Stuyvesant. Ninety-three of the colony's most important men sent Stuyvesant a letter, angrily demanding that he face reality. They expressed astonishment at Nicolls's patience: "that he should have granted us so long a reprieve, inasmuchas he could have delivered us as a prey and a plunder to the soldiery after one summons." Among the signers was Stuyvesant's eldest son, Balthazar. Stuyvesant finally relented.

Two days later—September 6, 1664—Dutch and English representatives gathered at Stuyvesant's Bowery estate to view the articles of capitulation. On September 8, "their Gouvernor with a silver leg" (so described by British travel writer John Josselyn, a contemporary) signed the papers. One of the stipulations read that from then on "this place is not to be called otherwise than New-York, on the island of

Manhattans, in America." Then came the ceremony marking the formal transfer of power: Dutch militia marched out of the fort that Cryn Fredericks had laid out nearly forty years earlier, beating drums and flying their colors.

Not a shot was fired. The terms of surrender offered to the Dutch were extremely generous. The English were acting purely out of common sense; suppressing their new subjects would only damage the colony's commercial value. There were no English merchants in their new territory, so they needed the Dutch to remain and keep the trade going. Therefore, as subjects of the Crown, the English granted the Dutch the right to live, worship, and travel freely within the former New Netherland, and to keep all their property. But the magnanimousness of the English did not extend to all inhabitants. The English were far less relaxed about matters of race than the Dutch, and they did not like that black people owned land along the Bowery. Indeed, soon after the Dutch surrender, they questioned Stuyvesant whether these freed slaves legally held title to their properties. Stuyvesant assured the new overlords that they did.

Stuyvesant, stripped of his title and job, retreated to his Bowery estate and buried himself in the considerable paperwork involved with the transfer of power. He and Richard Nicolls, whom the Duke of York appointed governor of England's new colony, got on splendidly. So even with the loss of New Netherland, life wasn't so bad for Stuyvesant. He still had his little paradise on the Bowery. Indeed, purchasing this land from the Dutch West India Company fourteen years earlier had been one of the best decisions of his life. Maybe the best. But Stuyvesant's reprieve was brief: in October 1665, he was forced to return to Holland at the Company's insistence to deliver in person to the States General his detailed report on his surrender of New Amsterdam to the English. The government took its time reading over his document, and in the meanwhile, he was not allowed to return to the place that had indisputably become his home. After two miserable, lonely years in the Hague, the Company finally permitted Stuyvesant to leave. He lived out his remaining years on his Bowery estate with his family. His

Bust of Stuyvesant, St. Mark's Church in-the-Bowery

friend, Governor Nicolls, was said to have visited him often there, and the village Stuyvesant had started continued to grow (in 1702, it had 400 residents). After his death, Stuyvesant's heirs remained on the family property for generations and enlarged it by buying up adjoining lots. (Two descendants built mansions on the estate.) Stuyvesant's remains are buried in the crypt of St. Mark's Church in–the–Bowery, the funky old Greek Revival church that was built in 1799 on the land where his private chapel once stood. And what a lovely place this is. During the past one hundred years, what began as a place to worship God evolved with the surrounding neighborhood to double as a performance space for all kinds of fringy artistic expression. In the 1960s, as the surrounding East Village became poorer and ravaged by drugs, St. Marks also became involved with local grassroots groups. Today, dance and poetry readings are still performed there regularly. People swear that sometimes they can hear the *tap-tap-tap* of Stuyvesant's peg leg at night in the sanctuary. Perhaps his ghost also steps outside and carefully picks its way between the worn-out gravestones in the courtyard. Or perhaps it was watching as a young Patti Smith, later regaled as the godmother of punk, first cut her performing chops there back in 1971. No doubt the old codger would have disapproved of her.

CHAPTER THREE

BOWERY LANE

Stand at the southern end of the Bowery today, at Chatham Square, where seven other streets also crazily converge—Park Row, East Broadway, Doyers, Worth, Oliver, St. James, and Division streets. Take it all in around you: the people, so many of them young and hungry and beautiful, the taxis and the cars—Uber!—the buses and the trucks, the energy and the noise. Then look north, where the Bowery begins, and follow your gaze uptown. Notice all the half-finished glass towers that are going up, some as high as sixty stories, imperiously dwarfing the old brick walk-ups (some of which predate the Civil War) that house artists, Chinese families, and small businesses. They remain vibrant fixtures of the neighborhood, give it its character, and are as beloved by neighborhood residents as ancient relatives with memories. But they are endangered. Hungry New York developers obsess over knocking them down and building in their places yet more skyscrapers, which they excitedly fantasize will net them hundreds of millions of dollars in profits. So they offer the owners of these shabby little structures handsome sums, to which many succumb. And soon their tenants, some of whom have been living in those buildings or running businesses there all their lives, get pushed out by the new owners eager to capitalize on their investments. Real estate in New York brings out the very worst in the people who profit the most from it, because while prices rise and fall, the value remains absolute. The Dutch founded New Amsterdam not as a religious refuge but as a place to do business, and this remains Manhattan's ethos to this day.* The British couldn't possibly have appreciated the value of the settlement—still mostly forest with farms carved out here and there—that they took from the Dutch in 1665 and renamed New York. To them, it was just one more addition to their growing empire.

The Duke of York was no fool. He knew that for his new colony's economy to keep moving, he had to keep Dutch businessmen happy. For their part, the businessmen were thrilled to be rid of Peter Stuyvesant and fawned over Governor Nicolls. Under "this intelligent and wise gentlemen," they wrote to the Duke of York one month after the English takeover, they would bloom "like the cedars on Lebanon." So the transition from New Amsterdam to New York was feeling like a win-win for everybody, and it proceeded as smoothly as cream pours out of a ewer and into a saucer. Nicolls immediately reestablished a municipal government, in which he—and also the governor who succeeded him, Francis Lovelace—deliberately included Dutch appointees, even to the mayorship.† Lovelace started a social club, which met weekly. "Its sixteen members—ten Dutch, six English—gathered at one another's houses to discuss matters of common concern and drink punch from silver tankards." Dutch businessmen, gratified by all this attention, showed their appreciation by hosting their English overlords at luxurious dinner parties in their homes— think of scenes right out of the old masters' paintings, with tables loaded with all those luscious local ingredients that chroniclers raved

---

* As Russell Shorto showed us in his beautifully written *The Island in the Center of the World*.
† Cornelis Steenwyck, who had been a leading businessman in New Amsterdam, was twice appointed mayor of New York: in 1668 and again in 1682.

about—oysters and shad and game birds—all served on lovely blue-and-white faience plates. Englishmen looking for business opportunities were immigrating to New York and marrying Dutch women. An Anglo-Dutch-Huguenot aristocracy of sorts—Knickerbockers these folks came to be called, after the pseudonym used by Washington Irving in his satire about Dutch New York—began to take shape. They built mansions inside the city—then bounded by what is now Wall Street—and began to eye the swampy, hilly properties along "the road to Sapokanikan," which they were soon calling Bowery Lane. These lands became even more valuable after 1673, when Bowery Lane became the southernmost leg of a comprehensive postal highway system that the British built to link New York to Boston via Connecticut. The King's Highway, a.k.a. the Boston Post Road, began at the tip of Manhattan and stretched north through the woods all the way to Nieuw Haarlem and through what is now the Bronx and beyond. As a result, traffic was increasing along the Bowery, which provided a further incentive for the wealthy to snap up the property along the road's flanks, which was mostly empty except for the few taverns and the area around the Collect, where a handful of families—black, white, and mixed race—were cultivating small farms. Within twenty years or so, nearly all the black owners were gone. They had either sold their plots or were pushed out by the racially intolerant British. In fact, the lives of all black people in New York, whether slaves or freemen, worsened after the British takeover. Slave trade increased, and slavery was codified into law. In the meantime, families whose names came to grace New York streets and parks—the Bayards, Rutgerses, Delanceys, Brevoorts, and Van Cortlandts—were building lovely country estates with mansions set far at the ends of tree-lined driveways on their newly purchased acreage. More taverns opened along the Bowery, foreshadowing what the street would become best known for. Besides the Half-Mile near the Collect, where everybody went to draw the famously delicious water from the tea pump, and Thomas Hall's Plow and Harrow at the bend, there was

Rebecca's House at the corner of Sand Hill Road, now Astor Place.* Rebecca was married to Adriaen Cornelissen, who was the official brander of all the horses and cattle in Manhattan. Passersby often stopped by Rebecca's for a glass of beer out of a barrel that the couple ordered weekly from a local brewer; but when the couple obtained a license to make their own beer and to also sell wine and liquor, their business soared. Their home brew tasted so good that Rebecca's became a destination, and just as the Bowery has ever since, it attracted a rowdy crowd. (Today, some 450 years later, places that offer fancy craft beers are a fixture along the Bowery.) Jasper Danckaerts, a member of a crazy evangelical sect who came to New York from the Netherlands in 1679 to start a religious colony, dropped in to Rebecca's one day, and he was outraged. The worst sort of people hung out there he afterward wrote indignantly in his journal. The place so offended him that he had to run outside into a nearby orchard "to seek pleasure in contemplating the innocent objects of nature." Danckaerts found Rebecca's through her aged parents, who ran the inn where he was staying. ("Don't you want to taste the beer of New Netherlands?" her father asked him.) Afterward, Danckaerts reprimanded the old couple for sending him to their daughter's tavern. He had to reprimand them: God, he believed, compelled him. Danckaerts did not remain long in New York, where, he complained in his diary, "the world and the godless hated and shunned us." He next went to Maryland, tried to set up his colony there, and failed.

On the other side of the Bowery from Rebecca's was John Clapp's tavern, where, every June 24, on Saint John the Baptist Day, Clapp hosted a feast exclusively for men named John, so that they "may find a hearty wellcome to joyn in consort with his namesakes." He also

---

* Early maps of New York reveal the presence of sandhills in the area from Lafayette to Hudson Street. The hills were leveled in the early nineteenth century, when New York's street grid was laid out.

operated a hackney coach service—according to him, New York's first—out of his tavern and rented out horses. He was also the Bowery's official poundkeeper (in charge of rounding up all stray animals). Clapp was a restless sort who had endless ideas on how to make money. In 1680, he'd immigrated from England to South Carolina, where he acquired three plantations in the settlement in Charleston. After being widowed twice in South Carolina, he moved to New York in 1690. By then all the goods from the southern colonies passed through New York to be shipped to England, and therefore it was the place for any businessman worth his salt. Clapp bought five acres along the Bowery, on which he built a house and his tavern. He married again, had two sons with his new wife, Dorothy, and acquired three slaves, which was nothing unusual; virtually all households in New York then had slaves. A few free blacks still owned small lots along the Bowery; in 1696 Clapp bought one of the lots from Daniel Bastiense, who'd inherited the land from his father. The lot next to Clapp's property belonged to Solomon Peters, a freed slave who was also a doctor. (In 1694, Solomon had made Clapp one of the executors of his will, so the two must have enjoyed a friendship together.)

Clapp sold his five-acre farm in 1697 and found himself with too much time on his hands. So he wrote an almanac ("having little else to do"), New York's first. It was published by William Bradford, the city's first printing house, which would also publish the *New York Gazette*, the city's first newspaper, which ran from 1725 to 1744. Clapp's almanac was filled with tasty and practical bits of information: "a plaine and easie table shewing the True time of high water in New-York City every day of the Moon's age," a description of the Post Road to Boston and inns "where Travellers may be accommodated &c." Soon, Clapp again grew restless and moved with his wife and children to parts north—Westchester and Connecticut, where he died sometime before 1725.

The gregarious Clapp moved in the same circles as Stephen De Lancey, a Huguenot refugee whose name was quickly Americanized to Delancey and was later conferred on a Lower East Side street. Delancey, who came to New York in 1686 and quickly amassed a fortune, was born Etienne De Lanci in Caen, in Normandy, in 1663, into a noble family. The De Lancis had served the French kings since the 1400s, despite the fact that they were Protestants. In 1685, after Louis XIV revoked the Edict of Nantes, which had protected French Protestants since 1598, Etienne, along with many other Huguenots, fled France, leaving behind his title and ancestral lands. He was an only child. His father, Jacques De Lanci, had died years earlier; his mother, Marguerite, was still alive, but she was too old to accompany her son. She went into hiding in Caen. Before Etienne departed, his *maman* gave him a stash of family jewels, which he hid in his clothing.

From France, Etienne went to Holland—long a refuge for persecuted Huguenots—but he did not stay. Instead he proceeded to England, where he swore allegiance to the King on March 11, 1686 (through a now long-obsolete process called denization). From then on he was known as Stephen Delancey. Two months later, he arrived at his final destination: the rough, young city of New York.

He immediately felt at home. New York's then openly expressed hatred of anything Catholic naturally warmed his heart, but for that alone he could have remained in liberal-leaning Holland, along with the many Huguenots who had found refuge there. What appealed to him most about New York was its free-for-all nature of doing business. Europe had guilds and restrictions based on class and whatnot, but in New York you did anything the hell you wanted.

So Delancey cashed in his mother's jewelry and jumped right into the game. His first major venture was in furs; as a native French speaker, he had an advantage when it came to trading with Canadians. He then branched into other lucrative commodities: cocoa, wheat, Madeira wine, West Indian rum, opium, and slaves. Delancey limited his slave trading (mostly) to Madagascar, the huge offshore trading hub off Africa's southeastern coast, because he could purchase Malagasy slaves for far less than those in the Caribbean or Africa.

Traders would then ship their human cargo to New York and sell them for a huge profit. Madagascar was also known for rewarding traders who brought merchandise there with outlandishly high prices, paid by pirates who had recently settled in Madagascar and acted as middlemen to slave dealers. For a time, Delancey had his own agent—"factor"—in Madagascar, one Giles Shelley, who parked his wife and son on his farm somewhere along the Bowery while he conducted his boss's affairs abroad. He regularly sailed his sloop, the *Nassau*, out of New York, loaded with all kinds of goods to sell to the Malagasy middlemen. They particularly loved those exquisite New York oysters. There were two kinds: those pickled in mace, allspice, black pepper, and vinegar, and the ones packed in earthenware vessels after being fried in butter, over which was poured more butter to preserve the oysters. Then Shelley would return to New York with human cargo to be sold at the slave market located conveniently at the harbor (at what is now Wall Street, between Pearl and Water).

Delancey's business acumen extended to his choice of a bride: in 1700 he married one of the nine daughters of Stephanus van Cortlandt, a member of one of New York's wealthiest and best-connected families. For himself and his new wife, Anne, Delancey built a luxurious mansion with a water view just north of the just-erected Trinity Church. Next to his house, he built a warehouse to store his merchandise.

Stephen Delancey then entered politics, which was usual for a man of his position. He served first as an alderman, then as a member of the King's Council (all positions were appointed by the Crown). Life in New York was so good for Delancey that France and the ancestral properties that he had been stripped of were receding from his memory. A portrait of him shows a big, fleshy man with small eyes and full lips, exuding a gouty, contented prosperity. Delancey, who was deeply religious, helped build L'Eglise du Saint-Esprit, a French Protestant church on Pine Street. But later he joined the Anglican Church, the final step in his assimilation to New York's merchant elite. Anne and Stephen Delancey had ten children, of whom only five survived to adulthood. When he died in 1741, bells rang in all the New York churches: Anglican, Dutch, and French. He was buried at Trinity Church, in his own vault.

Delancey passed his enormous wealth on to his four sons and daughter, along with his Anglophilia. He sent his eldest son, James, born in 1703, to England to study at Cambridge. When James returned to America, he entered politics and ascended the ladder: in 1735, then-governor William Cosby appointed Delancey second chief justice of the court. A few months later, James Delancey presided over the trial of John Peter Zenger, a German-born printer accused of publishing "false, scandalous, and malicious libel" in his newspaper against Governor Cosby. Zenger's lawyer, a silver-tongued litigator from Philadelphia named Andrew Hamilton, did not dispute that Zenger's paper had printed the articles in question. But he put forward what was, for the times, a shocking argument: in order for a statement to be libelous, it had to be false. Hamilton's stunning logic, coupled with his eloquence, flustered Judge Delancey. He told the jury that it was his—the judge's—prerogative to judge the law, not theirs. But the jury balked, and it took them only ten minutes to acquit Zenger. The Zenger trial established the principle of a free press in the English colonies. It also split New York into pro- and anti-crown factions; and Delancey got the plum job for his loyalty to the Crown in 1757, when King George II appointed him governor.*

All the while, James Delancey was accumulating properties along the Bowery. Most of his holdings were on the eastern side, extending through what is today the Lower East Side, through the salt marshes filled with cattails and herons and all the way to Corlears Hook and the water's edge. He acquired some land on the Bowery's west side, too, including Thomas Hall's Plow and Harrow at the curve. He changed the name of the tavern to the Delancey Arms, rented it to a

* His official title was: "His Majesty's Lieutenant Governor and Commander over the Colony of New York, and Territories depending thereon in America." *New York Mercury*, February 19, 1759.

proprietor, and introduced there the cruel but popular sport of bull-baiting, in which various animals—a dog bred to attack was a favorite choice—were set upon a bull, of which there was a ready supply from the nearby cattle farms. As the patrons stood around swilling beer, taking bets, and cheering, the two creatures went at each other until one was gored or bitten to death.

Altogether Delancey's holdings totaled some 300 acres, some of which he turned into his country estate. On one of the parcels—40 acres between what are today Delancey and Rivington streets—a previous owner had erected a brick house, set all the way back to what is now Chrystie Street, one block east of the Bowery. (Originally this piece of property consisted of three plots that Kieft had granted in 1643 to freed slaves; since then, it had changed hands several times.) Delancey enlarged this house into a mansion. He planted trees along the drive leading up to it. In back, he planted gardens; farther back, he built stables and a paddock for the many horses that he and his brother Oliver by then had acquired, which he raced on an adjoining private track. Next to the stables, Delancey planted orchards—and thus was derived the name of New York's Orchard Street, which some 200 years later would be crowded with tenement houses and Jewish immigrants, some of them commandeering pushcarts piled up with such homely necessities as old clothing, fish, cheap cooking utensils, potatoes, and onions. Delancey left the rest of his property as it was when he acquired it—fields, shipyards, rope walks—and leased it to entrepreneurs. This netted him a huge income.

James Delancey died of an asthma attack one stifling summer day in 1760. One of his sons, also named James, inherited the Bowery farm. Deciding it was time to develop the property, James had it surveyed. Then he had streets cut through it, according to a grid, as if anticipating the grid that would be imposed over the city some fifty years later that is such a proud point with New Yorkers. "It's so easy to find your way around Manhattan!" they love to brag. The new streets on Delancey's estate framed an English-style "grand square," and thus we have Grand, Orchard, and Delancey streets on the Lower

East Side. Delancey had other things on his mind then, too, such as trying to hold on to his family's political clout. But the political environment was changing: England's passage of the Stamp Act in 1765, which
imposed a tax on every piece of paper used in the colony, invoked a
furious reaction from the inhabitants. Loyalists were starting to feel
vulnerable, and Delancey, sensing which way the wind was blowing, aligned himself with the Sons of Liberty. Therefore the Delanceys regained control of the New York Assembly. But James's turnabout
was just a front: in reality, he remained a passionate loyalist, and he
made sure the King knew it.

Next to Delancey's estate, Dutchman Harmanus Rutgers owned a
farm that occupied the footprint of the original bouwerie number six
that Cryn Fredericks had laid out. Harmanus died in 1753. His son,
Hendrick Rutgers, inherited the farm. He had it surveyed and laid out
in rectangular plots at the same time as Delancey, and in 1765, the two
drew up a boundary—this became Division Street—between their respective lands. Rutgers built a mansion on his property with bricks
that were brought over as ballast from the Netherlands. (The mansion was demolished in 1885.) On the other side of the Bowery from
the Delancey estate were some 200 swampy, hilly acres that belonged
to Nicholas Bayard, grandnephew of Peter Stuyvesant. Like Delancey,
he was of Huguenot descent and a loyalist. Bayard's property included
what is now Soho, stretching from Broome Street—this was the driveway to his property—and ending at the northern edges of the Collect. His land included the 110-foot-high hill just north of where the
Werpoes settlement was, and he decided to name it Bayard's Hill.

The old tavern that everybody called the Half-Way House—it
stood just north of the old Dutch windmill—also stood on what was
now Bayard's land. Stagecoaches headed for Albany or Boston used the
Half-Way as a depot.

In 1749, Bayard was granted the right to operate the municipal
slaughterhouse on his property. He knew nothing about butchering,
but he nabbed it because he was an alderman and had clout. This
represented one sweet deal for him: by law, butchers could only

slaughter their cattle at the public abattoir, for which service they were charged a fee. This was galling to the butchers: the previous year they had petitioned the city to build and operate the abattoir but had been turned down.

Bayard's lease ran for twenty-one years, for which he would pay in rent to the city "the yearly fee of one peppercorn." All profits would be his, and they would be considerable: New York's population was then increasing and with it the demand for fresh meat.

Bayard's property provided a perfect location: it was far enough outside the city proper—where people were paying a lot of money for property on which to build homes—that the merchants delighting in the lovely sides of beef gracing their dinner tables didn't have to witness the actual butchering of the cattle, which was messy and ugly and smelled terrible.

Bayard built the new abattoir behind the Half-Way House, on the corner of Bayard and Mulberry streets—the latter so named for the trees that lined it, but Revolutionary-era maps label it "Slaughter House Street." He enlarged and fenced the surrounding pastures to accommodate the cattle being brought there for the kill and had a painted sign hung over the door of the Half-Way House depicting the head of a ferocious bull. Soon people were calling it the Bull's Head Tavern. Here, butchers who came up from the main food market at the marshy area at the tip of Manhattan Island where most of them operated their stalls—it was called the Fly Market, from the Dutch word *vly* or "meadow"—drank beer out of barrels and made deals with the cattle drivers who'd brought their herds to sell. Today, on the site of the Bull's Head, a twenty-one-story four-star boutique hotel stands, complete with a rooftop bar that sports a dress code: "Sorry no sweats, tanks, cargos, or flip-flops—think Downtown Chic." The actual slaughtering of animals was restricted to the middle of the night; and between one and six every morning, no matter how terrible the weather might be, butchers loaded their slabs of meat onto carts to the light of tin lanterns and pushed their haul down the bumpy surface of Slaughter House Street—a horrible road, but the shortest

Bull's Head Tavern

way to the Fly Market. Today, every September, for ten days, strings of bulbs gaudily light up the night along this same route as crowds gorge on all manner of artery-clogging Neapolitan-style goodies at the Feast of San Gennaro.

Bayard's abattoir made the Bowery synonymous with the meat business. Butchers were moving up to the Bowery and building wooden houses there in which they lived and operated their shops. Tanneries, an obvious outgrowth of slaughtering cattle, were also opening up around the banks of the Collect. The city's only source of drinking water, already being tainted by runoff from the nearby breweries, was now becoming a repository for the slimy throwaway of slaughtered livestock—blood, bones, whole carcasses—and the nasty by-products resulting from turning hides into leather. Then, as now, economic growth was polluting the environment.

The meat business was making Nicholas Bayard a whole lot of money, but he was doing a terrible job of running the public slaughterhouse. He refused to clean it or make necessary repairs, so butchers were forced to operate under filthy conditions. The water pump was always out of order, so they couldn't wash the blood off anything—the floors, the hooks, the knives—after they finished slaughtering the animals. Instead, it just collected in slimy red pools, feasted upon by flies. Then the next animal was killed and the next, adding more blood to what was already festering on the floor. The stench never got washed away. In 1760, twenty-two butchers delivered a petition to the city council with a list of complaints ("the pump having been out of order for six or seven years") about the deplorable conditions inside Bayard's. But once again, their voices were ignored. Bayard died a wealthy man in November 1765, one month after the British Parliament enacted the Stamp Act, which marked the beginning of a decade of unrest that would explode into full-blown revolution. In the meantime, life went on. Bayard left the bulk of his Bowery estate to his son, also Nicholas, who, like Bayard *père*, was a loyalist and an alderman. Nicholas fils immediately cleaned up the abattoir—one of the first things he did was to fix the pump—and hired Richard Varian, one of a family of butchers who operated in the Fly Market, to oversee it. He then added running the Bull's Head to Varian's job description. The butcher moved into the rooms above the tavern and invested some of his own money into Bayard's operation, which was making money hand over fist. So life was good for Nicholas Bayard—until 1776, when he fled New York soon after George Washington and his troops arrived to ready the city for war with the British. This was a smart move for Bayard, because Washington's soldiers were having a great time torturing any loyalists they came across, and the general was doing nothing to stop them. Their preferred methods included tarring and feathering and "riding the rail," which consisted of forcing a victim to straddle a spiked wooden fence rail, preferably one with lots of splinters, hoisting it up on their shoulders, and marching around to the cheers of onlookers. Bayard spent the war on Long Island, where he joined a loyalist brigade led by James Delancey's uncle, Oliver Delancey.

Back in Manhattan, the Continental troops immediately seized the Bayard estate. An entire brigade—Stirling's Fourth—moved in, set up camp in the marshy fields, and pockmarked them with barricades. Then another, Lasher's New York Independent, came in and cut down all the cedar trees that covered Bayard's Hill. At the top, from which you could see all of Manhattan, they constructed a fort: "a powerful irregular heptagonal redoubt, mounting eight nine-pounders, four three-pounders, and six royal and cohorn mortars." It took the men six months to complete the job, which they executed so beautifully that when they finished, Washington thanked them personally. The abattoir and Bull's Head, though, were allowed to keep operating: the troops after all needed to be fed and boozed. Richard Varian had skipped town to join a privateering operation against the British. But he was soon captured and sent to a Halifax prison.

Varian's wife then stepped in for him to manage the Bull's Head, which must have presented quite a challenge: the couple had sixteen children.

Troops also built a fortified line along Grand Street, across the Bowery and right through the Delancey estate. General Washington moved into James Delancey's mansion—the latter had fled to England—and used it as his country headquarters. His army numbered about 10,000. With New York's population then totaling around 22,000 souls, the soldiers' presence made for a sudden and drastic increase in the city's numbers. The soldiers were billeted in the mansions of other wealthy New York merchants; some of these places, one of them wrote in a letter home, accommodated six hundred men— "sickly, filthy, divided, and unruly . . . If the owners ever get possession, they must be years in cleaning them." Smallpox broke out among some of the troops. With all the extra mouths to feed in New York, essential goods—sugar, molasses, flour, pins—were becoming scarce and causing merchants to raise their prices. Every day, rumors flew that the invasion was imminent, and panicked civilians were fleeing the city.

But in September 1776, after two back-to-back defeats for Washington—first in Brooklyn, then at Kips Bay—the general ordered the troops to evacuate to Harlem Heights. Before leaving, he considered burning New York down rather than leaving it practically empty and newly fortified—like a shiny new gift—to the British, but the Continental Congress vetoed the idea. Ironically, Washington got his wish anyway, when on a hot September night just six days after the British took New York, a fire—said to be started by patriots who had stayed behind, perhaps for that very reason—broke out in a British-frequented whorehouse at Whitehall Slip, on Manhattan's southern tip. A southeast wind pushed the flames quickly through the city and to the north. By the time British soldiers put out the fire, one-quarter of the city was reduced to smoking, charred detritus. It was then that most of the structures that the Dutch had built were lost, including nearly 500 houses, which, made of wood, fed the flames like kindling. Trinity Church also burned down.

Besides turning the city into a smoldering hell, the fire created a logistical nightmare for the British: with some 26,000 of their troops now occupying New York, there were few places to billet them. Tent cities sprung up in the burnt zone, which extended west as far as Broadway. The flames had spared the Bowery, but it was a wasteland anyway. All the structures along the sides that the American troops had been occupying, from grand mansions to the crude wooden taverns and butchers' houses, stood empty once more, their insides filthy and abused; and the Bowery's packed-dirt surface had been so trampled by thousands upon thousands of soldiers—first Continental and now British—that if it were a living being, it would have been bruised black-and-blue. But nothing stayed empty for long. A company of cavalrymen, the Seventeenth Dragoons, filled many of the houses, one of which was used for storing gunpowder. Another house was appropriated by a group of prostitutes attached to the Thirty-seventh Regiment. It became known as the Casina. The British were now piling more rocks along the defense line that the bluecoats had built six months earlier that went along Grand Street, across the Bowery, and through the Delancey estate's gardens and orchards. The properties had been neglected since the previous spring and were full of weeds, and the fruit trees that hadn't been cut down to accommodate the barrier had been stripped by hungry soldiers. The mansion was turned into a military hospital, as was the nearby Rutgers mansion. So was the Plow and Harrow, across the way from the Delancey farm. But the

Bull's Head continued to operate as a tavern—Mrs. Varian, as a patriot, was relieved of her duties—and it became a center for recruiting loyalist volunteers. Just behind the Bull's Head, Hessian troops were using Bayard's Hill to conduct exercises. Bayard's abattoir stayed open, but with the British occupation all the old laws that governed New York no longer applied. So nobody was overseeing the abattoir; nor were butchers compelled any longer to slaughter their cattle there. The butchers were now doing their own slaughtering anywhere they liked; and the bloodstained abattoir, in a macabre example of readapting unused space, was being used mostly as a bullbaiting arena: that is, a torture chamber for animals.

For seven years, the British held on to New York. When they finally evacuated the city on November 25, 1783, the redcoats travelled down the Bowery and through Chatham Square, traversed Pearl Street, and continued to the docks at the East River. There, they piled into rowboats, which carried them to the waiting fleet. A few hours later, the American soldiers, led by General Knox, followed the same path the redcoats had just taken down the Bowery to Lower Manhattan. At Bowling Green, two patriot soldiers shimmied up the flagpole, with difficulty—in a final act of spite, the retreating army had greased it—hauled down the Union Jack, and replaced it with the new American flag. General Knox then turned his horse around, rode back up Broadway to Chatham Square, and continued north, along the Bowery. Thousands of people crowded along the sides of the road, cheering him on. Knox and his party came to a stop at the Bull's Head Tavern—Mrs. Varian by then had resumed her duties as hostess—where General Washington and New York governor George Clinton were waiting for them. A procession then formed, led by Washington and Clinton on horseback, and followed by army officers and citizens, eight abreast. They proceeded to Fraunces Tavern to celebrate the victory over the Crown.

The British occupation had destroyed New York's infrastructure, along with its economy. But with destruction comes opportunity to regroup and make money—and nowhere more so than New York.

After the war, New York passed a series of harsh forfeiture laws, some of which targeted specific loyalists. Nicholas Bayard was allowed to return to the city and managed to hold on to his property—at the end of the war it lay in ruins—but James Delancey was singled out for special punishment. All his properties were seized. His Bowery estate was carved into lots and sold to the highest bidders to develop as they pleased. A few of the purchasers were Jews, descendants of the Sephardim who'd immigrated to New Amsterdam from Dutch colonies 150 years earlier. But the lion's share of Delancey's lands were snatched up by a young German named Heinrich Ashdore, who would later change his name to Henry Astor. He had a younger brother named John Jacob, and "Astor" would soon become a synonym for New York money.

CHAPTER FOUR

THE ASTORS

John Jacob Astor made his first fortune by trading in furs. After that he did business with China: he started with tea and segued into opium (as the saying goes, behind every great fortune is a crime). And then he invested heavily in New York real estate. He was following the example of his older brother Heinrich, or Henry, who accumulated a lot of properties in Manhattan after the Revolution, mostly on or next to the Bowery.

Heinrich Ashdore was born in 1754, the second of four sons, in the area called the Palatinate, now in southern Germany. His father was a butcher. Astor came to America as a Hessian in the Revolutionary War. He worked as a sutler, that is, he followed the troops around and sold them provisions. He soon realized that he had a talent for selling things, which he was wasting by limiting his customers to British soldiers. So he deserted. We next catch up with Henry in 1784, when he became a naturalized citizen and married Dorothy Pessenger, a butcher's daughter. Her father, a German born in the then-English colonies, came to New York via Stone Arabia, an upstate town founded in the early 1700s by German Anabaptists (yet another one of Europe's many persecuted Protestant sects) in the gentle hills near the Mohawk River. (These were the first Europeans to colonize the area, which today is home to an Amish population.) In New York, Pessenger found an apprenticeship with a German butcher in the Fly Market, where he soon obtained his own stall. He then built a house on the Bowery on a lot he'd bought from among the forfeited properties of James Delancey.

For a while, Henry Astor worked at his father-in-law's butcher shop along with his wife, Dorothy. Henry adored Dorothy and kept her decked out in gorgeous clothes. The couple had no children. Astor soon made enough money to open his own butcher stall at the Fly Market and shortly after figured out a way to undercut his competition: He'd hang out at the Bull's Head with the other butchers while they were waiting for the cattle drivers to arrive with their livestock to be slaughtered at the abattoir. As soon as he heard the sounds of lowing cattle being led down the Bowery, Astor offered to buy drinks for everybody. When the butchers got good and drunk, Astor would quietly slip out the back door, mount his horse, and ride up the Bowery to intercept the cattle drivers before they arrived at the Bull's Head to conduct their business. This gave Astor the opportunity to choose which cattle to buy before the competition had a chance to look over the beasts. Word soon spread that Henry Astor's market stall had New York's best meat, which, along with the food shortage brought on by the war and its messy aftermath, enabled him to command sky-high prices for his beef.

Astor used the profits he made from butchering to buy up land. Along the Bowery, he followed his father-in-law's lead and snapped up some of Delancey's forfeited properties. He also bought most of Nicholas Bayard's war-ravaged estate. The latter was flat broke, so even though he managed to reclaim his land, it was impossible for him to bring it back to life with its tramped-down fields and denuded woods. He was resigned to losing it, but he was happy to see that shithole of an abattoir become somebody else's problem. By then the place had been operating—unregulated and never having been cleaned—for some nine years, mostly as a venue for animal fights.

Astor did not have enough cash to buy the Bayard properties outright, so the two men struck a deal: in 1785, Bayard leased his land to Astor for one year "for one peppercorn." In return, Astor promised to find the money to buy the property. In the meantime, he started cleaning it up. He even got some help from the Common Council: that same year they deemed the abattoir on his new property a health hazard and voted to move the public facility to Corlears Hook, on the East River. The following year, Astor bought most of Bayard's land outright. Richard Varian, who had been released from prison in Nova Scotia and was back in New York, still owned a piece of the Bull's Head, but in 1825 Astor acquired that as well.

People thought Henry Astor was nuts to buy all that depressed land. What was he going to do with it? How could his investments make him any money in their current state? Astor did not have enough cash on hand to improve his new properties, and nobody had any to lend him; New York's economy stood paralyzed by war loans. One newspaper wrote: "Cash! Cash! O Cash! Why hast thou deserted the Standard of Liberty? And made poverty and dissipation our distinguishing characteristic?"

But Henry's instincts were right on the mark. Not only were land prices low, but rents were *high*, indeed twice as high as before the war. This was due to a severe housing shortage resulting from the war and the 1776 fire. At the same time, New York's population was exploding. In 1783 it totaled around 12,000; three years later, it had doubled; by 1820, it had risen to 124,000. Most of the new immigrants were German or Irish, and they all had to live somewhere, as did the artisans in the city proper at the tip of Manhattan who were now getting priced out as the city's economy was recovering: *plus ça change, plus c'est la même chose.** And there was Henry Astor, sitting with all that empty property along the Bowery. He had a gold mine on his hands, and he knew it. He also had competition in the form of a younger brother who had landed in New York just as Henry was closing the deal on the old Bayard estate. Henry was not happy at the arrival of John Jacob

---

* The more things change, the more they stay the same.

Astor—yes, *the* John Jacob, whose eponymous descendants would embody the Gilded Age in New York. John had been living in London, where he and another Astor brother, George, had a successful business manufacturing woodwind instruments. But New York beckoned. John's first job there consisted of peddling donuts and cookies from a basket for a German baker named George Dieterich, who'd known the Astors back in the old country. From there, he graduated to beating the moths out of animal skins for a fur dealer, which is how he got started in the fur trade. During those first hard days in New York, he asked his big brother Henry for a $200 loan. Henry balked. Finally, he offered John half the amount—on the condition that he never asked him for money again. John accepted Henry's mean-spirited offer and used the loan to acquire his own pelts, which he peddled from a backpack, along with cheap jewelry and toys. Soon John was travelling up to Albany and Utica to buy furs from Indians. He then shipped the furs to London, thereby earning four times the price that New York paid. All the while, he was shipping woodwind instruments from London and selling them in New York.

Buy and sell, buy and sell—John Astor saved all his money. In 1789 he bought his first property: a few Bowery lots, for which he paid 47 pounds. The seller was his brother Henry. At that point, as much as the two brothers resented each other, they grudgingly understood that partnering would benefit them both financially. (Think of the Koch brothers today.) John then began investing in land simultaneously with Henry, along and near the Bowery and around Manhattan.

The Astor brothers' credo was to buy land when prices were low, hold on to it, and wait for their holdings to appreciate. Occasionally they flipped their properties, but only so as to buy more. They were not only patient but also cheap: they spent as little as possible on their investments. Once in a while they built on their lots, but most often they left it to their tenants to make improvements. Soon they owned a good chunk of Bowery properties and others all around Manhattan. They also left behind a meticulous paper trail of their real estate transactions. Their detailed ledgers document all their expenses, down to the last nail and plank. They carefully staggered their leases so that all would not terminate simultaneously. They squeezed every possible cent out of their tenants: besides rent, the latter also had to pay the owner's real estate taxes and property repairs—a custom that persists in New York to the present day.

No wonder they developed a reputation for stinginess.

These "customary and standard" practices in today's overblown New York real estate started with the Astors.

Besides collecting rents and not paying for improvements, the brothers found other creative ways to make money off their land. Sometimes they financed mortgages to buyers of their property, which, because of the interest paid, netted the Astors more money. Often these were "balloon" mortgages, meaning that the new lessee was paying off only the interest on the property until the loan came due, at which point he had to come up with a big payment to be applied to the principal. If he couldn't come up with the cash, the lender repossessed. Voila! A win-win for the Astor brothers.

As the Astor brothers were building their real estate empire, Henry held on to his butcher stall. But he didn't run it; he left it in the care of a journeyman—that is, somebody who was not licensed. Other butchers complained formally to the Common Council in 1801 about Henry Astor's habit of riding into the country to meet the droves of cattle before others had a chance to have their pick. This gave him an unfair advantage, they said, and caused the price of meat to go up. But there was nothing illegal about Astor's habit, which he had been engaging in ever since he was a young butcher eager to get a leg up on his competition. Granted, he didn't need his butcher stall anymore, what with all his land deals. But he couldn't bring himself to give it up. It was just too profitable. (He finally gave it up in 1807.)

The Astor brothers constituted a new breed of land-rich New Yorker. The old Anglo-Dutch merchant families participated in public life out of civic responsibility, but the Astors shunned civic involvement. Instead, they devoted all their energies to making money. As for philanthropic matters, apart from John Jacob's establishment of the

Astor Library in the mid-1800s—Henry died childless in 1833—it was Vincent Astor, a member of the family's fourth generation, who finally set up a family foundation in the 1950s.

To maximize their profits, the Astors during the 1780s and '90s were dividing up all the Bowery lots they were accumulating and renting them out to small tradesmen, who then built small structures on them, in which they both lived and worked. Astor tenants included sash makers, box makers, cordwainers, hairdressers, grocers, confectioners, wheelwrights, ship caulkers, joiners, washers, carpenters, and blacksmiths—all providers of basic services for the Bowery's growing population. More bodies also translated into increased demand for meat, so butchers continued to operate shops along the Bowery, even though the public abattoir was banished to Corlears Hook in 1785. In fact, butchers were now slaughtering cattle right on the Bowery, in the yards behind their shops. Before the poor beast was slain, it was a local custom for a band to play and follow an animal up and down the thoroughfare. The cruel sport of bullbaiting also continued to draw crowds in the taverns, providers of entertainment for the masses and a perennial Bowery staple. For refined sorts, there was a new place to go and have a good time, also on the Bowery. Vauxhall Gardens, the latest of identically named pleasure "resorts," as places of entertainment were then quaintly called,* occupied a large swathe of land owned by John Astor, just south of the Stuyvesant estate. (Today this is Astor Place, an intersection in the middle of which a black steel sculpture that everybody calls the Cube whimsically perches.) James Delacroix, a Frenchman who'd fled the Reign of Terror during the 1790s, designed and operated Vauxhall Gardens, a genteel confection of graveled paths and colorful gardens adorned with latticework and statuary. In summer, you could dine there al

---

* The original Vauxhall was in London.

fresco on a terrace in front of the greenhouse and watch the firework displays offered there every night along with your champagne and roast duck. There was even an outdoor theater at Vauxhall, where plays were performed by members of New York's most prestigious company, the Park, half of which, incidentally, was owned by John Astor.

As the Bowery's population density increased, its property got chopped up, and its pastoral ambience vanished. Virtually anybody could do business and live there, as long as he could scarf up the rent. Peter Stuyvesant's heirs continued living on his estate at the northern end, but boundaries were drawn between parcels as the generations multiplied. A 110-acre farm along the Bowery next to the Stuyvesant estate—today this area corresponds to the area from First to Fifth streets, including Tompkins Square, once the center of East Village subversiveness—was divided into nine slivers among the descendants of the owner, Philip Minthorne, in 1793. This venerable Knickerbocker clan included, along with Philip's son Mangle, an alderman, and Mangle's son-in-law, who was a governor of New York and then vice president to President James Monroe, his sister, Frances Minthorne. She grew produce on her bit of property and took it by cart every morning before sunrise to a market at the foot of Maiden Lane. She recycled whatever vegetables weren't pretty enough to sell into a compost pile that she let ripen over the winter and then used to fertilize the next year's garden. Everybody knew about Aunt Frankey's gorgeous vegetables. She married and had a lot of children, among them two daughters who also became famous as market women— Aunt Fanny and Aunt Katy. Market women were known to be tough babes; this was hardly the life that the genteel classes of late eighteenth-century New York imagined for their daughters. "Frances," a now-forgotten writer penned in the 1860s, "taught them to know how to earn their livelihood, instead of *not to know how,* as is the fashion of the present day."

As the nineteenth century approached and the Bowery's population grew, so did its land values. Development was happening fast and haphazardly. The Common Council had the power to fix or alter New York's streets or to assess owners to do the same but only on a case-by-case basis. As yet, there were no land-use regulations or zoning laws; New York's grid plan would not be implemented until 1811. So owners did as they pleased. They cut streets through their properties and built whatever structures they wanted on them—until somebody stopped them. However, the absence of regulations sometimes worked against their interests: for example, the physical condition of the Bowery was disgraceful. The road surface was uneven, and in bad weather sections of it were so muddy as to make it impassable. This was, simply, unacceptable: except for Broadway, the Bowery was the only road that led into and out of the city. Finally, after years of complaints to the Common Council by the Astors and Mangle Minthorne, the Bowery was fixed and graded in 1791. Ten years after that, it was paved—"turnpiked"—with cobblestones. And three years after that, owners were assessed to gravel the sidewalks and plant trees along them. (They fought hard against footing the bill and lost.)

Besides the dismal state of the Bowery—along with other roads—there was a myriad of other urgent infrastructure issues in New York that the Common Council, post-Revolution, was attending to. Water was a chronic problem: the Collect to the west of the Bowery, once a sparkling body of water filled with fish and the city's source of drinking water, had become a fetid puddle, surrounded by tanning yards that used it as a dump for their noxious waste. The Collect had started deteriorating after 1730, the year Anthony Rutgers was granted title to it, along with a putrid nearby swamp, on the condition that he drain the latter. He accomplished this within a year, thereby turning the swamp into a lovely meadow. But this project so lowered the Collect's water level that it was no longer connected to its outlet. So for sixty years, the water had been stagnating, its filth leaching into the springs that supplied and drained it. One of those springs supplied the tea water pump at the Bull's Head; but now even the tea water tasted bad. Somebody signing his name as "A Citizen" in the *New-York Gazeteer and the Country Journal* (August 25, 1785) compared the Collect to "a common sewer. It's like a fair every day with whites, and blacks, washing their cloth blankets and things too nauseous to mention; all their sudds and filth are emptied into this pond, besides dead dogs, cats, etc. thrown in daily, and, no doubt, many buckets from that quarter of the town."

Everybody knew that the Collect had to be reckoned with; and within a few years after the British withdrew from New York, people were weighing possible solutions. A French surveyor named Joseph Mangin, who, together with another surveyor, Casimir Goerck, was working on what was to be New York's first real estate map,* proposed building a dock in the pond's deepest area and using it as a shipping depot, reaching from either river via a forty-foot-wide canal. But his idea was soon abandoned and not merely because of the expense. The fact was that the Collect, besides posing serious health issues, was standing in the way of uptown development. As were all those softly rolling hills that surrounded the pond and continued up the Bowery along its western flank.

So the Common Council passed a resolution to drain the Collect. The project began in 1803. Workers dug a forty-foot-wide canal, below street level, along one of the slow-moving streams that flowed from the Collect to the Hudson. Along the stream was a street called Duggan Street after a nearby landowner, but now everybody began calling it Canal Street. (There was talk of making the street a permanent canal, but in the end it was covered with brick and turned into a sewer.) It took five years to complete the task. The draining turned the surrounding area into a stinking miasma. Nearby property

---

* Goerck died in 1798, and Mangin finished the map by himself, which he presented to the Common Council in 1803. But it was, by Mangin's own admission, an idealized plan of a future New York and therefore useless. Nevertheless, it was so beautiful that a few copies survived. See Robert T. Augustyne and Paul E. Cohen, *Manhattan in Maps* (New York: Rizzoli, 1997), 96 ff.

owners—among those whose houses fronted Canal Street was John Jay, Esq. (the first Supreme Court justice and second governor of New York)—complained to the Common Council that their cellars were inundated with water and mud, and the ground around them sinking. After the Collect was emptied, street urchins stood around amusing themselves by throwing stones through the windows of nearby houses and watching carters haul up piles of muck from the pond's bottom. The Council committee tried to figure out how to use this nasty stuff—"decomposed vegetable matter, similar to peat or turf"—as fuel or fertilizer. But for now, it lay about in huge, smelly piles; meanwhile, workers were tearing down the surrounding hills with pickaxes. They shoveled the earth into wheelbarrows, which they emptied into carts that workhorses and oxen then dragged to the chasm that was once the pond. Workers there then emptied the loads, painstakingly, one after another until the Collect was filled. Finally, the swamps surrounding the Collect were covered with sand, in order to make streets and lots. Houses were erected on top of the landfill, but immediately it began to sink. The area had no storm drainage, so it always stayed muddy and wet and provided breeding grounds for mosquitos. Only the poorest people—most of them Irish immigrants or black folks—lived there. By the mid-nineteenth century, this slum—known as the Five Points—was notorious. "The streets are narrow and dirty, the dwellings are foul and gloomy, and the very air seems heavy with misery and crime," James McCabe Jr. lamented in his 1872 guidebook *The Lights and Shadows of New York Life*. "This is the realm of Poverty."

Throughout the draining and than re-filling of the Collect—the entire process took eight years—the Astors continued buying property along the Bowery. And in the middle of the trauma being inflicted on Lower Manhattan's landscape, the state legislature, acting at the behest of the Common Council, in 1807 passed a law requiring that a grid be imposed on the entire island, from North—today Houston—Street, all the way up to 145th Street. Most of this was still open area. But New York was growing so rapidly that the city fathers felt it was urgent to have a blueprint to follow for further development. No longer would

Five Points, 1872

New York's streets be allowed to meander any which way, nor would owners be able to cut streets through their properties however they liked. Landowners naturally objected to limits on what they did with their private property. They must have applied pressure on lawmakers: the plan that John Randel, the engineer who was hired to survey the city, drew up—it took him four years to complete—specifically skirted John Jacob Astor's Vauxhall Gardens and the Stuyvesant estate. Thus, the Bowery and its immediate flanks were spared the imposition of the grid.

John Jacob Astor, however, soon realized that the grid increased property values, because it made the lots uniform and therefore easier to buy and sell. (In 1826, he asked the city to cut Lafayette Place—now Lafayette Street—right through his Vauxhill property.) By then his holdings included the Park Theatre. John Jacob Astor bought the theater, which was built in 1798, in 1806 with a partner, John Beekman, a member of an influential New York family. The Park—located on Park Row—was the place where New York's merchant elite went to be seen. It served up mostly Shakespearean plays, along with the occasional opera (the latter genre had yet to take hold in the New World). The place was a dingy wreck, entered through a filthy alleyway. It was bleeding money when Astor and Beekman purchased it, but within a few years they made it profitable.

By then, John Jacob Astor far exceeded his big brother Henry in wealth, and Henry naturally resented it. Henry had landed in New York first and had lent his little brother the money that got him on his feet. Henry decided to give John Jacob some competition: in the early 1820s, he made plans to build his own theater. It was a dicey business move. By then, New York had two other theaters besides the Park—the Chatham Garden and the Lafayette Circus—but both were struggling. (There was also the African Grove Theatre, at the corner of Bleecker and Mercer, for New York's large black population. There, white patrons sat in a separate section, as did blacks in mainstream theaters.)

But Henry was determined to see his idea through. The question was, Where would he construct his theater?

He chose the Bowery.

CHAPTER FIVE

SHAKESPEARE AND JIM CROW COME TO THE BOWERY THEATRE

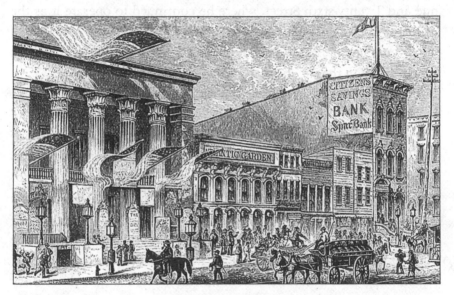

The Bowery Theatre

Next to the glamorous new Hotel 50 Bowery, which rises twenty-two sparkling glass stories up, squats an ugly brown toad of a three-story structure that houses several Chinese-owned stores and restaurants. Three hundred years ago, Bayard's stinky abattoir and adjoining Bull's Head Tavern filled these two sites, both of which Henry Astor bought in 1825 to use for his new theater venture. He then formed a corporation with several of his wealthy friends to finance it. The thought of Henry's theater project irked his brother John Jacob so much that the latter immediately purchased a bunch of parcels from the Stuyvesant heirs' estate at the northern reaches of the Bowery. He would use them to establish a new enclave of wealthy residents.

Oh, those two Astor brothers! As they continued to slug it out over each other's real estate deals, Henry's latest project moved forward. He kept the structure that housed the Bull's Head, on which site the new hotel stands; although he evicted the existing business because he planned to reconfigure it as an inn to go along with his new theater. (The Bull's Head proprietor moved his tavern uptown, to Third Avenue and Twenty-sixth Street, where he continued to operate it as the meeting place for horse and cattle dealers.) But Henry Astor razed what remained of Bayard's abattoir, and good riddance, the neighbors surely said. On the site, he planned his new theater.

Construction began in June 1826; completion of the theater took a mere six months. At the groundbreaking ceremony, Astor's buddy and New York's then-mayor, Philip Hone, laid the cornerstone. The stone had been hollowed out, and inside had been placed several lead boxes filled with newspapers and other memorabilia "to be preserved for the examination of future antiquarians," the New York Mirror wrote on June 24, 1826.*

Hone came from humble beginnings: he started out as a teenage peddler on the docks. From there, he moved into auctioneering, which made him a fortune. When he was forty, Hone took a Henry Jamesian grand tour of Europe, where he acquired expensive tastes and the pretensions of an English gentleman. He entertained visions of Astor's new theater raising New York's artistic and moral stature. At a banquet in Morse's Hotel held immediately after the groundbreaking, Hone made a short speech to attendees, reminding them that it was "incumbent upon those whose standing in society enables them to

---

* The time capsule has yet to be found.

control and direct the opinions of others, to encourage, by their countenance and support, a well-regulated theatre."

The official name of Henry Astor's new venture was the New York Theatre. But as people are apt to cling to any strong associations that they have with a particular place, everybody called it the Bull's Head Theatre. But that association faded away after the Bull's Head relocated, and soon everybody was calling Astor's new structure the Bowery Theatre. The exterior was Greek Revival, a style then all the rage. It had the form of a simple Doric temple, but with only two columns set rather close together on either side of the entrance. This gave the structure a funny look, like a person's face with eyes set too close together. No European city would have allowed a major theater to be designed in such a careless way, but New York didn't care much about style: Size mattered more. Size was what caught peoples' attention, and the just-completed Bowery seated 3,000 people, which made it the biggest theater in America. Moreover, the technology inside was state of the art. Gas lines ran along the walls and at the foot of the stage, from which jets enclosed in individual glass tubes protruded. This arrangement was a recent energy innovation; it was safer and gave much better light than candles.

No question, Henry Astor's new theater was going to steal audiences away from his brother's dingy old Park Theatre. Henry cast about for additional ways to undermine John Jacob Astor, at which point Charles Gilfert, Henry's manager, came up with an idea: All the seats at the Bowery would be priced at fifty cents, whereas the Park charged $1 for box seats and fifty cents for the pit. (At both, the gallery went for twenty-five cents.) Gilfert's plan was a success. On the Bowery's opening night and in the weeks following, the theater was packed. But there was a downside: the poorer folks sat themselves in the upper boxes—right among the genteel classes—and such democratic seating gave pickpockets ample opportunity to ply their trade. One man discovered after the first night's show that somebody had used scissors to remove his wallet from his waistcoat. The well-heeled patrons naturally complained. Two weeks later, Gilfert published an announcement in the newspapers that the theater was ending the one-price policy. He upped box tickets to seventy-five cents, thereby still undercutting the Park's price tag but making this section beyond the reach of poor folks. He kept the fifty-cent price tag for the pit, and the gallery would remain at twenty-five. So the hoi polloi continued coming to the Bowery Theatre, but now they were confined to the cheap section, far away from the rich folks who were still getting the best ticket price in town. Pickpocketing remained a problem, but it was happening only during intermissions, when everybody rushed to the basement to quench their thirst at the saloon and buy snacks at the concession stands. No doubt about it, Astor's new venture was a winner. Not only was it making money, but it was also drawing on an increasingly large—and formerly ignored—audience: the working classes.

In November 1826, six weeks after the Bowery Theatre's opening, an unknown twenty-year-old American actor named Edwin Forrest made his debut there. The next day, newspapers were ebullient over him; but at the same time, they noted his unpolished talent. Wrote the *Evening Post*: "The house was full and respectable. This young man, with study and perseverance, will reach the very highest rank of dramatic fame." The *New York Mirror* wrote: "For a true and vivid picture of conflicting passions, Mr. Forrest's Othello is superior to any in this country's except Kean's." The *Mirror* was alluding to the most celebrated English actor of that time. "Mr. Forrest's acting has no resemblance to that of any performer whom we recollect." The young man's gorgeous looks and passionate acting grabbed audiences by the throat. But everybody agreed that he still had much to learn. He was, after all, an American actor and therefore had no formal dramatic training, unlike his English counterparts. In fact, Forrest's unschooled freshness was part of his appeal. His lines, read in his beautiful, booming voice, needed work, but they packed a punch. Wrote another newspaper: "We trust he will persevere in his present plan, for almost anything is preferable to the drawling cant of the old school."

"He has great personal, physical, and intellectual advantages," the *Post* said.

> His conception is peculiarly his own, and with study he may be the means of uniting the fire of Kean and the dignity of Kemble in his own person. His form is singularly beautiful. He is no copyist of any singular actor. Let Mr. Forrest study—let him be prudent—let him copy the best models, and there is no degree of theatrical fame that is not within his reach.

Forrest, a native of Philadelphia, had learned the acting craft as a teenager, playing whatever role was offered to him in little theater companies that travelled up and down the East Coast, as far south as New Orleans. In the summer of 1825 he found work in Albany, where he performed at the Pearl Theatre with the great British tragedian Edmund Kean. Forrest played Richmond to Kean's Richard III, and Iago to the latter's Othello. During their time together, a relationship developed between them, and Kean became his mentor.

In Albany, Forrest had caught the attention of Charles Gilfert, who was then manager of the Pearl. Gilfert soon left for New York to take up the reins of Astor's new Bowery Theatre, and it was he who hired Forrest. (Forrest, during a gap in time between his Albany and Bowery Theatre gigs, played one performance of Othello at the Park without telling Gilfert. The Bowery manager was at first furious, but then he used Forrest's one-time Park appearance as a teaser to the Bowery opening.)

After his bit as Othello, Forrest performed often at the Bowery. In fact, during the first two years of this theater, he was the main draw, and he especially appealed to the working-class folk who lived in the immediate neighborhood. (So much for Philip Hone's "well-regulated theatre.") New Yorkers with aspirations of grandeur had their Park

Theatre, with its English actors and Anglophile pretentions. As a young man, Walt Whitman regularly attended performances at the Bowery Theatre. More than fifty years later, he reminisced about Forrest in an essay he wrote for the *New York Tribune* on August 16, 1885. Forrest, Whitman wrote, was "tabooed by 'polite society' in both Boston and New York at the time; it found him too 'robustorous.' But no such scruples affected the Bowery." Whitman recalled the receptions that Forrest received

> any good night at the old Bowery, pack'd from ceiling to pit with its audience mainly of alert, well dress'd, full-blooded young and middle-aged men, the best average of American-born mechanics— the emotional nature of the whole mass arous'd by the power and magnetism of as mighty mimes as ever trod the stage—the whole crowded auditorium . . . bursting forth in one of those long-kept-up tempests of hand-clapping peculiar to the Bowery—no dainty kid- glove business, but electric force and muscle from perhaps 2000 full-sinew'd men . . . There never were audiences that paid a good actor or an interesting play the compliment of more sustained atten- tion or quicker rapport.

But along with their enthusiasm, Bowery audiences had bad manners. (We might arguably point to Henry Astor as unintentionally planting the seeds of Bowery low culture, which then entered into American vernacular.) "With their slang, wit, occasional shirt-sleeves, and a picturesque freedom of looks and manners, with a rude good-nature and restless movement," wrote a reporter in the *New York Mirror* (December 12, 1835), "they kept the pit in a constant uproarious state of fermentation." Patrons yelled out during performances, drank hard liquor—a customary accompaniment to a night's theatrical en- tertainment at that time—and chomped on peanuts (from whence we get the expression: "no comments from the peanut gallery"). All the while, prostitutes serviced johns on the third tier, another then- customary practice in theaters, even at the Park, the purlieu of New

York's elite. Sometimes audiences got completely out of control. A performance of *Richard III*, starring Forrest's chief rival, the great Junius Brutus Booth (the father of John Wilkes Booth, Lincoln's assassin), "was everything, or anything, but a tragedy," the patrician newspaper *Spirit of the Times* wrote.

> In the tent scene, so solemn and so impressive, several curious amateurs from the audience went up to the table, took up the crown, poised the heavy sword, and examined all the regalia with great care, while Richard was in agony from the terrible dream . . . The Battle of Bosworth Field capped the climax—the audience mingled with the soldiers and raced across the stage, to the shouts of the people, the roll of the drums and the bellowing of the trumpets; and when the fight between Richard and Richmond came on, they made a ring around the combatants to see fair play.

The success of Henry Astor's new theater pumped life into the southern stretch of the Bowery, where today, that sexy high-rise boutique hotel with the dress code in its penthouse bar imperiously dwarfs nineteenth-century brick walkups—most of which house Chinese mom-and-pop businesses—that wait in fear for developers' wrecking balls.

The economic growth that began during the 1780s and '90s was snowballing. The population density was growing and the increased foot traffic made the surrounding area desirable for conducting business. People were renting Henry Astor's lots and improving them, building little wooden houses where they lived and worked, producing and selling all manner of merchandise: clothing, dishes, hats, glass products. They might sublet unused space to other small businesses—pawnshops, grocers, brothels. Some owners ran boardinghouses, a pressing need for which arose as immigration to New York continued. People were living, working, manufacturing, and playing on the Bowery. They were creating a microeconomy, which caused land values to increase. Henry Astor began dividing his Bowery lots as a means to squeeze more money out of them. He turned the two lots next to the southern end of the Bowery Theatre into three: 42 Bowery was rented to a bandbox maker, Sylvain Bijotat, no doubt one of the many Frenchmen who fled the Reign of Terror that had accompanied the Revolution years earlier and found refuge in New York. An Italian named Cipriano Carraciole operated a confectionary business out of 44, and a grocer operated his business at 46. On the northern side of the theater, Henry Jones, the new proprietor of the Bull's Head Tavern—he also owned the Vauxhall Gardens—enlarged it and renamed it the New York Theatre Hotel. The number of taverns increased, oyster bars and ice-cream parlors opened, and peddlers sold street food. Day and night, little girls hawked boiled corn. These waifs became such a common sight along the Bowery that a *New York Tribune* reporter in 1853 wrote a series of stories about one of them and then published them as a book. Poor Little Katy the Corn Girl, age twelve, was beaten to death by her alcoholic mother late one night on the street, because the child had not managed to sell all her ears of corn.

Amid this hustle bustle, a youth culture peculiar to the Bowery came into being. It was expressed in the behavior of young, white working-class males, or b'hoys as they were called, probably a mocking allusion to the Irish pronunciation of "boy," which de facto shows that many were of Irish extraction. But the young men fiercely identified as Americans. A "Bowery b'hoy" had a rude and slightly dangerous edge but a mighty heart. He spoke a Bowery slang that enriched American English with expressions like "pal" and "going on a bender." (And how appropriate that the term "going on a bender" originated on the Bowery!) During the day, he worked, "a stout clerk in a jobbing house, a junior partner at a wholesale grocery, and still more frequently a respectable butcher with big arms and broad shoulders." Or he worked at physical labor, digging ditches and lifting heavy loads. After work, he donned a distinct uniform—tight black pants, a red flannel shirt, a tall silk hat—and work boots, which announced to the world that he was working class and proud of it. His hair was carefully styled, cut short in the back with two long, curled soap locks—so called because he greased his hair with soap—flopping over each ear. He carried a cigar, casually perched between his second and third fingers. He valued loyalty above all other qualities—to his family, to his country, and to his fire brigade. New York did not yet have an official fire department, so firefighting was a strictly local and volunteer affair. Every b'hoy belonged to a company and sported the number on his shirt. Each brigade claimed its turf, and sometimes rival brigades went at each other over which of them had the right to put out a burning fire. Whoever arrived first would put a barrel over the hydrant—"plug" in Boweryese—and sit on it to mark his territory.

Bowery b'hoys also loved theater. It was them Walt Whitman was talking about when he later recalled those wildly enthusiastic and ill-mannered audiences at the Bowery Theatre.

After Forrest's debut at the Bowery Theatre in 1826, he was no longer just an actor: he was a star—the first *American* star—with all the accoutrements that went with stardom. His success marked a real shift on the American stage. All his competition up to then—Junius Brutus Booth (the father of two sons, also actors, in addition to John Wilkes) and Edmund Kean—were English. England was where actors learned their craft and the place where bona fide literature came from, or so the thinking went: the concept of American culture did not yet exist. The English looked down on America for its crudeness, but the absence of tradition there also allowed for a sense of freedom that was impossible to enjoy in England. So for many artists, America beckoned: Booth had emigrated to America in 1821 and stayed; even before he left England he was a die-hard Republican. His father had come to America during the Revolution to fight against the Crown! When he returned to England he kept a portrait of George Washington in his drawing room, and no one was allowed to stand beneath it without taking off his hat. Booth surely felt more American than British.

Forrest's popularity was also due in no small part to his explosive sex appeal. Women in the audiences were mad for him. With his strong features, shock of black hair, and beautifully toned body—he worked out daily—he resembled one of those young Greek athletes depicted on ancient vases. When the actress Fanny Kemble (member of a celebrated British acting family) saw him for the first time, she is supposed to have said: "What a mountain of a man!" Forrest and his wife Catherine would later go through an acrimonious divorce, each accusing the other of infidelity. That he was guilty is inescapable: a diary he kept in 1835 of a trip to Russia includes a lovely description of a drunken tryst he enjoyed with a Dutch woman while travelling through Germany.

When Gilfert hired Forrest in 1827 for a second season at the Bowery, the young actor asked for—and received—an unheard-of salary for that time: $200 a night. Gilfert had no choice: Forrest had become the theater's main draw. Forrest performed eighty times at the Bowery Theatre that year. Most of his roles were Shakespeare, who was then, hands down, everybody's favorite playwright, across class lines—including the Bowery b'hoys. That year, Forrest played Othello and Iago, King Lear, Shylock, Richard III, and Macbeth to packed houses. But, ironically, his astronomical success was killing the golden goose: Forrest's huge salary was eating up the theater's profits.

On the evening of May 26, 1827, a stable on Bayard Street between the Bowery and Elizabeth Street caught fire. A wind, blowing from the west, helped spread the flames through a wide swath of the Bowery and some of the wooden houses that lined the street. The fire then reached the Bowery Theatre. The theater was not completely destroyed: its front and side walls remained, but they were so warped and cracked that they had to be demolished. Despite the theater's recently dwindling fortunes, Astor and the other shareholders immediately put up the money to rebuild. It took only three months. The number of columns on the front portico was increased to six, which greatly improved the look of the façade.

Forrest had decamped for engagements elsewhere, not to return to the Bowery Theatre until 1833, so Junius Brutus Booth took his place as the leading man. According to Walt Whitman, the masses loved Booth as much as Forrest, but the Bowery Theatre continued to struggle financially. It was mostly closed from 1828 to 1829.

Then, in August 1830, a hard-living English immigrant and actor named Thomas Hamblin took over the management of the Bowery Theatre. He'd had some measure of success as an actor in England—more than once he'd played Shakespeare in London's Covent Garden—but he remained obscure there. This left Hamblin feeling dissatisfied, and in 1825 he departed for New York with his wife, Elizabeth Blanchard, an actress, and their four young children.

Hamblin found work at the Park Theatre, but when he took the reins of the Bowery Theatre, he discovered his real gifts: great business instincts and a razor-sharp awareness of the zeitgeist. This was Jacksonian America, a time of rampant nativism, in ways shockingly similar to our own Trumpian dystopia. People—some of them mere second-generation Americans—back then were yelling: Too many immigrants! They are taking away our jobs! They are corrupting our religion! Newspapers all over the country broadcast that the pope was plotting to take over America, and Irish immigrants, in the words of the *Ohio Observer*, were his "sacerdotal agents . . . who come, not like others, guided by individual enterprise, but with their location agreed upon by the Pope and his advisors before they embark." This is what the working classes—the people who constituted the Bowery Theatre's audience—were feeling.

Consequently, as soon as Hamblin took the reins at the Bowery Theatre, he set out to make it more American. He changed its name to the American Theater—though people continued referring to it as the Bowery—and while he and Elizabeth both performed there regularly, he set out to hire American actors. He made a big deal about it: there was a persistent anti-British sentiment among Americans, and Hamblin tapped into it. When the great British actor Charles Kean was appearing at the Park Theatre in *Barbarossa* or the *Pirate of Algiers,* Hamblin mounted his own production at the Bowery with a young, barely known American, George Hazard. Hazard, Hamblin announced in an ad that he placed in the *New York American,* represented NATIVE TALENT. As did all the eager young actresses he was then promoting, some of whom he found in the whorehouses he frequented. Hamblin's sexual appetites were so notorious that everybody referred to his theater with the irresistible double entendre "the Bowery slaughterhouse." He knew exactly how to exploit his actresses, sexually and otherwise. Often he didn't pay them, insisting that the experience and the exposure he was providing more than made up for the money they weren't earning. He marketed them specifically as Americans, in contrast to the many English actresses then playing New York, such as the grande dame Fanny Kemble and his own long-suffering wife, Elizabeth. The latter, Hamblin then decided, was of no use to him, and in 1831 he sent her back to England. In her absence he assigned Elizabeth's parts at the Bowery to Josephine Clifton, the niece of one of his favorite madams—all for the cause of encouraging "native talent," he insisted—and to another young woman, Naomi Vincent. When word of Hamblin's treachery reached his wife in England, she decided that she'd had enough. Upon her return to America, she sued for divorce. The settlement in 1832 stated that Hamblin was never to marry again as long as Elizabeth was alive. Perhaps Elizabeth insisted on this condition out of sheer spite. Or the judge could have made this call based on Hamblin's increasing disregard for what society then considered acceptable behavior: by that time he had discarded Josephine Clifton but continued his liaison with Naomi Vincent. Elizabeth received a huge divorce settlement, $2,500, in exchange for which she relinquished any further claims on Hamblin's estate. She also had to swear that she would never visit the Bowery Theatre, nor the neighborhood streets "under any pretense whatsoever." Elizabeth took her settlement, kept her husband's name—for all Hamblin's unsavory reputation, it carried tremendous value—and continued acting in New York and around the country. In the meantime, Naomi Vincent— whom the papers also referred to as "Mrs. Hamblin"—died in 1835 giving birth to Hamblin's child. She was only twenty-one. Elizabeth, the de jure Mrs. Hamblin, also had a few stints managing theaters, during which time she met a much younger actor, J. S. Charles. She married him in 1836, which de facto stripped her of her former married name. Going forward, she was identified as Mrs. J. S. Charles. But by then, her star had waned. The sad truth was that divorcing that scoundrel Thomas Hamblin had badly hurt Elizabeth's career. Two years after she remarried, she got her revenge by collaborating with Mrs. Mary Clarke, a struggling journalist and playwright who supplemented her income by writing salacious tell-alls. The two wrote a pamphlet outlining the peccadillos of Hamblin, the "Great Seducer," in vivid detail: "Everything he touched turned to gold, which he extracted from the vilest filth of the earth in the human form: the scum of brothels became candidates for public favor in his form." Copies of *A Concise History of the Life and Amours of Thomas S. Hamblin* were quickly snapped up. When one of the pamphlets was listed in an 1869 estate auction, it was described as "excessively rare, having been rigidly suppressed."

Shakespearean drama continued to play at the Bowery Theatre, but Hamblin was soon presenting more and more of those crowd-pleasing extravaganzas known as melodramas. One such play was titled *The Cannibals; or, Massacre Islands*. Billed as a "nautical drama," it was based on a true story about a voyage to Antarctica, where thirteen travellers on a ship to the aptly named Massacre Islands were eaten by natives. Another was *Mazeppa; or, the Wild Horse of Ukraine*, based on a poem by Byron about a young man who is strapped, naked, to the back of a wild horse as punishment for his love affair with a countess. (Hamblin also came up with other ideas for increasing revenue, such as using the theater to host benefits for firemen.) Under Hamblin, the Bowery soon became New York's most popular theater, and it was making him a lot of money. But theaters in New York were multiplying, and he had competition. So Hamblin began actively looking for novelty acts that he was sure would please the masses. He found one in a strange little song-and-dance number that debuted on November 12, 1832. That evening, a tall, skinny performer named Thomas "Daddy" Rice, his face blackened with burnt cork, stepped onto the stage and performed a number that for the last few years he'd been doing in theaters all over the Ohio Valley and the East Coast to great acclaim. It was called "Jump Jim Crow," and it went like this:

> Come, listen all you gals and boys, Ise just from Tuckyhoe,
> I'm goin' to sing a little song, My name's Jim Crow.
>
> Weel about and turn about and do jis so,
> Eb'rey time I weel about I jump Jim Crow.
>
> I went down to the river, I didn't mean to stay;
> But dere I see so many gals, I couldn't get away.
> And arter I been dere awhile, I tought I push my boat;
> But I tumbled in de river, and I find myself afloat.
>
> Weel about and turn about and do jis so,
> Eb'rey time I weel about I jump Jim Crow.

The next day, "Jim Crow" was on nearly everybody's tongue; "boys whistled it in the streets, ladies sang it in parlors, while it was heard in the mart of trade and in the workshops." Rice repeated the act every night at the Bowery Theatre during the 1832 season. It marked the triumphant return of "Daddy" Rice to New York. He'd first cut his acting teeth as an extra at the Park Theatre, where, in a production of *Bombastes Furioso,* he once so mesmerized the audience in a strange falsetto voice and sporting a bizarre pointed hat that the two leading actors felt sidelined by him. (We don't know if Rice played this in blackface.)

Rice then left New York for the travelling circuit, doing blackface

Daddy Rice as Jim Crow

at every two-bit theater in the Ohio Valley and thereabouts. Note that there were never blacks among the audiences: segregated theaters—indeed, segregated *everything*—were the only normal across America.

Rice was said to have based his Jim Crow routine on an elderly slave whom he met in Louisville. The slave, who was all bent over from arthritis and scoliosis, worked in a stable where Rice liked to go riding, and he had a habit of singing snatches of a folk ditty about Jim Crow when he was rubbing down the horses. At the end of each stanza, he gave an awkward little jump. Rice was transfixed. He asked the slave to perform the song and the movements for him over and over, until he had both down pat. Then Rice added "Jump Jim Crow" to his repertoire. He took the act to theaters all over—everywhere, it was a hit—before bringing it to the Bowery stage, the very place where American popular culture was starting to emerge. From that point on, the Jim Crow character, as we would say, went viral. Audiences everywhere recognized and laughed at him. Later, "Jim Crow" became a moniker for the violent racism of the postbellum South and remains very much part of our American lexicon; it appears in headlines and packs quite a punch.

The figure of Jim Crow today makes us cringe, but context is everything: in the early nineteenth century, slaves were not considered human. This malignant idea was literally enshrined in the Constitution's three-fifths clause. Therefore, white audiences felt no empathy for a character on a stage representing an old, crippled slave—played, no less, by a white man in blackface. Laughing at ol' Jim Crow made people feel good; whereas honestly confronting slavery, America's most urgent and sickening moral dilemma, did not.

By the time Daddy Rice brought Jim Crow to New York, the state had outlawed slavery—in 1827—and abolitionists were starting to make some inroads. The New York Anti-Slavery Society, founded in 1833, was holding regular meetings a few blocks south of Hamblin's theater, at the Chatham Street Chapel. In addition, two houses owned by the Delaplaines, at 134 and 136 Bowery—they were an old Huguenot family with abolitionist leanings—housed Quakers who ran a bookstore and library filled with anti-slavery leaflets and books that they were churning out on their printing presses.

But these people were an exception in New York. The city did not embrace abolitionism, and the reason was mostly economic: without slaves, how else could plantations produce all those commodities—rice, cotton, tobacco—that had to pass through New York's harbors, banks, and exchanges? Ending slavery in the South would cause severe economic pain to New York. And despite our perception of New York as the perennial beacon of liberalism, the reality was different. New Yorkers felt the same ugly prejudices toward black people as whites did everywhere. In the early nineteenth century, segregation was a fact of life in their city as much as anywhere in America. African Americans in the 1830s comprised 18 percent of New York's population, but only in the poorest neighborhoods did the races mingle: in the Five Points, African Americans and Irish lived on top of each other and fought, drank, and played music together in "disorderly houses." Everywhere else, custom dictated strict segregation. Black people were banned from theaters and other places of amusement (for example, Vauxhall Gardens). On steamboats, African Americans were restricted to the outside decks. The Sixth Avenue El had signs on certain cars: COLORED PERSONS ALLOWED IN THESE CARS. In horse-drawn omnibuses, they could only stand, never sit. And African Americans in New York could not vote.

Daddy Rice performed *"Jump Jim Crow"* at the Bowery Theatre forty-nine times during the season of 1832 to 1833 and twenty times the following year.* He even took the act to London and performed it at Covent Garden. (The *New York Mirror,* October 5, 1833, wrote: "The original song of Jim Crow itself, whether we consider the delicious poetry, the delicate sentiment, the chaste and racy wit of its numbers, or the flood of divine music which forms the air, is a production which must take rank with the first compositions of the age. Mr. Rice as Jim Crow is positively enchanting.")

Daddy Rice was not unique. Performers everywhere were "corking up," and it was now customary for a blackface number to bookend the main play. In New York, a funny duck of a guy named George Washington Dixon, who was probably both gay and mixed race, was playing a character he called Zip Coon. He was the counterpart to Jim Crow, the Kentucky plantation slave: Zip Coon was a free black man and sharp dresser. He lived up North, and had a higher opinion of himself than he merited. Zip had a signature song (which Dixon probably did not write, but was forever associated with):

O ole Zip Coon he is a larned skoler,
O ole Zip Coon he is a larned skoler,
O ole Zip Coon he is a larned skoler,
Sings possum up a gum tree an coony in a holler,

---

* By 1837, New York had nine theaters—this figure comes from Philip Hone's diary—and the Bowery was by far the most popular.

Possum up a gum tree, coony on a stump,
Possum up a gum tree, coony on a stump,
Possum up a gum tree, coony on a stump,
Den over dubble trubble, Zip Coon will jump.

[Finish to each verse.]
O Zip a duden duden duden zip a duden day.
O Zip a duden duden duden zip a duden day.
O Zip a duden duden duden zip a duden day.
Zip a duden duden duden zip a duden day.

Disney studios used Ole Zip Coon in the song "Zippety Doodah" in the animated film *Song of the South*, which came out in 1946. Today, the movie, with its use of racist stereotypes, rightfully offends us.

Dixon was well known for this and other outré performances, which he took to theaters all over the country and even inspired a songbook: *Dixon's Oddities: A Collection of Nerve-Working, Side-Cracking, Care-Destroying, Mouth-Tormenting Songs, As Sung by Mr. George Dixon, at New York, Philadelphia, Boston, Baltimore, and New-Orleans Theatres.* When he wasn't onstage, he was writing fringy publications; indeed, Dixon considered journalism his real profession. He first tried his hand at it in Massachusetts, where he also served time in jail for forging a signature. He then landed in New York in 1838 and started a new publication: *Polyanthos and Fire Department Album* (the subtitle being a hook for working-class males). It had pretensions of being a literary magazine, but it was mostly a scandal sheet, filled with hysterical exposés of rich people's sexual dalliances and diatribes against women who either provided or had abortions. In the first issue, Dixon wrote about—yes!—Thomas Hamblin and his affair with a sixteen-year-old ingénue with the charming name of Louisa Missouri Miller, whom he'd taken under his wing at the Bowery Theatre. Hamblin, who liked to settle things with his fists, retaliated by beating up Dixon. The performer-cum-editor, undaunted, acquired a pistol and continued churning out unsavory stories about

Hamblin and other unfortunate New Yorkers, especially the high and mighty. One of his victims committed suicide by jumping off a roof after Dixon exposed his affair with a married woman. As a result, Dixon made a lot of enemies and became so notorious that when the papers ran scandalous stories about him, they didn't even have to mention him by name; everybody knew who that "certain gentleman" was. In the meantime, circulation numbers for *Polyanthos* were increasing, and Dixon insisted that he was writing those exposés for only one reason: moral reform, which was, in fact, very much on people's minds. As America, that brash young republic, was struggling to find its footing, its citizens were obsessing over anything having to do with sex; forming temperance groups as women wept over their alcoholic husbands; and getting "born again" at revival meetings led by evangelical preachers who were roaming the country by horseback. Most of all, Americans were grappling with the largest ethical question of all: slavery. What a clever rogue Dixon was! By tapping into all the surrounding anxieties, the man papers called the American Melodist had made himself into a celebrity.

One Sunday morning in 1832, Charles Finney, the most influential evangelical of the time—he was tall and strikingly handsome, with piercing blue eyes so clear that sparks seemed to emanate from them—preached a fiery abolitionist message at the huge Chatham Gardens Theatre on Park Row, just a few blocks south of the Bowery Theatre, where audiences were going wild with delight every night watching Daddy Rice jump Jim Crow. The Chatham Garden—the site today is a municipal jail—had been rented specifically for this occasion by the wealthy merchants and brothers Arthur and Lewis Tappan, members of a prominent abolitionist family from Boston. Finney began holding weekly revival meetings at the Chatham. He drew thousands of people, both black and white, and refused communion to anybody who did not support abolitionism. The following year the Tappans purchased the theater and turned it permanently into a church. This became the Chatham Street Chapel, and Finney continued to preach there until 1836. The preacher's presence in the city, and the Tappan brothers' open support of him, had a lot of merchants in New York worried. No question about it, abolitionism was bad for business. And for Finney to be thundering about the evils of slavery under the auspices of two of the city's richest citizens—the Tappans founded a mercantile business that later became the firm Dun and Bradstreet—was making the business community very skittish. The Tappans were not merely anti-slavery; they actually believed in equal rights for black people. Their truly radical position for the time scared white people. Newspapers in New York were railing against the Tappans, and rumors were spreading that the Anti-Slavery Society they'd helped found was advocating interracial marriage or "amalgamation." (The rumor was false: the Tappans' progressivism did not extend to the acceptance of blacks and whites marrying each other.) As tensions in New York further ratcheted up, Tappan loaned the Chatham Street Chapel to a group of abolitionists, who, along with a choir of African Americans, were to celebrate a special occasion on July 4, 1834: the seventh anniversary of full emancipation in New York. The state had taken its time to free its slaves. What could have been achieved in one piece of legislation had instead dragged on for twenty-eight years, beginning in 1799 with the Gradual Emancipation Law, which freed only the children of slaves born after July 4th of that year, until that same date in 1827, when slavery was finally abolished.

When the group arrived at the Chapel on that July evening in 1834, they were met by an angry anti-abolitionist crowd. Things got so ugly that they postponed the meeting until a few days later; and when the group reconvened—the date was July 7 and the heat was unbearable—members of the New York Sacred Music Society, arriving at the Chapel for their usual weekly practice, were incensed to find themselves displaced by a black choir. A fight broke out. The police came and arrested six African Americans. The remaining black choir members, feeling threatened by the angry crowd that had formed around them, fled.

The next day, newspapers defaulted to that vicious, racial canard: they claimed that gangs of black men were threatening the safety of white men and, especially, their women. In the meantime, the heat was growing fiercer. On the night of July 9, anti-abolitionist crowds formed at several places in the city, spoiling for a fight. One group trashed Arthur Tappan's beautiful home in Lower Manhattan, on Rose Street, though he and his family fortunately were not there (aware of the danger, they had left the city). The mob then met up with another, which had started its rampage at the Chatham Street Chapel on a tip that an abolitionist group would be meeting there that night. When nobody showed up, the men moved on, spoiling for a fight. The two groups combined and, moving through the streets, rushed up the Bowery until they found another target: the Bowery Theatre. That night, the great Edwin Forrest was performing *Metamora*, one of his favorite plays. Written for him by an American playwright, it was a tragedy about the eponymous chief of the Wampanoags, who dies at the hands of the Puritan settlers. The crowd, by then numbering some 4,000 angry white men, burst into the theater and redirected their fury to the Bowery Theatre's British stage manager, George Farren, for whom this performance of *Metamora* was a benefit. Farren was targeted because the previous day a butcher who was attending a performance at the Bowery heard Farren say that Yankees were jackasses "and I would gull them if I could." (Later the butcher told his account to the police under oath.) Accounts of what happened next vary, but the gist of it was that when Thomas Hamblin tried to calm the crowd by going onstage waving two American flags, he was pelted with rotten vegetables and booed off with shouts of "Down with the Englishman!" Then George Washington Dixon stepped onto the stage—he was billed that night as an entr'acte—and the mob cheered. They yelled: "We want Zip Coon!" As Dixon performed his signature number, the 4,000-strong crowd calmed down. Afterward, they dispersed, but for the time being, the atmosphere in New York remained tense.

That same year, 1834, the Bowery Theatre burned down for the second time. As it was being rebuilt, Thomas Hamblin began buying shares of it from John Jacob Astor's corporation. (His brother Henry had died the previous year. Henry had no children, and he left the theater to his brother.) The Bowery Theatre burned again for a third, then fourth time in quick succession: 1836 and 1838. Perhaps the fires were caused by gas—the Bowery, remember, was the first theater to use gas pipes—but we don't know for sure. By then, Hamblin was sole owner of the Bowery Theatre, and he'd turned it into New York's biggest, most popular entertainment palace. Along the way, he had also acquired a few other theaters and was deeply in debt. So he was looking especially hard for new talent to bring in the crowds. He found it one day in 1843 when he wandered into the Bowery Amphitheatre, a lowbrow venue right across the street from his Bowery Theatre: four young white musicians in blackface who called themselves the Virginia Minstrels were making strange, irresistible music with a banjo, a fiddle, a tambourine, and knucklebones. Hamblin was intrigued, and he hired them. Once again, his instincts were right on target.

CHAPTER SIX

THE MOB TAKES THE STAGE

O h, that Thomas Hamblin. As always, he was onto something: with the Virginia Minstrels, the strange phenomenon we call minstrelsy, with its edgy and shame-inducing racial content, immediately took New York by storm.

By the mid-1840s, theaters all over New York were headlining minstrel groups with names like the Kentucky Minstrels and the Ethiopian Serenaders. This was especially so around the Bowery, where on any given night at least one and probably several of the many theaters—the Chatham Theatre, the showman Barnum's American Museum down on Broadway and Ann Street, Hamblin's Bowery Theatre, White's, the Melodeon, the Bowery Amphitheatre—offered a chance to escape into white fantasies of how much the slaves down South enjoyed their lives on the plantations.

Minstrel groups were made up of white musicians only—blacks then were not allowed to perform in front of white audiences— pretending to be black.* They corked up, donned wooly wigs, and portrayed horrible slave stereotypes: the mammy, the mulatto wench,

---

* Interesting fact: after the Civil War, blacks formed minstrel groups, and they, too, performed in blackface.

the old darky, the dandy. Their acts consisted of back-and-forth banter, dancing, and singing, performed to the twang of the banjo and the rattle of the bones. Sometimes the material had a raunchy edge, or one of the characters sang in female drag. This highly stylized and lowbrow entertainment was devoured by all, across the class spectrum. Mark Twain adored, as he called them, "nigger shows." So did the great Edwin Forrest, who on occasion himself "blacked up." Even the high-and-mighty Park Theatre, forced by economic reality, featured minstrel shows. From there, they spread throughout America—though not to the slave states until after the Civil War—and then across the Atlantic, to London.

Minstrelsy was a spectacular cultural phenomenon, and to most people of that time it felt benign. But abolitionists condemned it. Frederick Douglass, writing in the *North Star* on October 27, 1848, called blackface performers "the filthy scum of white society, who have stolen from us a complexion denied to them by nature, in which to make money, and pander to the corrupt taste of their white fellow citizens." After the civil rights movement, minstrelsy was agonized over by cultural historians and experts in Afro-American studies, and to this day continues to be. We still don't fully understand it; but that it became so wildly popular in prebellum America shows that it mattered, immensely. It revealed something profound about race, a subject that nearly 200 years after Thomas Hamblin discovered the Virginia Minstrels we have barely begun to talk about.

Minstrelsy, a fun house mirror version of segregation—white people playing black characters to white-only audiences—started on the Bowery. What is more, the Bowery was one of the few places in segregated antebellum New York where the races mingled. Whites and blacks drank, danced, caroused, and banged out music together in the numerous basement-level song-and-dance dives or "concert saloons" then flourishing along the Bowery and nearby Five Points. Today, the federal courthouse, a smart-looking gray granite structure, rises twenty-seven stories high on the site of this once-notorious neighborhood, which was built on top of the filled-in Collect. Nothing remains

of the Five Points, then so named because of the five streets that inter-
sected there: Anthony (now Worth), Center, Orange (now Baxter),
Little Water (which no longer exists), and Mulberry. But if you stroll
the streets surrounding the courthouse, you'll notice that the street
dips down in places, as a kind of gentle reminder of how the terrain
once was. When Charles Dickens visited the Points in 1842 during
his first trip to America, the filth and poverty stunned him ("all that is
loathsome, drooping and decayed is here"). But when he dropped into
Almack's, a "disorderly house"—the then-universal term for a seedy
place that offered such enticements as drinking, gambling, watching fights, whoring, music, and dancing—his tone changed. Like many
a white person going slumming, Dickens was charmed: "A buxom fat
mulatto woman, whose head is daintily ornamented with a handker-
chief of many colors," he wrote in *American Notes,* an account of his
1842 adventures that chronicles his awe and disgust for this then-new
nation. "The landlord attired in a smart blue jacket, like a ship's stew-
ard, with a thick gold ring upon his little finger, and round his neck a
gleaming golden watch guard. How glad he is to see us! What will
we please to call for? A dance? It shall be done directly, sir." And
then, Dickens continues, "the greatest dancer known" appears and
works his magic:

> Instantly the fiddler grins, and goes at it tooth and nail; there is new
> energy in the tambourine; new laughter in the dancers; new smiles
> in the landlady; new confidence in the landlord; new brightness in
> the candles. Single shuffle, double shuffle, cut and cross-cut: snap-
> ping his fingers, rolling his eyes, turning on his toes and heels like
> nothing but the man's fingers on the tambourine; dancing with
> two left legs, two right legs, two wooden legs, two wire legs, two
> spring legs—all sorts of legs and no legs—what is this to him? And in
> what walk of life, or dance of life, does man ever get such stimulat-
> ing applause as thunders about him, when, having danced his part-
> ner off her feet, and himself too, he finishes by leaping gloriously
> on the bar-counter.

The dancer was a sixteen-year-old named William Henry Lane, known on the street as Master Juba ("juba" was the name of a dance). So electrifying was his hoofing that he was allowed to perform before white audiences, which was unheard of in the 1840s. He even competed in dance contests staged at the (new) Chatham and Bowery Theatres with John Diamond, an Irish American famous for his rendition of the jig. Juba's talent was copying another dancer's steps and then adding flourishes that made the dance his own. The consensus was that Juba won. Thus was "tap dancing" born—on the Bowery.

In 1848, Frank Chanfrau, an actor who grew up on the Bowery with his three brothers—his French-born father owned a tavern—created a stage character named Mose, based on a real fireman named Moses Humphreys, whom he'd admired as a child. Everybody called Humphreys the king of the Bowery. He was a printer by trade and, like all genuine b'hoys, a devoted member of a fire brigade. One day Chanfrau saw the guy eating lunch at a Bowery hashery. Humphreys bellowed so loudly that Chanfrau nearly jumped off his chair: "Gimme a sixpenny plate of pork and beans; and don't stop to count dem beans, d'ye heah?" Moses Humphreys embodied all the traits of the urban thug, a real rough, tough American, hard drinking and always ready for a fight. Moses Humphreys, a huge bear of a man, fought hardest of all. He ruled the Bowery with a combination of fists, hobnail boots, chutzpah, and charm. He rode the Lady Washington engine of brigade No. 40. Finally, Moses met his match in 1838 in a terrible battle between No. 40 and the Old Maids, a rival brigade. It took place on Chatham Square, and it was over who had the right to douse a fire burning on South Street. No. 40 was creamed, and Humphreys was beaten bloody by Henry Chanfrau, Frank's brother. The Old Maids seized the Lady Washington as booty and trashed it. The disgraced Humphreys never showed his face on the Bowery again. People said that he relocated to Hawaii, where he ran a pool hall in Honolulu and had thirty children.

Chanfrau first played Mose in a skit at the Olympic, a popular theater on Broadway, in 1848. The curtain rose on the actor dressed in the familiar Bowery b'hoy attire, complete with red shirt and skin-tight trousers, stovepipe hat, soap locks, and a cigar stuck in his mouth. Chanfrau/Mose removed the cigar, spit on the ground, and, in a reference to his defunct Lady Washington, snarled: "I ain't a-goin' to run wid dat machine no mowah!" Chanfrau's Mose brought down the house. The real-life b'hoys in the pits, seeing and hearing themselves caricatured onstage complete with their peculiar Bowery-accented lingo—"fust" for "first," "waudewille" for "vaudeville," "arn't dere goin' ta be any fitein'?," "now look a-here," "she's a gallus girl, she is, I'll have to get slung to her one uh dese days," "take de butt [fire hose]"—made them feel deliriously proud. Apparently, the Mose character also charmed the swells sitting high up in the boxes, because a month later the skit was expanded into the full-length play *A Glance at New York*, which ran for the rest of the 1848 season. The character acquired a girl, Lize, the Bowery g'hal, and a devoted sidekick named Sykesy. In New York, wrote theater critic William Northall in his 1851 book *Before and Behind the Curtain*, "nothing was heard, sung or talked about but Mose":

> The theater was crowded from pit to dome nightly, and the hi-his of the pit testified how happy they were to see a congenial vulgarity thrust under the nostrils of a better class of people. The piece was the town's talk, and few could resist the inclination to go and see for themselves what had produced such an extraordinary excitement all about them. When the public curiosity had been somewhat satisfied, and Mose no longer drew the crowds after him, the boxes no longer shone with the elite of the city; the character of the audiences was entirely changed, and Mose, instead of appearing on the stage, was in the pit, the boxes and the gallery. It was all Mose, and the respectability of the house *mosed* too.

When the season ended, the Olympic manager, William Mitchell—determined that his theater not remain indefinitely déclassé—did

F. S. Chanfrau as Mose

not renew Chanfrau, who had no problem finding another venue: the Chatham Theatre,* which by then was depending almost entirely on minstrel acts for its survival. But after Chanfrau-as-Mose appeared there, it was packed full every night. Soon the Chatham restricted its repertoire entirely to the Mose plays. As for the Olympic, Mitchell's decision was a business disaster. Without Mose, the theater's revenue plummeted. In the meantime, the Mose character was spawning an entire industry of Mose-centered plays and dime novels, in which Mose sometimes travelled out of New York all the way to California. Sometimes the story line centered on a terrible fire that Mose heroically fought; sometimes he rescued babies. Chanfrau played Mose over 1,000 times in cities throughout America and sometimes twice in one

---

* Built in 1839, and later known as the National. Not to be confused with the Chatham Gardens, which was by then a church.

night, one after another, in two different theaters. There were so many Mose-themed productions that actors besides Chanfrau began taking on the role, although it would forever be associated with its originator. And Mose's image was everywhere, in posters, cartoons, and advertisements.

When British author William Thackeray visited New York in 1852, he insisted on being taken on a Bowery tour, so he could meet a real b'hoy. Once there, he approached a kid who looked the part—he was, appropriately, sitting on a fire hydrant—and asked him for directions just so he could hear the boy talk "Bowery flash." "Please, sir, I want to go to Brooklyn," Thackeray said. The boy answered: "Den why de hell dontcha go?"

In all the Mose stories, this idealized b'hoy had a heart of gold. But on the real street, the young men going crazy over Frank Chanfrau's character probably belonged to one of the gangs then proliferating on the Bowery and Five Points. The most famous of them were the Bowery Boys—spelled without that strange *h* between the *b* and the *oys*—who one hundred years later were scrubbed and repackaged by Hollywood into silly movies. The Bowery Boys developed out of those fire brigades, which had all the characteristics of street gangs: obsession with turf (differences over which they settled with violence) and an intense code of loyalty. Additionally, New York had no official fire department yet—it would not be established until after the Civil War—so the brigades operated with complete autonomy.

The Bowery Boys had a clubhouse at 40–42 Bowery, next door to the Bowery Theatre, and their bitterest rivals were the Dead Rabbits, an Irish gang over at Five Points. In 1857, the Rabbits attacked the Boys in their headquarters, which escalated into a riot that spread to the surrounding area and later became famous. The Boys were aggressively nativist. Never mind the Irish ancestry of so many of them; no, they felt cockily American and probably felt disgust at the hordes of starving Irish potato famine refugees that ships were dumping on New York's shore during the 1840s. Added to the nativism, already on the rise the decade before, was now xenophobia, and both were poisoning the air like the gas from a leaky pipe in a theater that bursts into flames during intermission as soon as somebody lights up a match.

There was a popular minstrel tune that was being performed in New York theaters in the mid-1800s. It went as follows:

> *Music now is all de rage*
> *De minstrel bands am all engaged*
> *Both far and near de people talk*
> *'bout Nigger Singing in New York*
>
> *Barnum's Museum can't be beat*
> *De fat boys dar am quite a treat*
> *Dar's a big snake too wid a rousing stinger*
> *Likewise Pete Morris, de comic singer*
>
> *De Chatham keeps among de rest*
> *Entertainments ob de best*
> *In public favor dis place grows*
> *'specially on account ob Mose*
>
> *De Astor Opera is anoder nice place*
> *If you go thar, jest wash your face!*
> *Put on your "kids" an fix up neat,*
> *For dis am de spot of de elitet!*

The Astor mentioned in this song—"the spot of the elite"—was a grand neoclassical theater. Built in 1847, it served as a monument to the eponymous family, many of whose members lived in the surrounding enclave that John Jacob Astor had created for wealthy New Yorkers along the northern stretch of the Bowery—it then extended all the way to Fourteenth Street—on land he had purchased from the

Stuyvesant estate. (John Jacob, remember, had deliberately done this in order to one-up his brother Henry, who at the time was building the Bowery Theatre down at the thoroughfare's southern end.) The Astor Theatre stood on a slight elevation at the triangle where East Eighth Street, Astor, and Lafayette Places intersect. (Today, an eleven-story brownstone structure dating from 1890 occupies the Astor's footprint.) Its site had been chosen specifically for its location; its raison d'être was to create a haven for New York's aristocracy, far away from the riffraff and their nightly carryings-on in the theaters to the south along Broadway and the Bowery. The managers believed they would accomplish this goal by imposing a strict dress code: to gain entrance, you had to be freshly shaved and wear kid gloves and a white vest. The good seats were by subscription only, and to keep the prostitutes away, single women were denied admission. The Astor was, wrote *Herald* columnist George G. Foster, the only theater in America that could be rightly called elegant.

This grand marble edifice was built specifically for opera. But at that point the art form had not really taken hold in New York; in order to stay solvent, the Astor's schedule included a lot of Shakespeare. The theater's intended audiences, still clinging to their fusty notions about "culture"—that for drama, literature, and music to be considered seriously, it had to come from Europe—expected all roles at the Astor to be performed by British actors. One of whom, the great William Charles Macready, stepped onto the stage on the evening of May 7, 1849, to play the role of Macbeth. Macready had performed in America many times and was always warmly received. This was to be his farewell engagement.

That same night, his rival—the great Edwin Forrest, darling of the American stage—was also playing Macbeth just a few blocks away at the Broadway Theatre.

Macready's first tour to the States, in 1826, corresponded with Forrest's debut at the just-opened Bowery Theatre (which Macready deemed "handsome and commodious" but not enough to compensate for its slum-infested location). He admired Forrest's vigorous performance but was critical of the younger man's rough—that is, American—acting edges. Rivalry festered between the two ever after, which the newspapers assiduously covered. On Macready's second American tour in 1843, Forrest trailed him from city to city, performing the same Shakespearean roles.

So now: two competing Macbeths on the same evening. What a treat! In fact, there were three. That son-of-a-bitch Thomas Hamblin—he had never stopped performing, even as he managed the business end of things and his very complicated personal life—was not about to let the Bowery Theatre be sidelined during this nineteenth-century version of a media event. So he was playing Macbeth that night at the Bowery Theatre as well.

As the date of the Macbeth performances drew near, two sleazy public figures who were aligned with the nativist cause put their heads together to turn the feud between two actors to their political advantage.

Isaiah Rynders was the political boss of the Sixth Ward—which included parts of the Bowery and the Five Points—and as such he acted as a liaison between the gangs and Tammany, the city's powerful and graft-infected Democratic club. Founded after the Revolutionary War and originally nativist in outlook, by the early 1800s Tammany was embracing the thousands of immigrants flooding into New York, most notably the Irish, for an obvious reason: votes. But Tammany had recently lost the mayoral election to Caleb Woodhull, the candidate of the Whigs, who were then the main rival of the Democrats. Woodhull represented the interests of New York's merchant class, and the political atmosphere in New York was feeling tense. The Forrest-Macready brouhaha, with its subtext of xenophobia, was adding to the tension, and Rynders saw this as a moment to be exploited. He would manipulate it and pick at it like a scab to make trouble for Woodhull's administration.

Rynders had a hanger-on, a twenty-six-year-old dime novelist who, after working as a cabin boy on a ship that journeyed to South America and then as a midshipman in the war against the Seminoles in Florida, travelled about the country, writing pulp fiction about sailors and big game hunters. He also published his own newspaper under his pen name, Ned Buntline (his real name was E. Z. D. Judson) in which he expressed obsessively patriotic views. Buntline was, in the words of a contemporary, a "radical Americanist." He was addicted to taking risks: the previous year, 1848, he'd escaped a lynch mob in Nashville after killing in a duel the husband of a sixteen-year-old girl whom he'd seduced. He then moved to New York and fell in love with Chanfrau's Mose the fireman and his personification of the working-class patriotism that Buntline embraced. He began churning out dime novels about the imaginary Bowery character and at the same time became cozy with the Bowery Boys gang in the flesh. (He continued to publish his newspaper, *Buntline's Own*, which he now filled with lurid stories of New York's underbelly, by whom he meant "foreigners.")

Rynders and Buntline bought up hundreds of gallery tickets at the Astor, distributed them to the Bowery Boys, and instructed them to boo Macready off the stage. The boys did more than that: They pelted Macready with rotten eggs, vegetables, pieces of wood, and a bottle of asafoetida, a foul-smelling elixir that broke all over Macready's costume. And the boys booed so loudly that during the first two acts, nobody could hear the actors' lines. At the beginning of the third act, after people began throwing chairs onto the stage, Macready decided he'd had enough. He left the stage and went home.

(Forrest's performance at the Broadway, incidentally, was scantily attended. But down at the Bowery Theatre, Hamblin's Macbeth played to a house "crammed to suffocation almost," wrote a reporter from the *Baltimore Sun* who attended the performance.)

Macready was scheduled to play the Astor one more time, on May 10, 1849.

Rightfully disgusted by the behavior of his American hosts toward him, though, he decided to return to England without finishing out his American engagement. Only after forty-seven prominent American men of letters—including Washington Irving and Herman Melville—sent him a letter begging him to see it through, did Macready relent.

Over the next three days, tensions in New York ran high. Buntline again gave out hundreds of tickets for Macready's farewell performance to would-be hecklers, and Mayor Woodhull implored the managers of the Astor Theatre to cancel the performance. They refused. In the meantime, Bowery toughs were plastering broadsides all over the city:

WORKINGMEN! SHALL AMERICANS
OR ENGLISH RULE IN THIS CITY?

New York's police chief told Woodhull that even the full force—it totaled 800 men—would not be sufficient to handle a riot. (Some of his police were guarding the homes of wealthy New Yorkers, who were afraid of looting.) So Woodhull called up several regiments of state troops to help keep the peace and hoped for the best. On May 10, some 200 musket-bearing, spiffily uniformed infantry and cavalrymen—Greyjackets—assembled at Washington Square and waited for orders.

On the evening of May 10, 150 policemen stood guard outside the Astor Theatre, and 100 more policemen were inside, scattered among the audience. The curtain went up at 7:30—right on schedule. The three witches uttered the opening lines of *Macbeth,* but nobody could hear them over the racket coming from the hecklers, who were seated throughout the audience. When Macbeth—Macready—made his appearance in scene 3, the heckling escalated into booing, which grew louder and louder until finally, at scene 4, act 1, one of the policemen inside the theater gave a signal to those outside and more police stormed in and "closed in upon the scoundrels occupying the centre seats and furiously vociferating and gesticulating, and seemed to lift them or bundle them in a body out of the centre of the house, amid the cheers of the audience."

By then, thousands of hooligans spoiling for a fight had lined the streets around the theater. Among them was Ned Buntline, there to lead on his boys. They began throwing stones against the theater's windows on the Eighth Street side, and "the volleys of stones flew without intermission." Stones smashed through the windows, one hitting the huge crystal chandelier, which broke into a thousand shards. Other stones knocked out streetlamps. Some stones were aimed at policemen, who ran for cover inside the theater, where hecklers were sitting in the cheap (gallery) seats, keeping up "the din within, aided by the crashing of glass and boarding without." Meanwhile, the crowd outside kept getting bigger. (Newspapers estimated the number at 10,000.)

The theater was under siege, and everybody inside was growing nervous.

The actors keep at it, but at the end of act 2, the theater manager approached Macready "and much frightened, urged me to cut out some part of the play and bring it to a close." Macready grew angry. "I said that I had consented to do this thing, to place myself here, and whatever the consequence I must go through with it. The audience had paid for so much and the law compelled me to give it; they would have cause for riot if all were not properly done." Macready got through the banquet scene. When he went down to his dressing room to change his costume, "the battering at the building, doors and windows was growing, and water was running down fast from the ceiling to the floor of my room. The stones hurled in had broken some of the pipes."

It was time to call out the troops. Around 9:00 p.m., the 200 Greyjackets who had assembled earlier at Washington Square marched up Broadway to Astor Place, to confront the mob. They fired their muskets, first into the air, then into the crowd. Twenty-two (to thirty-one) people died, more than 150 were injured and 117 arrested. And all the while, inside the theater, Macready finished the play. "And in the very spirit of resistance I flung my whole soul into every word I uttered, acting my very best, whilst these dreadful deeds of real crime and outrage were roaring at intervals in our ears." Then he went to his dressing room and quickly undressed to the sound of soldiers firing on the rioters. At the insistence of a friend, he donned a disguise—some of the rioters, his friend said, were out for his blood—and hurried out the back door and through the crowd. By then, several rioters had been killed. "You must leave the city at once!" his friends told him. At 4:00 a.m. a livery carriage conveyed him to safety in New Rochelle. On May 22, 1849, Macready sailed for England, never to return to America.

The next day—May 11—the major newspapers lambasted the rioters, while pamphlets issued by an unknown group calling itself "the American Committee"—no doubt the work of Rynders and Buntline—flooded the city, urging vengeance for the killings. ("Americans! Arouse, The Great Crisis has come!") The mayor urged people to stay home and avoid crowds. Rich people, fearing looting, bolted their doors. It took two days before order was restored.

As for Edwin Forrest, he stood to gain from Macready's humiliation. Therefore, he did not speak out against the actions of the rioters. But neither did he castigate the authorities for their use of brute force. In the end, it worked out well for him: after calm was restored, Forrest received bundles of fan mail congratulating him for winning the contest with Macready.

The Astor Theatre shut down after the riots and reopened the following September. But the affair had sullied not only its name but the surrounding area as well. People joked about the "Massacre Opera House" at "Disaster Place," and the moneyed people living nearby, on the upper flank of the Bowery—among them John Jacob Astor fils—decided they could no longer stomach a Bowery address. The street's cachet had already been steadily devolving for the last twenty or so years as New York's gentry increasingly moved uptown. Or the former were moving a few blocks west to Broadway, the "great promenade and thoroughfare," wrote Charles Dickens in 1842 in *American Notes*. He admired Broadway, "that wide and bustling street" with "its glittering shops" and gorgeous ladies. "Heaven save them, how they

Astor Place Opera Riot

dress! We have seen more colours in these ten minutes than we should have seen everywhere in so many days!" Broadway, Dickens observed excitedly, was crowded with every kind of vehicle: "hackney cabs and coaches too; gigs, phaetons, large-wheeled tilburies, and private carriages," driven by "negro coachmen and white; in straw hats, black hats, white hats, glazed cabs, fur caps." But, he added, move a few blocks over to the Bowery and "the stores are poorer here; the passengers less gay; and the lively whirl of carriages is exchanged for the deep rumble of carts and wagons."

So in late September 1849, four months after the debacle of the Astor Place riots, a group of wealthy upper-Bowery residents petitioned the Board of Aldermen to rename the section of the Bowery where they lived, which ran from the Astor Theatre to Fourteenth Street. The new name they requested—Fourth Avenue—was outstanding in its blandness. The city elders immediately approved the change, which made the poor Bowery, with its northern section lopped off, suddenly one-third shorter. It was as if the city were cutting off a gangrenous limb, lest the infection spread to parts north.

The Astor limped along for another three years before closing for good.* It was demolished in 1890, and the Mercantile Library erected that lovely brownstone building, now housing condos worth millions, on the site. But on the southern stretch of the Bowery, there remained a vibrant theater scene. In 1852, the Chatham Theatre presented a new play. It was called *Uncle Tom's Cabin,* and it changed the world.

---

* Vauxhill Gardens also closed around that time: Charles Haswell, *Reminiscences of New York by an Octogenarian, 1816 to 1860* (New York: Harper & Brothers, 1896), 121.

CHAPTER SEVEN

THE CIVIL WAR ON THE BOWERY

Uncle Tom's Cabin started out as a weekly serial by Harriet Beecher Stowe in the abolitionist newspaper the *National Era*. By the time it was published in book form in 1852, her story of the noble slave and his evil master was already being used—without her permission—as the basis for a play. (Stowe was powerless to control the co-opting of her work, as copyright protection in America did not extend to the stage until 1856.) It was probably first performed in Troy, New York, in 1852. After a short run, it migrated to New York to the Chatham Theatre (also called the National), a few blocks south of where the Bowery began, and it caused a sensation. Audiences were electrified by the characters Stowe had created: Tom, the humble old slave; Eliza, the desperate mother; little Eva, the saintly child; Topsy, the poor orphan; and Simon Legree, Tom's cruel owner. They loved them, hated them, and wept over them. Even the pit audiences in Bowery theaters—"the newsboys, candy-sellers, factory hands, and homeless children who had never been to Church or School"—listened silently, without jeering or laughing, when Tom, informed that he had been sold, says, in that exaggerated "negro" accent that white actors assumed on the stage and was always associated with the comic: "No, I can't run away. I can't run away. Let her go, it's her right. If I must b'sold, le'b be sold—Mass'r allers found me on the spot. I nebber hab broke my trust, and I nebber will!" The *Times* noted how strange it was to witness such respectful behavior by the dregs of New York society. The effect of the play, the *New York Times* stated, was to elevate the black man; and the newspaper doubted that United States officers would get any assistance from Bowery b'hoys in chasing runaway slaves.

Soon versions of *Uncle Tom's Cabin* were playing in just about every New York theater and spread to cities across the country and on to England. Concurrently, Stowe's novel was outselling every book but the Bible. Abolitionists were ecstatic, and the anti-abolitionists were terrified. (The play's purpose, ranted the *Herald* [September 1852], whose owner, James Bennett, was an unapologetic racist, was "to poison the minds of our youth with the pestilent principles of abolitionism.") By some estimates, millions of people were flocking to see all those "Tom plays," and because copyright laws did not exist to protect Stowe's work from being pirated, it soon fragmented into multiple and often crude stage adaptations. A production at Barnum's Museum, the *New York Times* wrote, was so far from the written work as to be a sham and a disgrace. Uncle Tom characters were even incorporated into minstrel shows. But all had something in common: all were played by white actors in blackface, because in 1850s antebellum America, black actors were still barred from performing in front of white audiences.

By the mid-1850s, the height of the Uncle Tom craze, at least four different versions of the play were playing simultaneously in theaters on and near the Bowery. The Bowery Theatre in 1854 featured the famous Daddy Rice, inventor of the Jim Crow character twenty-two years earlier, as Uncle Tom. It was extraordinary, really: the actor who'd for years made audiences crack up with his lampoon of the poor, crippled schlemiel had progressed to portraying a serious character, the grandfatherly Tom, whose humility and dignity aroused in them profound feelings of shame, perhaps, or simply empathy. For the first time, a blackface actor was not playing for laughs. No, in Uncle Tom's presence, white audiences shut up and listened.

Playwright George Aiken wrote what was considered the authoritative script for *Uncle Tom's Cabin*. Its accompanying music included a song by a young composer that became wildly popular. It went like this:

Way down upon de Swanee Ribber, Far, far away,
Dere's wha my heart is turning ebber, Dere's wha de old
folks stay.
All up and down de whole creation Sadly I roam, Still
longing for de old plantation, And for de old folks at home.

[Chorus] All de world am sad and dreary, Eb-rywhere I
roam; Oh, darkeys, how my heart grows weary, Far
from de old folks at home!
[2nd verse] All round de little farm I wandered When I
was young,
Den many happy days I squandered, Many de songs I sung.
When I was playing wid my brudder Happy was I;
Oh, take me to my kind old mudder! Dere let me live and die.

[3rd Verse] One little hut among de bushes, One dat I love
Still sadly to my memory rushes, No matter where I
rove. When will I see de bees a-humming All round de
comb? When will I hear de banjo strumming, Down in
my good old home?

The composer was Stephen Foster, the Pennsylvania native who wrote music for the Christy's Minstrels. His songs were being performed in all the New York theaters. Life should have been good for Foster, but it wasn't. He was selling his songs to publishers for a pittance.* Or he gave them away for free: "Oh Susanna!" for example, which turned out to be one of the most popular songs ever written.

Foster was perennially in debt. He was an alcoholic, and his marriage was unhappy. His wife, Jane, had no feeling for music, and the two quarreled constantly. Jane left him in 1853, two years after Foster composed "Old Folks at Home." She took their only child, a daughter

---

* At that time, the customary practice for composers and writers was to sell all the rights to their works to publishers.

named Marion, with her. While pining for his absent wife, Foster wrote "Jeanie with the Light Brown Hair." Foster was always sad, longing for what he once had or some idealized form of what he never really had or for things that never really existed. Such as, perhaps, his marriage. Some have speculated that Foster was gay: he married a woman with whom, it seems from what we know, he shared nothing. Not his music, nor, perhaps, intimacy: Marion, their only child, was born exactly nine months after Foster and Jane married, which raises the question of whether the couple had sex only once, on their wedding night.

Jane and Marion rejoined Foster in Manhattan in 1854. The three then moved to Hoboken, where Jane left her husband again, this time for good. Foster went back to Pennsylvania.

Foster grew up in a well-to-do Pittsburgh family listening to blackface minstrel music. His father went bankrupt when he was a teenager, and he moved to Cincinnati as a young man to work in his brother's shipping business. The office was right on the river, where Foster could hear African American stevedores singing as they worked the docks. The music found its way into Foster's compositions, which people played in their parlors all over America and which became permanent fixtures in American songbooks: "My Old Kentucky Home," "Old Folks at Home," "Oh Susanna," "Jeanie with the Light Brown Hair." The sheer passion of his melodies still moves us; but the syrupy lyrics about slaves longing for the old plantation, try as we might to contextualize them, are hard to listen to.

Uncle Tom's Cabin reached deep into America's soul, down to places nobody dared confront before. Eight years after the publication of Stowe's novel, the first shots were fired at Fort Sumter. In the interim, the Missouri Compromise failed, and each side of the slavery debate hardened its position. In the mid-1850s, the passionate abolitionist John Brown, who had spent years in Boston among the elite voices being raised against the immorality of slavery and was exasperated by those who soothingly counseled "patience," went to Kansas to raise hell against bands of thugs who were fighting hard and dirty to keep it a slave state. There Brown, along with four of his sons and a handful of followers, waged ferocious acts of guerilla warfare. Their feats included hacking five men to death at Pottawatomie in 1856, in supposed retaliation for the attack and burning of Lawrence, Kansas. As the violence in "bleeding Kansas" escalated, Brown returned East and started planning for what he is best known, the raid on the federal arsenal in Harpers Ferry, West Virginia.* His goal was to procure arms to distribute to slaves and thereby help jump-start a slave rebellion. By then he and his outlaw escapades in Kansas were an object of fascination to the American public.

In October 1859, Brown and twenty-one other men, of whom five were black, raided the federal arsenal in Harpers Ferry. This audacious move ended quickly: Brown was captured, tried, and sentenced to death. During his time in jail and on trial, only pro-slavery reporters—most of them came from nearby—were permitted to talk to him. (The only exception was an undercover reporter from the anti-slavery *New York Tribune*.) Their accounts were then picked up by newspapers around the country, so much of what was printed about John Brown during his last days was spun through a pro-slavery lens and no doubt inaccurate.

As his time of execution grew near, newspapers all over the country were weighing in on John Brown. Democratic newspapers accused the Republicans, with their anti-slavery rhetoric, of causing the Harpers Ferry insurrection. Republicans, among them presidential hopeful Abraham Lincoln, insisted they were not to blame.

In New York, "the *Tribune* and other Republican papers treat the John Brown case, the Harpers Ferry insurrection, too sympathetically; they disapprove in words, and do all they can to elevate that fanatical law-breaker and homicide into a martyr . . . The *Post* and *Tribune*

---

* In 1859 Harpers Ferry was in Virginia; West Virginia did not become a separate state until 1861.

and our Brownists generally put their sympathy on the ground of their martyr's insanity, and talk of its being shameful to hang an insane man . . . [But] it is unwise to give fanaticism a martyr," wrote George Templeton Strong in his diary two days before Brown's execution. But Brown was not insane. The label was pure calumny, spread by the pro-slavery faction.

On December 2, 1859, in Charles Town, West Virginia, a wagon pulled by two white horses carried John Brown—he was seated on the wooden coffin that would afterward hold his body—to the field behind the prison where he had been held. There, gallows awaited him. Brown's cortege was escorted by three companies of soldiers. In addition, several corps of troops were lined up about the field, and cavalrymen on their horses guarded the flanks. Altogether, the troops numbered about 1,500. The effect, an eyewitness afterward wrote, "was most imposing, and at the same time, picturesque." When the wagon reached the gallows, Brown stepped to the ground and walked up the steps to the platform. His demeanor was calm. Even when a white hood was placed over his head and the noose around his neck, his knees did not tremble. For fifteen minutes, he stood there, waiting to die, not moving, while the troops who'd escorted him arranged themselves in proper formation. Finally, somebody cut the rope that held the trapdoor from falling. John Brown, "man of strong and blood hand, the terrible partisan of Kansas, the demi-god of the abolitionists," immediately dropped three feet, and the noose squeezed the life out of his body. Soldiers then cut down his body and placed it in the coffin on which Brown had sat during his final journey. The coffin was then transported by railroad, first to Baltimore and then to Philadelphia. From there, it was sent by boat to New York and to the care of Jacob Hopper, a Brooklyn undertaker and relative of a well-known abolitionist and Quaker minister, Isaac Hopper, who lived just off the Bowery. Isaac Hopper accompanied the coffin to the undertakers Graw and Taylor at 163 Bowery at eleven o'clock at night. It was a fitting address to deliver John Brown's body: just across the street, abolitionist material was being composed and printed in the Delaplaine houses at 134–136 Bowery.

The undertakers opened the coffin to find the rope still strung around the neck of the corpse. They removed Brown's clothing—his coat and vest had been stabbed through with bayonets—and placed his corpse on ice. His face was black-and-blue, and the mark of the noose was visible on the left side of his neck and under his ear. When the body was frozen enough to bury, they laid it out in a white shroud "with pleated trimmings and white cravat." The abolitionist's body was then placed in another coffin, this one of solid rosewood. When word went out that John Brown's body was lying in a Bowery funeral home, hundreds of people came out to pay their respects. Brown had visited New York and had celebrity status there. Visitors came from across the spectrum. "I never had such illustrious guests, the very biggest bugs and make no mistake," Louisa Williamson, who worked for the undertakers, wrote in a letter a few days later to her brother. People were clamoring for relics, so Louisa distributed bits of the rope and screws from the coffin. But she kept a rifle cap that she found in the pocket of his pantaloons. ("I guess when I realize any real benefit from it I shall be extremely fortunate.")

The next morning, Brown's remains were carried by train to Vermont, unloaded at Lake Champlain, taken across the lake by ferry, and carried by wagon to the farm where he and his wife and some of their children—he fathered a total of twenty-two, with two wives— had lived, in North Elba, New York, in the Adirondacks. There, he was buried.

John Brown had pushed the slavery question so far into the open that the country could no longer avoid a resolution. And he knew this. On the morning of his hanging, he had given a jail guard a piece of paper on which he had scrawled the words: "I John Brown am now quite certain that the crimes of this guilty land will never be purged away; but with Blood."

Two weeks after Brown's execution, the Bowery Theatre presented a play about him—no copy of it survives—that the *Herald* described as "an original drama, written by a lady of Brooklyn, called *Insurrection, or Kansas and Harpers Ferry.*" Americans all over had strong feelings about John Brown. For some he was a martyr and a saint; others condemned him as a terrorist. And Harpers Ferry became a talking point in the 1860 presidential campaign.

On a cold, snowy day at the end of February in 1860, Abraham Lincoln stepped in front of the lectern in the Great Hall of the Cooper Union. (The grand Italianate-style school, built entirely of brownstone, had just been constructed at the Bowery's northernmost end, just south of the then-defunct Astor Theatre.) Onstage with him were some of the city's leading Republicans, among them William Cullen Bryant and Horace Greeley. This was Lincoln's first trip to New York; he'd come at the invitation of the Young Men's Central Republican Union of New York. They were seeking a presidential candidate as an alternative to the presumed favorite, the state's own William Henry Seward, a U.S. senator. They feared that Seward's anti-slavery views, which he took every opportunity to express loudly and clearly in the Senate, were too radical for him to win the election.

Lincoln opposed slavery on moral grounds and was against its expansion, but he was far more conventional in his beliefs about race than Seward, who took the then-outlying position that every human being, black or white, should have the same rights. In 1858, the incumbent Democratic senator in Illinois, Stephen A. Douglas, accused Lincoln numerous times of being an abolitionist during the famous series of debates between the two candidates. Lincoln's response was clear and, in the context of today, shocking: not only was he no abolitionist, he said, but he also did not believe that blacks should vote or serve on juries. Whites, he stated clearly, were inherently superior to blacks: "There is a physical difference between the white and black races which I believe will forever forbid the two races living together on terms of social and political equality."

Lincoln, "the great rail splitter" as people called him, seemed the antithesis of Gotham. But the oratorical brilliance he'd displayed two years earlier in the Douglas debates had elevated him into a public figure. Hence, there was a great deal of curiosity about Lincoln in New York, and despite the nasty weather on that February day, Cooper Union's Great Hall was packed with a crowd of some 1,500 people. An eyewitness later wrote: "When Lincoln rose to speak, I was greatly disappointed. He was tall, tall—oh, how tall!—and so angular and awkward that I had, for an instant, a feeling of pity for so ungainly a man."

Lincoln began to speak. "His face lighted up as with an inward fire; the whole man was transfigured," the eyewitness wrote. "I forgot his clothes, his personal appearance, and his individual peculiarities. Presently, forgetting myself, I was on my feet like the rest, yelling like a wild Indian, cheering this wonderful man."

Afterward, in the *Brooklyn Evening Star* of February 28, 1860, a reporter wrote:

> Nature has endowed Mr. Lincoln with few exterior oratorical graces. His voice is often harsh and shrill, his action nervous and angular, his address marked by many provincialisms . . . [But] he does not call to his aid the vehement declamation or anecdotical resources so liberally drawn upon by stump speakers. Raising no side issues he meets the question fairly and fully, and goes straight to the substance of the matter. As an effort of pure reasoning and a direct appeal to the intellect of the hearer, it is not often that such a speech is listened to.

Lincoln's Cooper Union speech quickly and smoothly dispensed with the troublesome subject of John Brown and Harpers Ferry. ("That affair, in its philosophy, corresponds with the many attempts, related in history, at the assassination of kings and emperors. An enthusiast broods over the oppression of a people till he fancies himself commissioned by Heaven to liberate them. He ventures the attempt, which ends in little else than his own execution.") It was printed in newspapers across the country, and in May, Lincoln won the Republican nomination.

In the meantime, the Democrats had split bitterly into northern and southern factions over the slavery question, and a Republican victory in the November presidential election seemed inevitable. The morale of New York's Republicans, who were very much a minority, soared; and in September, they celebrated with a procession of their political club, the "Wide Awakes." They marched through Astor Place and down the Bowery; the sight was "imposing and splendid," the Republican George Templeton Strong wrote in his diary on October 31. "The clubs marched in good order, each man with his torch or lamp of kerosene oil on a pole, with a flag below the light; and the line was further illuminated by the most lavish pyrotechnics. Every file had its rockets and its Roman candles, and the procession moved along under a galaxy of fire balls—white, red and green. I have never seen so beautiful a spectacle on any political turnout."

Three weeks later, Democrats counterdemonstrated with their own mass meeting at Cooper Union. They declared themselves the White Man's Party. In New York, Democrats greatly outnumbered Republicans, and when Lincoln won the election in November 1860, he lost every ward. New York still hoped to avoid a war, even as southern states began to secede before the inauguration in March 1861. But one month later, when the Confederate army bombarded the federal garrison at Fort Sumter in North Carolina, the city broke out in war fever. When Lincoln called for 75,000 volunteers to join up—"to possess the forts, places, and property which have been seized from the Union"—males as young as fifteen, all dying to get a gun in their hands, crowded into the recruitment offices that were opening all over the city. Of them, thousands came from the slums flanking the Bowery; probably this street sent more young pups into battle than any other. Billy Wilson, a thug and ward heeler for the Tammany organization—where William M. "Boss," who would make "Tammany" a synonym for graft, had just taken the helm—assembled the Sixth Regiment out of 850 thieves and other assorted Bowery riffraff. He led his smelly army of recruits into Tammany Hall one morning, squeezed them into the meeting room, and announced that three-quarters of them would be dead within three weeks if they followed him. But, he said, with sobs breaking out of his throat, he would die before any of them. The men cheered. Then Wilson made them kneel and swear to support the flag, which they obediently did and after which Wilson paraded around the room waving a Union flag and brandishing a sword, as the poor schmucks chanted: "Blood! Blood! Blood! We swear!" Immigrants had their own units: the Irish, who had been flooding New York in gigantic waves ever since the 1840s potato famine, joined the Sixty-ninth Infantry; the Germans, the Seventh "Steuben Guard," with its fifteen-piece brass band, and the Eighth, the "German Rifles." Lincoln's friend, Colonel Elmer Ellsworth, formed a unit of 1,100 New York firemen. He specifically wanted these men for his new regiment, he wrote to Lincoln, "because there are no more effective men in the country. I want men who can go into a fight now." The Fire Zouaves, so-called after their uniforms based on the French colonial army, behaved very badly when they arrived in Washington on May 2, 1861, burning fences, carousing, and scaring women. Until they were ultimately disbanded—in 1863—they had the well-deserved reputation of being hard to control. The two German regiments were far more disciplined; the recruits had been trained as soldiers in Europe, during Germany's bloody 1848 revolution against the monarchy. German immigrants were feeling wildly patriotic toward their adopted country in 1861 and enthusiastic about preserving the Union. "They love the flag which has honored and sheltered them," the *New York Times* wrote admiringly of the German regiments. "They are American citizens now, and they desire to show their citizenship by offering their lives for their country."

So imagine, if you will, the Bowery during May of 1861. The weather was balmy and spirits were high: war, especially in its preparatory stages, excites people, and it's good for the economy. The Bowery was engulfed with soldiers and civilians, and its businesses were booming. Tailors stitched up uniforms in blues and reds and grays—each unit had its own colors and style—as quickly as they could, and shoemakers cut leather and hammered nails into soles to make boots, trying to meet the sudden demand to outfit all the new

Colonel Ellsworth's Zouaves

enlistees. The newly uniformed soldiers strutted around, dropping into saloons and beer gardens. They also patronized the many photographers operating along the Bowery—every time you looked, another enterprising man with a camera had opened another shop—to have their pictures taken to give to their families to treasure after they were shipped off. Every day, another column of soldiers was marching down the Bowery, through Chatham Square, and then along Pearl Street all the way to the docks, where they piled onto ships that took them south, where they debarked and began what the Union thought would be a lickety-split campaign.

But two months later, the unexpected defeat of the Union army at Bull Run shocked the North. The patriotic feelings that engulfed New York after Fort Sumter fast changed to fury at Lincoln. Nevertheless, the war was profiting New York's economy enormously because all kinds of war supplies—ships, hay, horses, cattle, rifles, canons, bread, uniforms—were either made in New York or passed through it, as did the Union militias from everywhere.

The immigrants kept coming, too. In 1850, the city's population totaled half a million; in 1860, it topped 800,000, of whom one-quarter were foreign-born. They came from everywhere, but most were European, including "famine Irish" and German refugees from the political uprising of 1848; a good many among the latter were Jews. During the Civil War, European immigration plummeted. Yet even during those terrible years, people continued to be drawn to New York, but now the newcomers were mostly Americans: veterans too emotionally broken to return home, or, if they did, they found their wives, thinking they were dead, living with other men; deserters; men whose farms had been burned down by the invading army; young girls who, in the chaos of wartime with so many of the men away at war, found a window of opportunity to run away from abusive, alcoholic homes. In 1865, close to 800,000 people lived in New York; and even with the slowing of European immigrants during the war years, nearly half of the city's denizens had been born in a foreign country.

The immigrants were concentrated mostly in the "Bloody Sixth" and Tenth wards. Both synonyms for poverty in New York, they encompassed the Bowery—that is, the actual thoroughfare—the Lower East Side, Mulberry Bend, and the Five Points. With not nearly enough places to house them, these desperate people piled into every wretched wooden shanty or brick tenement house—the latter term, denoting housing for the urban poor, was already part of the American lexicon by the 1820s—elbowing themselves into every available space. Cellars and attics and rooms were partitioned into tiny spaces with clotheslines or pieces of wood; one newspaper reported that forty or fifty people were living in a room meant to accommodate five. People pissed and defecated into buckets; they slept piled up together on straw pallets or filthy rags. The slop pails, filled with garbage and human waste, were emptied from windows or, if more convenient, on the roof. There was no indoor plumbing; people got water from public pumps on the street. Sometimes the pumps were located in a building's courtyard next to privies so covered in filth as to be unapproachable. (One, described by the *New York Times* on October 10, 1865, "oozed a thick filthy mass of emerald colored material, disgusting to the eye, oppressive to the nostril, and dangerous to health.") Incredibly, New York had yet to construct public baths, an institution that Greeks and Romans took for granted thousands of years earlier. So the poor of New York had no place to wash their bodies. The one exception was a small bathhouse at Grand and Mott streets. Opened in 1852, it charged a five-cent fee, which most people could not pay; it closed down in 1862.

With such utter lack of sanitation, diseases festered. Every summer brought outbreaks of typhoid and dysentery, and twice—in 1832 and again in 1849—the city was hit with cholera epidemics. At the same time, following the Civil War, New York's economy exploded even more, which translated to more tenements being built to house the endless influx of impoverished immigrants. And with no laws regulating their construction, tenements were built right up to the lot line— the standard size of the New York lot, imposed by the 1811 grid, was 25 by 100 feet—or they were squeezed into backyards not only on top of the contaminated soil, but also as close to the neighboring structures as humanly possible. The result was that tenements admitted no outside air or light, making them foul and dark and reeking inside. Charles Dickens wrote in 1842 in *American Notes* that "dogs would howl to lie in them" and "rats move away in quest of better lodgings." Outside offered no relief because the alleys and lanes—all unpaved— were knee-deep in mud and human excrement.

Only one place offered escape from this existence: the Bowery. Once this road belonged to New York gentry, who lived the grand life in mansions set among the adjoining fields. But the Revolutionary War had destroyed that ambience almost a century ago, and New York's rich folks had moved uptown, leaving behind the Bowery to the poor, who made it theirs, completely. The Bowery in turn took care of them like some poverty-stricken, foul-mouthed, tough, self-sacrificing mother. On summer nights, when the heat made it impossible to sleep inside their packed, airless rooms, men, women, and children went to the Bowery and squatted on the curbs—yes, by then the Bowery was paved with stones!—or on the doorsteps of the dowdy little wood and brick houses that were jammed tightly into all those lots owned by the Astors. The sidewalks functioned as a huge open marketplace, where, day and night, merchants hawked heaps of cheap clothing, shoes, crockery, hardware, and other household goods. Even when it was cold out, the Bowery never slept: at night, long after the stores had gone dark, gaslights shone inside the theaters and minstrel halls. The Bowery understood how much its inhabitants needed a good time, and it gave it to them.

The Bowery also gave them booze.

Since Dutch times, the Bowery was a natural location for taverns, and the huge numbers of Irish and German immigrants who called the Bowery home caused drinking establishments along it to multiply. In the 1850s and '60s, so many German beer gardens opened that the Bowery acquired a moniker: Kleindeutschland. In 1858, a German named William Kramer bought the New York Theatre Hotel—formerly the Bull's Head Tavern, flush by the Bowery Theatre—enlarged it, and turned it into a beer hall that held 3,000 people. Most of the patrons of the Atlantic Gardens were German—on Sundays, this was the place where German fathers brought their wives and children for a family outing—but the rest of the crowd was of every nationality, even American. What they all had in common was a taste for lager beer—"even that made in Gotham," wrote one Junius Henri Browne in his 1869 guidebook to New York, *The Great Metropolis*. (Guidebooks to New York were then big business.) "The Americans sit at the little tables, and look like doomed spirits beside their round-faced, square browed, jolly neighbors." Across the street from the Atlantic, Germans turned the Bowery Amphitheatre—where Hamblin saw his first minstrel group—into the Stadtstheatre, for plays and operas in German. George Templeton Strong in 1861 saw a production there of Offenbach's *Orpheus in the Underworld*. ("Went to the plebeian Stadtstheatre in the Bowery, where we saw *Orpheus in der Unterwelt*, a funny extravaganza that has had a great run in Paris," Strong wrote on March 12, 1861, a week after Lincoln's inauguration. "Music by the celebrated Offenbach, whoever he is; rather piquant and Frenchy.")

The southernmost stretch of the Bowery offered a different kind of drinking experience. The concert saloons—usually located in basements—offered cheap booze, rinky-dink piano music, and dancing, along with "pretty waiter girls," some of whom turned tricks in back rooms. The first concert saloons opened in the 1850s along Broadway and the Bowery and then multiplied "like immoral mushrooms," Junius Henri Browne wrote. "They at once found patrons innumerable. Their illuminated transparencies, their tawdry display, their jangling music, their painted and bedizened wantons—such is public taste—made them immediate pecuniary successes." Concert saloons were considered such a danger to public morals that a grand jury convened in 1861 to investigate them; the following year—1862—the New York legislature passed a law meant to shut them down. But this proved impossible: all the troops gathering in or passing through New York made vice the city's number one industry. A police census taken in 1866 showed that the city had seventy-five concert saloons that employed 747 "waiter girls," 621 houses of prostitution, and 2,670 streetwalkers.

In 1860, Stephen Foster returned to New York, took a room in a Bowery boardinghouse and continued composing music in the back room of a nearby "liquor grocery." Liquor groceries were vicious places that sold cheap, sometimes poisonous booze along with groceries, thereby helping to ruin the already miserable lives of the poor families who patronized them. The reporter and flaneur George G. Foster in one of his New York in Slices columns for the *Tribune* compared them to "a venomous toad upon the corner of a block of miserable poor men's dwellings who disseminates its venom all around." It was an apt place for Foster to work: his drinking had spiraled out of control. Dressed in hand-me-downs and living on a diet of turnips and potatoes from the grocery, he wrote his compositions on pieces of brown wrapping paper. Then the young poet and Foster's friend, George Cooper, added lyrics. Foster hawked his music sheets along the Bowery to passersby, or he sold them to theaters. One of the pieces went like this:

> *Beautiful dreamer,*
> *Wake unto me*
> *Starlight and dewdrops*
> *Are awaiting thee*
> *Sounds of the rude world*
> *Heard in the day*
> *Led by the moonlight*
> *Have all passed away*

"Beautiful Dreamer" became a standard in American songbooks and, as sheet music, must have sold millions of copies. But most of the songs Foster produced during the Civil War years used the war as a subject and have been forgotten: "Was My Brother in the Battle?" "We're a Million in the Field," "I'm Nothing But a Plain Old Soldier," "Willie's Gone to Heaven." These were, need we say it, terrible times. New York was far from the corpse-strewn battlefields, but as with any war, the conflict was played out everywhere and took its own peculiar shape depending on thousands of factors—among them, locality. New York remained divided over the war. Abolitionists were increasingly speaking out; in July 1862, William Lloyd Garrison addressed a crowd at Cooper Union. But anti-abolitionist newspapers—most egregiously among them Bennett's *Herald*—howled that it was an outrage to be sending off young white men to fight "nigger wars," when all the while, fresh troops, so young, all uniformed up and carrying guns, kept arriving in New York from all over the Union. So the air was perpetually charged with excitement, as well as anxiety and resentment, as the young soldiers partied and whored, and finally got back in formation and marched down Broadway or the Bowery to hop on a ship or a train that would take them to Virginia or Tennessee or

Georgia, where they were probably going to die, either in battle or from disease. In July 1863, two weeks after 8,000 men died at Gettysburg, a lottery for the nation's first-ever draft was held in New York, and the tension that had been building in the city burst like a pus-filled boil lanced with a needle. What started out as an attack on a conscription office by a crowd of about 500 men quickly became a riot that spread through the city and was impossible for the metropolitan police to handle on their own. On the second day, some 5,000 troops were transported from Gettysburg to help contain the disturbances; by the third day, the newspapers were talking about the "Great Draft Riots." Groups of white men, most of them Irish, poor, aroused by fears of losing their jobs to emancipated slaves, resentful of the draft, and unable to pay the government the $300 required to get out of it, roamed the city, out for the blood of black New Yorkers. Mobs, some including women and children, chased, tortured, lynched, and killed black people at random. In between, they pulled down telegraph wires, looted stores, smashed windows, and burned down buildings—among them, and on the very first day of the riots, July 13, the Colored Orphan Asylum. Fortunately, the children inside got out safely. White thugs set fire to the homes where blacks lived and murdered entire families within them, even little children—in one instance a three-month-old infant. Three men kicked down the door of a room and found Abraham Franklin, a young, physically deformed man who worked as a coachman. He was kneeling at the side of his old mother, praying for God to protect her. She stroked his head and said, "I feel the good angels here in this room." The men seized the man, beat him with their fists and clubs, and hung him from a beam, all in the presence of his mother. They then ran back out to the street to find more victims, returning to the scene of their crime a few hours later to find the mother still seated in her chair, keening over her son's body, which by then was lying on the floor, the noose still around his neck, because some policemen had rushed in in the interim and cut it down. The thugs hung Franklin's body up again and mutilated it.

It took New York five days to put down the Draft Riots. At least one hundred people died, and for months afterward the city remained traumatized. Some civic organizations and wealthy individuals, ashamed by the violence that had been unleashed on the city's black residents, counteracted with expressions of goodwill and monetary donations to charities, whose stated purpose was to help African Americans. But many blacks fled New York after the riots.

Among the buildings the rioters destroyed was an army recruitment office on Grand Street, just off the Bowery and steps from where Foster was working at his music. Did he notice the chaos around him during those five terrible days in July, or was he by then too malnourished and ill from the effects of alcoholism? We don't know. But in January 1864, six months later, this poignant bard of the Bowery died at Bellevue Hospital four days after collapsing in his room, where he was found naked and bleeding from a gash in his neck.

At two o'clock on a beautiful April afternoon in 1865, as bells rang from City Hall and fire trucks around the city, a funeral cortege carrying the remains of Abraham Lincoln began moving up Broadway from City Hall. The coffin had lain open during the previous twenty-four hours, through the night, as people wishing to pay their respects to the slain president stood in lines stretching for blocks. Since the president's assassination ten days earlier, the city had been in mourning, and today it completely shut down. Every building—from churches to grand department stores such as Stewart's to expensive restaurants like Delmonico's to the lowliest shops and saloons—was draped in black crepe. From roofs, flags flew at half-mast, and over each streamed a thin black pennant. People crowded the sidewalks, hung out windows, or stood on roofs, quietly watching the procession as it trudged up Broadway to Union Square Park. There, a memorial service took place, after which the coffin continued its journey uptown to the Hudson River Train Depot on Thirty-fourth Street (where the main post office now stands) to be reloaded on the funeral train that had begun its journey from

Washington. New York was just one stop along the route to the train's final destination in Springfield, Illinois.

The South was destroyed, 750,000 people had died in the war, and the president had just been assassinated. What would America be like moving forward? In this atmosphere of fear and confusion, people were constantly passing through New York, and many of those who had no place to call home were ending up on the Bowery. There, they camped out on the sidewalk or a stoop or, if they had ten cents, found a night's shelter in one of the many cheap lodging houses. People were referring to these men by a term that had become popular during the Civil War: "bummers" or "bums" (the word was a synonym for "hanger-on" or "straggler" and was associated with General Sherman's march through Georgia); and the awful places where they slept were an evil peculiar to postbellum New York. They opened every night around ten, shut their doors at three in the morning, and in between a panoply of lost, ragged souls straggled inside. For the price of a dime, they got a bedbug-infested straw pallet, often with no cover, in a room stuffed to the rafters with other dirty, sweaty men. The rule was "first come, first served" and the last man in got the worst spot. You kept your clothes on while you slept and put your hat and your hobo pack under your head. Otherwise, you'd wake up to find everything stolen. Then, early the next morning, you got kicked out. Lodging houses were highly profitable, and remained a Bowery institution. Although by the late nineteenth century, everybody was calling these places flophouses.*

In 1865, a friend of George Cooper named Tony Pastor opened a theater at 201 Bowery, across the street from the Atlantic Gardens. Pastor was the son of a Spanish immigrant who made his living by playing the violin. The short, chubby, and slightly cross-eyed Pastor made his performance debut when he was six, singing at meetings of the Hand-

---

* The term "flophouse" originated with hobos, who had their own distinct slang.

in-Hand Temperance Society. From there he graduated to P. T. Barnum's museum and then to minstrel shows and finally circuses, where he worked as a clown. During the Civil War, he landed at a Broadway theater, where he concocted an act in which he sang a patriotic song while waving an American flag, urging the audience to sing along. It was a hit.

Pastor had a bold marketing idea: his new theater would offer variety shows with strictly family-friendly content. The idea was to attract women and children. They were a vast, untapped market: Broadway and Bowery theaters, except for the prostitutes who worked the upper tiers, were frequented overwhelmingly by men. The saloons customarily attached to theaters offered all kinds of booze. But at Tony Pastor's Opera House—he advertised it as "the Great Family Resort"—there was no drinking. You couldn't smoke there, either.

At first, the ladies didn't come. Pastor then tried to lure them in with free bonbons, dolls, and flowers. When that didn't work, he made Friday "ladies' night," when husbands and young men could bring their wives and girlfriends for free. Then he gave away bags of flour, hams, and sewing machines. Finally, he advertised that he would give away silk dresses to the first twenty-five ladies who showed up for a particular show.

That did the trick. The lobby of Pastor's Opera House was so swamped that twenty-five policemen had to be called in to keep order. From then on, entire families flocked to Pastor's for a night of song, dance, and minstrel shows. (He was credited with inventing vaudeville.) Pastor himself frequently appeared on the stage. The *New York Times* wrote: "He is really a capital comic performer, and the uproarious applause which greets him when he appears in a neat but not gaudy attire, comprising a white silk hat, a sky-blue velvet coat, and a vest and trousers of immaculately white linen, is proven by his spirited delivery of half a dozen songs, to be well deserved."

One of Pastor's signature numbers was a valentine to the Bowery; the refrain went:

> *In the Bowery, in the Bowery,*
> *For beautiful girls with bright eyes and dark curls*
> *In the Bowery, in the Bowery,*
> *That's where I reside when I'm home.*

Followed by stanzas that extolled the Bowery's virtues:

> *No butterflies of fashion there,*
> *Or idlers may be found,*
> *But men with open hearts and hands*
> *With honest labor browned*
> *Men who to help a friend in need,*
> *Would their last dollar lend*
> *Who never live on other folks,*
> *But earn the cash they spend.*

One stanza acknowledged how much the Bowery contributed to the Civil War:

> *The dark rebellion raised its head*
> *And war o'er the land spread*
> *When rushed into Columbia's aid*
> *Each gallant hero band,*
> *Among the foremost on the field,*
> *Upholding still our starry flag*
> *Was found the Bowery boys.*

Then, as a piano tinkled in the background, Pastor recited:

When the call came for soldiers in the hour of danger, the Bowery was the first to send its volunteers, and nobly did they do their duty. Who does not remember that incident at the Battle of Antietam, when the enemy charged in full force, our brave regiment bravely stood its ground, under a terrific fire and changed the tide of seeming defeat to one of glorious victory. This was noticed by General McClellan, who exclaimed: "What regiment is this?" "New York Volunteers," was the answer. "Where do they hail from?" Why, of course—

In the Bowery, in the Bowery,

By the time Pastor was performing this number—sometime during the 1870s—the distinctive Bowery culture the song invoked, as embodied by Mose the Fireman, no longer existed. The Bowery boy ("b'hoy") had disappeared after the Civil War, when New York first established a municipal fire department and the volunteer companies disbanded. Mose vanished from popular culture, and whoever was left of the Bowery boys went West to find gold or south to fight in the Mexican War. Or if they stayed put, wrote Junius Henri Browne in his 1869 guidebook to New York:

> You saw them in degenerate forms and with shorn glory, about the famous theater, and in the cock and rat-pits near Houston and Grand Streets. But his crimson shirt, his oiled hair, and his peculiar slang, and his freedom of pugnacity, and his devotion to the fire engine, are things gone by. The places that knew him know no more. He was a provincial product, the growth of a period. The increase of the city, the inroad of foreigners, the change in customs, and especially the disbanding of the volunteer fire department swept the Bowery boy from his fastenings. He is a waif now under many other names—a thief at the Five Points, a blackleg in Houston Street, a politician in the Fourth or Sixth Ward, a sober-settler in the great West, or a broker in Wall Street.

Guidebooks like Browne's were a thriving industry in postbellum New York, which was, hands down, America's center of sin: After textiles, prostitution was the city's second largest industry. Amid a growing fascination with the city's underbelly, the Bowery was so notorious that most guidebooks devoted an entire chapter to it. James

McCabe Jr. wrote in his 1872 *Lights and Shadows*: "Respectable people avoid the Bowery as far as possible at night. Every species of crime and vice is abroad at this time, watching for its victims. Those who do not wish to fall into trouble should keep away."

In 1875, Tony Pastor moved his theater to 585 Broadway. He'd had a good run on the Bowery. But by then, just uttering the word "Bowery" conjured such tawdry images that the address had become a liability.

CHAPTER EIGHT

THE DEVIL'S WORK

N ew York's economy exploded after the Civil War. Technology was fast advancing, and New York's bankers provided the necessary capital to build the factories, trains, ships, and skyscrapers that characterized the Gilded Age. In the 1870s, New York's population reached, and then topped, 1 million; fully half of its denizens were immigrants, and three-quarters had at least one foreign-born parent. Immigrants were New York's life force, providing the labor needed to build and run all these new inventions. It seemed there was no limit to New York's growth or to how many immigrants it could take in. Irish and Germans continued to comprise most of the foreign-born population, amidst smatterings of other European nationalities.

Into this sea of white European faces, some Chinese—perhaps 1,000—arrived during the 1870s. Almost all were men—typically they left their families behind in China, with the intention of returning after making money in America—and some were coming directly from the mainland. But others were refugees from the West, where anti-Chinese violence was then breaking out all over. With the railroads completed, the Chinese who'd built them were now toiling at whatever menial jobs they could get, and the sight of them infuriated white working-class males. "The Chinese," they screamed, often referring to the immigrants with vicious racial epithets, "are taking away our jobs!" (How familiar these crude expressions of racism ring in today's xenophobic world.) In New York, the new arrivals joined a small enclave of their countrymen—they numbered perhaps 250—most of whom, historians say, first arrived in the 1840s and lived along Mott and Doyers streets, which were part of the Five Points. As attacks against Chinese in the western states continued and violently escalated during the mid-1880s, many more fled for their lives to New York. In 1880, the city's Chinese were estimated to number around 2,000, and about 400 of them lived in a 300-yard stretch of Mott Street that began at Chatham Square. "This small space," the *New York Times* reported on March 22, 1880, "has come to be known as 'China Town.'" The men found shelter in boarding-houses run by compatriots, sleeping on wooden bunks—sometimes crammed three to a board—that reached all the way up to the ceilings. Chinese immigrants worked as servants and cooks and porters and at other menial jobs, or they operated laundries or manufactured cigars, which they peddled along the Bowery from little stands. Some had been merchants in China and used their know-how to open stores, from which they sold food items, herbs, teas, chopsticks, porcelain tea sets, paper fans, toys, slippers, and silk. Some operated restaurants; by 1885, Chinatown had six. They were patronized by both Chinese and white customers and even then offered white patrons way more than chop suey (a group of tourists in 1896 sampled a dish of chicken with preserved pineapple, pea pods, mushrooms, bamboo shoots, and deep-fried noodles). And there were the vice businesses: gambling joints and opium dens, hidden away in damp cellars and foul-smelling back rooms. There, lonely, homesick men paid ten cents for a pipe stuffed with opium. After inhaling the blue, sweet-smelling smoke, they'd start dreaming. But their sleep only lasted half an hour at the most before they had to wake up and return to the misery of life on Mott Street. Chinatown was a source of often-prurient and racist-tinged fascination to outsiders. The world of these immigrants felt opaque and inaccessible, although some white women, mostly Irish, gained access through marriage to Chinese men. These women formed their own in effect expat community in this tiny world.

In the 1880s, a gigantic new wave of Europeans arrived in New York, and they completely changed the landscape. Unlike their predecessors, these people came from eastern and southern parts of the continent: Jews fleeing the violence of Russian pogroms, and Italians. They flooded into the already packed slums around the Bowery. The Jews colonized the Lower East Side, and the Italians clustered mostly on the other side of the Bowery, around Mulberry Bend, which adjoined the Five Points. The arrival of these two groups overwhelmed the existing German and Irish populations, some of whom then moved on to the far west side, which today we call Hell's Kitchen, or uptown along the East River. As the number of souls living around the Bowery increased, hungry real estate speculators jumped in, building as many tenement houses as they could fit on every available piece of land and squeezing in as many people as possible. The Lower East Side became the most densely populated place on earth at the beginning of the twentieth century, which meant that the city's slums had gotten worse. How was that possible! Since the 1850s, pressure was mounting on officials to mitigate the desperate living conditions of New York's poor, yet to date nothing concrete had been done. There were still no public baths; the first did not open until 1901. Occasionally the city took a few baby steps: in 1879, a law was passed that required all rooms in new tenements be ventilated. Builders fulfilled this requirement by carving out a three-foot indentation between abutting buildings. But this proved the opposite of a solution: rather than improving air circulation, these spaces—air shafts, they called them—created miniature versions of hell. People used them to toss out whatever nasty objects they didn't want to deal with, as if flushing their shit down a toilet, except that the bottoms of the shafts were inaccessible, so whatever fell just stayed there. Air shafts also acted like flues and made fires—which happened frequently in tenements—worse by causing the flames to shoot up to the floors above. And they carried every sound, so you were privy to the intimate details of your neighbors' lives. You heard couples making love, babies screaming, parents yelling at children, as if all were in the same room. The well-intentioned 1879 law only increased the claustrophobia of the tenements, which were now filled to bursting with Italians and Jews.

Everything about this latest group of immigrants fascinated and re-pelled New Yorkers: their strange customs, their exotic looks—Italians' black hair and dark skins, the distinct features of Jewish faces; their in-decipherable babble—Sicilian, Neapolitan, and dozens of other Italian dialects, and Yiddish, an amalgam of German and Hebrew. They and the Chinese along with all other new immigrants now getting off boats at Castle Garden by the thousands every day*—Greeks, Hungarians, Bohemians, Serbs, Syrians—all had something in common: poverty. They needed a place to escape to and to play on.

Their street was the Bowery.

In 1876, the Third Avenue El began running along the Bowery. The tracks were built right over the sidewalks, thereby blocking out all sun-light and turning the street into a perpetual and noisy night. Along the two tracks that ran on either side of the street, the trains, powered by steam, roared up and down all day and all night,

> shutting out light and air from the stores and subjecting pedestrians to annoyance and damage of clothing from the constant dripping of oil, water impregnated with grease and rust, and from melting ice and sleet in the winter season. The upper floors of buildings have been rendered almost uninhabitable for dwelling purposes by the din of passing trains within a few feet of the windows.

As a result, some businesses suffered and even moved away. But for others the El proved a boon, because it brought folks from all over the city eager to sample the cheap delights of the Bowery. Even more people were coming down there after another technological miracle arrived in 1882: electric lights, extending from the southern end of the Bowery to

---

* Ellis Island wasn't built until 1892.

just past Houston Street. The Bowery was the first major thoroughfare in New York to have electric lighting on such a grand scale.

Electric lights and fast and cheap transportation, coupled with the area's swelling population, fed the Bowery's economy. The area's denizens, poor as they were, needed food and shelter, and the numbers of hash houses and cheap hotels along the Bowery multiplied. Chinese immigrants sold cigars, in stores or from sidewalk stands. If you lived uptown and needed cheap kitchenware or secondhand clothing, the El now made it easy to get to the Bowery for an afternoon shopping expedition. Which meant that all those shabby little businesses were no longer serving only the locals; they were becoming in fact destination spots, and concurrently, bona fide destination businesses were opening up, and thriving, on the Bowery. Two hat stores, Callahan's and McCann's, supplied people all over the city, and the gorgeous floral arrangements of New York's best-known florist shop, Le Moult's, festooned restaurants, funeral homes, and the interiors of Fifth Avenue mansions. The Tammany Hall crowd hung out at Mike Lyons' restaurant between Prince and Houston Street, which fed up to 2,000 people a day.

But it was at night when the Bowery, now all lit up, was at its most gorgeous, most louche best. It became the number-one destination for that age-old pastime, slum tourism. People went to the Bowery for fun spiked with danger, because, along with the tired and the poor, the Bowery embraced just about anything connected with vice, the number one business of New York in the Gilded Age. There were plenty of other hot spots around the city: the Tenderloin, encompassing most of today's Midtown—it stretched from Twenty-third to Fortieth streets, bounded by Broadway and Sixth Avenue—was considered the epicenter of the city's sex industry. Most of the prostitutes there worked in brothels, some of which catered to wealthy clientele.*

---

* John F. Delaplaine, a member of the proudly abolitionist clan that owned 134–136 Bowery, also owned considerable real estate in the Tenderloin, and rented much of it to madams.

Saturday Night on the Bowery, 1871

But while the Tenderloin's major industry was sex, the Bowery's little economy was diverse. There, everything was for sale and at bargain prices. Women on the Bowery sold their flesh in the concert saloons or out on the street. There were so many ways to enjoy a wicked night out on the Bowery that people called it the devil's work. Nestled among its various entertainment options—theaters, dives, dance halls, beer gardens, shooting galleries—were strange little places called dime museums or anatomical museums. When P. T. Barnum's five-story-high American Museum—it stood at the south end of Park Row, a ten-minute walk from the Bowery—burned down in a spectacular fire after the Civil War and Barnum left New York and took his show on the road, it left a huge gap in the city's entertainment options. After all, Barnum's had entertained crowds for some twenty-five years with a panoply of wonders and hoaxes: freak shows, fortune-tellers, cute baby contests, minstrel shows. There were exotic animals: cages of tigers, lions, and monkeys, one water tank holding hippopotami and another with two white beluga whales—the newspapers said the poor creatures were boiled alive during the fire—and aquariums filled with fish. Finally, there were the miscellaneous "curiosities": mostly dead creatures preserved by stuffing or varnishing or, as in the case of human fetuses, pickling in formaldehyde, and skeletons, the most famous touted to be a real mermaid named Feejee but was really a monkey's body and a fish's tail sewn together. Barnum's message to Americans was that it was fine for everybody, rich and poor, to be entertained by peoples' deformities and weirdnesses. People bought it. And today cultural historians describe his museum—the huge structure was dirty and "ill-shaped," according to the *Times* of July 14, 1865—as the birthplace of American pop culture.

True enough. And so was the Bowery, where all forms of artistic expression for the masses found a home. So too, naturally, did dime museums, which provided the same sleazy entertainment that people had grown to love at Barnum's, but on a much smaller scale. The city had dozens of these places; besides the Bowery, they clustered on Broadway and later in Brooklyn, at Coney Island. Freaks, some of whom first cut their chops at Barnum's, were the main attractions, especially if they were famous—many were—which gave them a lot of clout with their employers. Freaks had a tightly knit community, a high sense of worth, and were protective of each other. There were so many kinds of freaks: people who, because of medical conditions that caused their bodies to waste away, were advertised as "living skeletons," the original of whom was Isaac Sprague, a Barnum's alumnus; giants, the best known of whom was Patrick O'Brien—he measured seven feet five inches—and his wife, the giantess Annie, whose height topped her husband's by two and a half inches; albinos; dwarfs; the Davis brothers, a pair of tiny, mentally disabled brothers with unusual physical strength, born two years apart, who were claimed to be the Wild Men of Borneo; bearded ladies and young men whose faces were covered with hair due to a rare genetic disease called hypertrichosis, perhaps the most famous of whom was the Russian-born Fedor Jeftichew, a.k.a. Jo-Jo the Dog-Faced Boy, who was brought to America by Barnum; the ubiquitous fat ladies, who were sometimes used in staged marriages to living skeletons. Some dime museums displayed children with physical deformities: Bunnell's, at 298 Bowery, billed a child who was no doubt hydrocephalic as "double-brained" and another, who had severe eczema, as "Leopard Boy." These poor souls were victims—in contrast to the people who proudly displayed their bodies all covered with tattoos. Some of the latter were famous, such as Captain Costentenus, formerly a Greek sailor, and a woman named Nora Hildebrandt. (Today they would not be considered freaks at all.) The tattooed crowd could get their inking done right in the neighborhood; the Bowery by the 1880s sported at least one tattoo parlor. They also frequented a photographer, Charles Eisenmann, at 229 Bowery. He was a German immigrant who, together with his son-in-law, Frank Wendt, opened a studio in 1881. Soon, to supplement their incomes, all the freaks from the neighboring dime museums were going to Eisenmann's to get picture cards made, which people then traded and collected.

Some dime museums had something vaguely medical about them, in which case they were advertised as "anatomical museums." They were stocked with glass jars containing body parts preserved in formaldehyde or wax models of syphilis-ridden faces and deformed genitals. The more diseased the specimen or facsimile, the better: Americans then were fascinated by disease, especially the venereal kind, a common affliction of the times. Usually newspapers advertised anatomical museums as "For Gentlemen Only." The attractions there were notorious for built-in scams: for example, visitors might be suckered into paying extra to see "special exhibits," such as a naked woman who turned out to be a mannequin in flesh-colored tights. Doctors—usually with dubious credentials, or disgraced members of their profession—lured men into offices for free blood pressure tests. Once inside, the men instead were offered cures for "paresis"—the then-catchall term for sexually transmitted diseases—and sometimes masturbation, which in those prurient Victorian times was considered a form of sexual deviancy. During the course of this "consultation," a flap on the wall fell and exposed a sign saying the doctor's fee was $2 (or some other sum), and typically the victim was too embarrassed not to pay up.

The Bowery never slept. You could buy booze there night or day—

even on Sundays, in open defiance of the state excise laws, which were the only weapon the city had to shut down dives. But the laws were hard to enforce, especially since saloon owners often paid off cops to look the other way. Even when good cops tried to enforce the law, the legal system was so corrupt and Tammany infested that charges were often mysteriously dropped. The former bare-knuckled prizefighter Owney Geoghegan, whose saloon at 103 Bowery had the distinction of being the Bowery's worst dive during the early part of the 1880s, was indicted 102 times for violations of the excise law. But he had a lot of friends at Tammany Hall, so nothing ever happened to him. Unlike the surrounding dives, Owney's—a.k.a. the Old House at Home—had no light at the entrance, so if you didn't know it was there, you'd walk right past it. But everybody knew about Owney's place. No tourist felt he'd seen the real New York if he didn't stop off there; the darkness added to the cachet. Inside, Owney—"with his round head held down, his chin held back, and he seemed to be growling, if not audibly"—prowled the three floors of his dive keeping watch. He looked like a bulldog. The waiters at Owney's—men only, there were no waitresses—doubled as performers and boxers. On each floor, on sixteen-square-foot platforms furnished with stakes and ropes—boxing rings–cum–performance spaces—that had been constructed at the back of the room, the guys danced, sang, and sparred with each other. Often three shows were going on at the same time. The dingy walls of the establishment were plastered all over with pictures of boxers, a collection "probably as complete as any in America," from the cheapest prints to fine etchings. Owney's became the "fashion of the gilded youth of the town"; every night you'd see them there, all decked out in their white shirts and high silk hats, sharing tables with bank robbers and other lowlifes and, here and there, teenage girls as young as fourteen, who were waiting to get picked up. Yes, the Old House at Home was a paradise for slum tourists, complete with real slum violence. Sixteen-year-old Roxie McBride was stabbed there one night by her husband, "Stuff" McBride, as she was going out the door. She ended up in the hospital—and survived—but there were people who died after getting into fights at Owney's. One of the unfortunates was a tough named John Rose, who stupidly got into a fight with Owney himself, though no charges were ever filed against Owney.

Owney finally got nailed in 1883, when the New York Society for the Prevention of Cruelty to Children went after him for violating child labor laws: a ten-year-old kid was selling oranges to the patrons during nighttime hours. For this, Owney spent thirty days in jail. The experience must have traumatized him, because upon release, he never returned to the Bowery. He died of a stroke in 1885 and was laid out at the home of his brother-in-law, policeman Patrick McGinley, near the Bowery. On the morning of the funeral, some 3,000 "of the most disreputable frequenters of the Bowery" stood in front of McGinley's house to pay their respects. Owney's defunct resort was superseded by his rival's, Billy McGlory, who several years earlier had opened a place right next to Owney's and set out to destroy him. (Among the things McGlory, who previously had operated an infamous dive on the Bowery at Grand Street with the charming name of the Burnt Rag, did to harass Owney was send longshoremen over to the Old House to beat people into a pulp.)

McGlory needed a bouncer, so he hired a big brute named John McGurk, who had impressed him when McGurk worked next door at Owney's. In 1889, McGurk, having been taught by masters, opened his own dive, which became a hangout for sailors. By the mid-1890s, he'd started nine resorts. Six were soon shut down by the cops for violations of the excise laws, but the other three managed to party on. Hardly a day went by without a robbery at one or more of them: a common sight on Bowery streetcars was a man shivering in the cold, sans overcoat, because it had just been stolen at one of McGurk's places. McGurk's dive at 295 gained particular notoriety in March 1899 as the place where three teenage girls over a period of five days ingested carbolic acid. From then on, everybody called 295 Suicide Hall. (According to one newspaper account, somebody carved the words "Suicide Hall" into the plaster wall with a knife that he then used to cut his throat.) Bess Levery—she'd taken the poison on the sidewalk, just outside the door to McGurk's—died instantly. The other two—Florence Levine and Emma Hartig—were rushed to Bellevue Hospital, where their stomachs were pumped and they survived. Interviewed by the *New York World* right after these unfortunate incidents, McGurk said, "Such places as mine must exist. They keep women off the street." These poor young things were members of a suicide club: During the previous few years, twelve girls had killed themselves along the Bowery and Second Avenue. All were out-of-towners drawn to the lights of the big city and lured to McGurk's by his well-waxed dance floor and three-piece orchestra. There lay the road to ruin: "Rendered unconscious by drink, they are soon forever lost to family and friends."

Perhaps McGurk really did see himself as a savior: who else would let these desperate women, who held the lowest place in the pecking order of New York's prostitutes, through the door? Most of the prostitutes in the Tenderloin worked in brothels, but sex on the Bowery went at bargain rates. You bought it on the street or in concert saloons or in the balconies of the theaters—the Bowery Theatre was especially notorious as a place for hookers to find and service their johns—or in nearby tenement brothels run by Jewish and Italian thugs.

Gay sex was also for sale on the Bowery. In fact, a vibrant gay subculture existed there openly and comfortably and it drew men—and women too, although there is less documentation for their presence—from all over town. So when it came to matters of sexual identity, the Bowery was way ahead of its time. Gay men cruised along the Bowery and in its gay-friendly dives—an 1899 investigation by the state found at least six*—some of which they shared with straight patrons. This was probably the case with Owney's and certainly at one of McGlory's resorts, the Armory, on the corner of

---

* The Mazet Committee, so called for its chairman. It named Paresis Hall and, right across the street, Little Bucks, the Rabbit, Manilla Hall, the Palm Club, and the Artistic Club.

Hester and Elizabeth streets, where all the waiters were effeminate males dressed in drag.

Here is one account of such a place, the Rabbit, as told by a Columbia University student and after-dark frequenter of New York's gay underworld, which he documented in a series of memoirs under the nom de plume Ralph Werther:

As I walked the Bowery on that first spree, I was puzzling my mind as to which of the brightly lighted dance-halls or the dark and fearsome dives—through whose doors I saw pass only sailors, gutter snipes, and slovenly gangsters—would be the best stage for my virgin effort at female-impersonation. At last I slipped into the least prosperous-looking and, to the stranger, most uninviting, dance-hall, the notorious "Rabbit." And why the "Rabbit"? Because it looked to be the most crime-inviting of all the dance-halls. I had stood and watched as there passed in and out the most criminal-faced of the Bowery boys: coal-heavers, dock-rats, and fierce-and-cruel-stalking gunmen—not to speak of the poor, deluded fallen angels. I dropped into a chair. Almost in less time than I can tell it, four youthful coal-heavers came up grinning: "Hello Bright Eyes!"

Those three words were the most soulful, the most infatuating, that had ever fallen on my ears. I was also delighted because so lucky as to take in, right off, some of the many bewitching Bowery boys I had stared at that night, and cement them to myself. I smiled back: "Hello!"

For the next few hours, I was in hitherto undreamed-of bliss because of being wooed by all four in their delightfully wild and rough way. And they treated me as their sexual opposite. They danced with me in turn. Only after four hours, I had to own up that I was not an out-and-out female. But that knowledge seemed to count for nothing with these lovesick coal-heavers.

Then there were the more openly gay places on the Bowery: "fairy" resorts, also called slides, where men went to have sex with men who rouged their cheeks and lips and dressed in women's clothing. This is where closeted middle-class men from uptown—disparagingly called inverts by fairies—went for sex. ("There are plenty of them and they are good customers of ours," sniffed Queen Toto, who worked at the aptly named Slide, which the *World* insisted was New York's worst dive.) Sexual identities inside fairy resorts were fluid: straight men, too, patronized the effeminate male prostitutes, and female prostitutes also hung out in these places. When the Slide closed in 1892, Biff Ellison, a member of the Five Points Gang who occasionally worked for Tammany Hall as a hired thug, opened Columbia Hall on the Bowery at Fifth Street. Paresis Hall, as the outside world came to call it—paresis was a synonym for syphilis, which people then believed you could contract by being in the same room as a fairy—became the epicenter of the Bowery's gay scene. "Smooth-faced, high-featured, well-dressed, a Gangland cavalier, never married," the *Pittsburgh Press* (July 14, 1912) described him. "He was not a moll-buzzer: no one could accuse him of taking money from a woman." Ellison, no doubt, was gay. He employed boys as young as fourteen. Their photos adorned studio cards piled on tables near the entrance, like menus in a restaurant. Inside, beautifully attired young fairies made the rounds, chatting up clients and sitting down at tables with them. The clients then bought the boys drinks before heading to the second floor with their chosen ones to be serviced by them in curtained partitions. Paresis Hall was more than a brothel; it served as a safe haven for gay and cross-dressing men across New York's social spectrum. Like any Bowery place of entertainment, the Hall—this was what the gay community called it—operated only at night. During the daytime hours, when the place was quiet and empty, the young bucks who worked there used the upper floor as their own space to gather and discuss whatever they deemed important to them, including literary subjects. They called their group the Cercle Hermaphroditis.

In 1891, a musical called *A Trip to Chinatown* opened on Broadway. It was essentially a vehicle for song-and-dance numbers with hardly a plot, and it had nothing to do with New York. (The Chinatown of the title referred to the one in San Francisco.) The show featured a catchy song in three-fourths time:

> Oh! The night that I struck New York
> I went out for a quiet walk
> Folks who are "on to" the city say
> Better by far that I took Broadway
> But I was out to enjoy the sights
> There was the Bow'ry ablaze with lights
> I had one of the devil's own nights
> I'll never go there any more
>
> The Bowery! The Bowery!
> They say such things and they do strange things
> On the Bowery! The Bowery!
> I'll never go there any more

America immediately fell in love with this catchy song, which was soon circulating all over the place on sheet music (and piano rolls) and being played on every sort of piano, from the tinniest to the most sonorous. Everywhere—in parlors, dives, saloons, beer halls, theaters, drawing rooms of New York mansions—people were singing "The Bowery" and dancing to its tune.

One year later, a group of Bowery merchants petitioned the Board of Aldermen to change the street's name. Because of that darned song, they insisted, nobody wanted to come to the Bowery anymore. (Although nobody offered any evidence to prove their claim, and other merchants said it was absolute nonsense.)

They offered a few colorless suggestions for renaming the Bowery: South Third Avenue, Cooper Avenue (after Peter Cooper, the philanthropist who built Cooper Union), Central Broadway. Their request was denied, but they did not give up. Every couple of years, they repetitioned, but nobody offered sympathy for their request. " 'The

Bowery' is one of the historic street names in this city and ought to be cherished on that account," the *Real Estate Record and Builders' Guide* wrote indignantly in 1898. And a notorious Bowery denizen named Chuck Connors told the *Times* (March 13, 1897):

> Wot's der matter wid der "Bowery"? I suppose you guys would like ter see it called der Foubourg St. Germain? You take my advice and go blow snow off a ditch. Der song not'in! A grand opera couldn't kill der name of dis street!

Connors was the Bowery's resident philosopher and bullshit artist—"da Lane," he called his purview. He was pals with all the thugs, but, like the Bowery b'hoys of old, he had a heart of gold. Connors had no vocation and a reputation as a liar. He claimed to have grown up on Mott Street, but some said that he was really a black sheep from a wealthy family. Every day, he slept until four in the afternoon, got up, donned his old black suit and bowler hat, stuck a cigar in his mouth, and headed over to Barney Flynn's saloon at the corner of the Bowery and Pell Street. Then he sat there until four the next morning, drinking, smoking cigars, and feeding stories to eager reporters in his own version of Boweryspeak, which was so deliberately exaggerated that it became a parody of how people actually spoke on the street. The reporters then turned Connors's nonsense into articles that circulated all over the country. As a youth, the short, compactly built Connors did a turn as a lightweight boxer, but was mostly known for clowning around in the ring ("the Terpsichorean light weight pugilist of Mott Street," a sports writer at the *Salt Lake Tribune* [August 7, 1892] called him).

When he was not boxing, Connors did odd jobs for local people or gave people lessons in how to talk with a real Bowery accent. He was rumored to know Cantonese, and the newspapers called Connors "the [white] mayor of Chinatown." He led nighttime tours there that supposedly steered visitors up close to all the vices that it was famous for, like gambling and smoking opium. Most of the opium dens were staged, in which participants in the scam, usually a mix of Chinese men and white women, would take a few puffs on pipes filled with wax before pretending to fall over in a stupor. In one place, every night, at a certain stage of the exhibition, one of the women would toss her pipe aside and shout, "I am tired of all this." Then she would take a swig from a bottle marked "carbolic acid," and fall groaning on the floor. That was the cue for the guide to rush the visitors out of the den, so that, he told them, they wouldn't be arrested as witnesses.

Connors had friends in Tammany, which hosted an annual ball for him that was attended by all his thug friends (they had terrific names: Paddy the Fake, Cherrynose Jack Stew Johnson, Baldie Carroll, Blizzard) and Bowery politicians. His partner at these dances was always a six-foot-tall, 200-pound young woman who went by the name the Rummager.

Chuck Connors had a rival on the Bowery named Steve Brodie, who was equally famous, but on a grander scale. When he was a kid, and one of a group of seven bootblacks—shoe polishers—who worked the corner of Chatham and Frankfort streets, he was participating in and winning miles-long footraces he'd persuaded people to bet on. This made him famous among his fellow bootblacks, and from then on his goal in life was to remain famous. Brodie was an expert swimmer, so he came up with the idea of jumping off the recently completed Brooklyn Bridge. The drop measured 120 feet. A man had already tried this stunt and died, so there was already a lot of interest in the subject.

In 1886, Brodie made his attempt on a $200 bet. He survived, but he received a short sentence in the Tombs, New York's massive prison that had been built over part of the filled-in Collect, for attempted suicide, along with substantial newspaper publicity. (Many later said that the stunt was a hoax: supposedly, a dummy was thrown off the bridge as Brodie slipped into the East River from a strategically located rowboat.) After he completed his jail time, Brodie was offered jobs in dime museums, which he took for a while. Then he went around the country wagering bets and jumping off bridges.

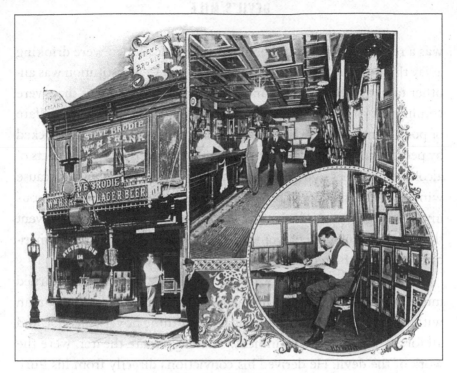

Steve Brodie's Saloon

Eventually he accumulated enough money to return to the Bowery and open his own saloon, which used his bridge-jumping feats as a theme.

He plastered the walls with pictures of bridges, as well as famous fighters: he used Brodie's for staging boxing bouts. Brodie's became a Bowery go-to place, and the owner's exploits were written into a play, *On the Bowery,* in which Brodie played himself. At the play's climax, Brodie jumps off the Brooklyn Bridge to save his girlfriend, Pearl, who has fallen into the East River. He emerges with her in his arms, as he sings: *My Poil Is a Bowery Goil.*

As the Bowery was becoming the national symbol of urban debauchery, moral reform movements, all under the auspices of old guard Protestants, were starting up throughout America. Many had good intentions, such as those having to do with temperance. Alcohol abuse was a real problem everywhere; many American men were drinking away their wages, leaving their families to starve. Prostitution was another target of these groups and a perfectly justified one if they were coming at it for the right reasons—that is, out of concern for the welfare of poor young women. But the purest of intentions often get hijacked by peoples' irrational hang-ups, and genuine concern over the effects of alcohol on families sometimes turned into code for xenophobia, because wine and beer and saloons played vital roles in the social lives of various immigrant groups. And what started out as honest attempts to prevent the sexual exploitation of women got all twisted up with some Americans' hysterical hatred of anything having to do with sex.

Such was the case with Anthony Comstock, whose name turned into a synonym for prurient aggression. Comstock, a short, bulky man with muttonchop sideburns, believed that dime novels, alcohol, and all forms of public entertainment, even legitimate theater, were the work of the devil. He derived his convictions directly from his Puritan forebears. He came from a strict Congregationalist family in Connecticut, one of ten children. Arriving in New York in 1864 as a young man after serving in the Union army, he found a room in a boarding-house on Pearl Street and a job as a shipping clerk. He also discovered New York's cornucopia of theaters, gambling dens, concert saloons, and brothels, racy tabloids like the *Police Gazette*, and dime novels with titles like *The Gay Girls of New York* and *New York Naked*. He was especially offended by the dirty postcards and brothel guides that were openly displayed at newsstands.

Comstock began tipping off police to where they could find obscene materials—"obscene" being a decidedly arbitrary label that in his mind included anything having to do with contraception. In 1871, this self-appointed arbiter of public morality found a perfect life partner: Margaret Hamilton, an eighty-two-pound wisp of a woman ten years his senior. She was a model Victorian "wifey," as he affectionately called her, who completely subordinated herself to her husband. The couple had no children.

Eventually Comstock insinuated himself into the YMCA. The

organization's mission—offering young men a place to go to that had good Christian values as an alternative to the temptations of the big, bad city—nicely dovetailed with his ideas. With the Y, Comstock started the Committee for the Suppression of Vice. He attracted the attention of the Y's president, the financier Morris Jesup (who later became a major philanthropist). He gave Comstock money to further his campaign. Thus armed, Comstock set off for Washington, D.C., in January 1873 to lobby for an anti-obscenity law.

To make his point, Comstock stood on the floor of Congress, where he displayed dirty pictures and other paraphernalia that he claimed were being sent through the mail and blabbered on about it for days. (The country was then in the midst of the latest of the financial panics that happened on a regular basis during the Gilded Age.) In March, an anti-obscenity law was passed, which Comstock had helped write. Congressmen did not dare to challenge his bill. "Every Congressman who presumed to ask what it [the bill] was all about, or to point out obvious defects in the bill, was disposed of by insinuation, or even the direct charge, that he was a covert defender of obscene books, and, by inference, of the carnal recreations described in them," the acerbic H. L. Mencken wrote in a 1913 essay. The so-called Comstock Act made it a federal crime to possess or disseminate anything of an "obscene, lewd, lascivious . . . or filthy" matter. (It is thanks to him that it is illegal to send porn through the mail: incredibly, the law today remains on the books.) Comstock also got a rider tacked on to the bill that created a new position just for him. As "special agent for the Post Office," he had absolute authority to enforce the new law. In other words, he could intercept mail and open it.

Comstock, triumphant, returned to New York. But his increasing visibility and big mouth were making the YMCA uneasy, so the organization cut its ties with him. No matter, he simply reincorporated the old Committee for the Suppression of Vice as the New York Society for the Suppression of Vice (NYSSV). Even though the Y no longer backed him, Jesup as an individual continued to give him money, and New York's other megacapitalists—Samuel Colgate and J. P. Morgan and John D. Rockefeller—followed suit. They felt that they had to, because Comstock was becoming a real political force in New York. Moreover, the vague language in the Comstock Act—adjectives like "obscene" and "lewd" were open to interpretation—made it possible for him, as Mencken put it, "to bring an accusation against practically any publication that aroused the comstockian blood-lust."

But with all that, Comstock was still not satisfied. His new law had given him the power to intercept mail. But there was also the matter of all the things he considered morally objectionable that were available to the public, which could be just about anything: theater productions featuring scantily clad women, books containing pictures of equally scantily clad Greek statues, and so on. The list of possible "obscenities" was endless. So the NYSSV pressured the state legislature to insert into New York's penal code its own version of the Comstock Act, one with real teeth. Albany obediently complied. The new law in effect gave society agents the right to arrest anybody at will.

Comstock, armed with both state and federal laws, began a crusade that lasted forty years. He had freethinkers arrested, contraceptive devices confiscated, and he made huge bonfires with piles of books and other printed matter that he'd collected with the help of local authorities. By the late 1880s, public opinion began turning against him—"That pyrotechnic crank," the *Times* of Richmond, Virginia, called him (January 26, 1888). But Comstock had the law—his law!—on his side and forged ahead, ruining peoples' livelihoods and sometimes their very lives. Some of his victims ended up in prison: the French-born Jules Dumont, for example, a.k.a. Jarbeau Fairy, who had a successful dressmaking business and worked nights as the floor manager of the Black Rabbit, a gay resort on Bleecker Street. "A foul bestial wretch," is how Comstock described Dumont, who was sentenced to fourteen years at hard labor in 1900. Four other drag queens were arrested along with Dumont during that bust of the Black Rabbit in 1900. All got prison time, but Dumont's sentence was the longest. One can hardly dare to imagine the torments these men suffered in jail, and it was all because of Comstock, for whom this amounted to a major accomplishment. He was proud of the havoc he wreaked: once he bragged that he'd burned fifteen tons of books and caused fifteen people to commit suicide (among whom was the abortion provider Madame Restell in 1878).

Comstock's crusade took him all over the country, but his focus was New York, the sin capital of America, with its cornucopia of targets. In September 1874, when the Metropolitan Theatre on Broadway mounted a production of *Paris by Moonlight*, which featured that delightful Parisian dance, the cancan, Comstock got the police—Captain Williams, of the Eighth Precinct—to arrest the entire troupe of forty-two people. (The next morning they released everybody but the proprietor of the theater, Samuel Shapter, who had to post $500 bail "for keeping a disorderly house.") He had newsstand owners arrested for selling dirty books and magazines. He barged into libraries and bookstores and seized the works of such giants as Emile Zola (*Nana*), Honore de Balzac (*Droll Stories*), and Thomas Hardy (*Jude the Obscure*). He made no distinction between the classics and pulp literature: in his view, any printed material that so much as mentioned sex corrupted youth. He felt the same way about publicly displayed paintings and statues that depicted nude figures. He kept obsessively detailed ledgers of the NYSSV's arrests: information about each "offender" included religion, address, education level, nationality, and the inventory seized, including the exact number of offending objects (from Max Rosenthal's cigar store "689 obscene cards, 24 pictures"). Comstock also noted the charge, the bail set—at the least $500, which few could meet—and, if there was a conviction, the sentence received. This, besides fines, often included jail time. (A peddler on the Bowery, for example, caught with two obscene books got sixty days in the Tombs. Another, Paul Deheerer, was arrested in front of 128 Bowery for selling obscene photos concealed in clam shells. Police seized fifteen photos displayed in the window of a photographer at 352 Bowery, along with 378 postcards and a bunch of negatives. The Singer brothers at 82 Bowery were fined $50 for selling obscene pictures out of their notions store. At 252 Bowery, photographer David Landau was fined $400 dollars for manufacturing obscene mirrors. Rosenthal's Curiosity Shop at 236 Bowery and David Hartsilver at 158 Bowery were each hit with a $50 fine for displaying watches with obscene pictures in their respective windows.)

In 1888, Comstock found a new target, thanks to his pal in the Eighth Precinct who'd helped him fourteen years earlier in the bust of *Paris by Moonlight*. As Inspector Williams—he'd been promoted from captain—was strolling down the Bowery one January day, he decided to check out a few dime museums. He entered No. 138—known as the Egyptian Musee—and found displays of naked wax figures, both men and women, as part of an exhibit on human anatomy, along with models of genitals. The inspector, gratified that his search for new forms of "obscenity" along the Bowery was so far bearing fruit, continued his walk. He next stopped in front of the window at No. 81— the European Museum of Anatomy—which displayed another wax figure—this one clothed—"about to be cut up with hundreds of knives, representing a method of old time torture." Since the statue was clothed, it didn't bother him. The inspector then went inside and found more statues—nude ones.

Bingo!

The police of the Eighth District spent the next few days along the Bowery, gathering evidence. They found additional naked wax statues in the Parisian Museum at 309 Bowery and at Kahn's Anatomical Museum, which was one block over on Broadway. (The latter had been operating for twenty years.) A few days later, the police, armed with warrants, raided the offending museums and arrested the owners, along with a few men who were working for them. Then they seized all the naked wax figures, loaded them onto horse-drawn trucks, and carted them off to the police station. REVOLTING SHOWS CLOSED, the *New York Times* trumpeted the next day. A week later, Comstock confronted the museum owners in the Court of Special Sessions in the Tombs, where New York's criminal cases were adjudicated. Comstock charged the defendants with "maintaining exhibitions tending to degrade the morals of their patrons." Kahn had the means to hire a lawyer, who managed to get his client's case postponed. But the other three owners could not afford lawyers, so they pled guilty and hoped for the best. The judge fined each owner $250, a large sum in 1888. He also threw in a $50 fine for each employee for good measure. Walter Price, proprietor of the Parisian Museum, who was nearly blind and also paralyzed—his disability was, to be sure, the reason for his interest in anatomical curiosities—asked the judge for leniency. The judge, moved by Price's plight, reduced his fine to $50. But Price could not come up with even this reduced amount. The other defendants could not pay their fines, either. So they were forced to shut their museums. As for the nude wax figures, a judge gave the police permission to destroy them. But he told them that the pieces taken from Kahn's—six cartloads of "wax figures of females life size, some pregnant and some otherwise, & 37 cases of filthy penises" were to be spared, to await the court's decision. Still, that left all the "disgusting-looking anatomical subjects," per the *New York Times*, that were taken from the Bowery museums. Police superintendent Murray and Inspector Williams watched as policemen chopped up the offending items with axes in the yard outside police headquarters, and then burned them in a huge bonfire.

When Kahn's case came up, the judge dismissed all charges against him. Apparently he had a great lawyer, because when Comstock tried to convince the judge to at least destroy Kahn's collection of offending wax objects, the judge refused. Kahn immediately reopened his museum (in 1888)—not on Broadway, but on the Bowery, No. 253. There, in 1897, one particularly repulsive exhibit featured a man named Rienzi di Colonna shut up inside a glass case, attempting to fast for thirty days. He died within a week. Comstock kept up his crusade against dime museums, and one by one they were closing. (The last one closed in 1911.) Ridding the Bowery of the dives, however, proved way more complicated.

As Comstock continued his war against the human libido, another son of New England jumped on the reform wagon. But the latter was of a different sort altogether, and pursued a wholly different angle. The

Reverend Doctor Charles Parkhurst was pastor of the fancy Madison Square Presbyterian Church, and his target was Tammany Hall. He was hell-bent on breaking the organization's hold on the municipal government and particularly on the police department. Parkhurst was tapping into something profound: the public—that is, New York's Anglo-Saxon Protestant public—was outraged over Tammany. Following the demise of William M. "Boss" Tweed in 1872—the Tammany leader, famously caricatured by cartoonist Thomas Nast, came to personify municipal corruption—the organization had regrouped and emerged stronger than ever, controlling New York's Democratic Party through a system of clubhouses and "ward bosses" (wards were then the city's smallest political units, equivalent to today's districts), all bound tightly together based on who was doing what favor for whom. Tammany's arms reached into the highest echelons of municipal government and extended all the way down to the gutters; along the way, money changed hands numerous times. Saloons and brothels had to buy "protection" from the police, who in turn had to hand a cut from their payoffs to Tammany.

But there was a subtext to Parkhurst's agenda. "Tammany" was such a loaded word: along with municipal corruption, it implied "Irish," "immigrant," and "poor." (Parkhurst hated the Irish and openly said so. He once remarked that if the country got rid of rum and the Irish, it could close three-quarters of its poorhouses and tear down half the prisons.) In Gilded Age New York, few social services existed for the swelling population of poor living in the squalor, and to them Tammany offered a lifeline. In exchange for votes, Tammany provided food, loans, jobs, and protection. Not just to the Irish, but Jews and Italians, too.

Parkhurst began his crusade on February 14, 1892, when he mounted his pulpit and devoted his Sunday sermon to Tammany. It was quite a Valentine's Day gift to the city: he told his well-dressed congregation that New York was mired in "the slimy, oozy soil of Tammany Hall." The police, he said, were on the take, and city officials were "rum soaked and polluted harpies that under pretense of governing this city are feeding day and night on its quivering vitals." His parishioners were mesmerized. The next day, Parkhurst's sermon was printed in all the newspapers.

The backlash was immediate, and the name Parkhurst was suddenly known all over town. How dare he! politicians complained. Had Parkhurst actually witnessed the corruption he described? One week later, District Attorney DeLancey Nicoll convened a grand jury to question Parkhurst. The jurors found no basis for Parkhurst's allegations: all his information, they said, was secondhand—it came from the newspapers—and everybody knew how untrustworthy the press was. The judge who had ordered the grand jury report formally censured Parkhurst, and the Tammany machine stopped worrying about the annoying pastor.

Parkhurst, humiliated by the political naïveté he had displayed, knew that the grand jury was right: he *hadn't* witnessed any evidence of Tammany's ties to sex and sin. So he decided he had to go and see for himself. He hired a private detective—a rather shady character named Charles Gardner—and told him: "Take me to the most notorious resorts that you know of!"

Over a three-week period, Parkhurst, Gardner, and a friend of Parkhurst's from his congregation disguised themselves as locals by dressing in ratty clothes and roamed New York's demimonde. They dropped in on an opium den in Chinatown, where they witnessed a fat lady from one of the Bowery freak shows "who lay on her tremendous back, her 300 pounds of flesh just tingling with the ecstasy of the drug." At a Bowery concert saloon, so filled with smoke that you could hardly breathe, heavily painted women, one by one, stood on a stage and sang popular tunes. Then they descended from the stage, sat on men's laps, and "in no way rejected any advance, no matter how vile it was." A fancy whorehouse in the Tenderloin—a burly cop stood on the steps, swinging his club, as if bragging to passersby that this place was under police protection—offered a stable of French women who performed various sexual acts on each other. Gardner took careful notes of everything the men had seen. After their slum tour was finished, each man delivered dozens of sworn affidavits to D.A. Nicolls—all of which made irresistible newspaper copy. Parkhurst, invigorated by the publicity, ratcheted up his crusade with more sermons. He so raised the public's ire that, in 1894, the state legislature put together a special committee to investigate police corruption in New York. What the Lexow Committee—named for the state senator who chaired it—found was so sensationally damning to the police that Tammany Hall lost the mayoral election to the reform candidate. Mayor William Strong then appointed Teddy Roosevelt as police commissioner.

At the same time, Anthony Comstock, pariah though he was, was continuing to pound the sidewalks in his compulsive search for anything he deemed pornographic. Between him and Parkhurst and Roosevelt, the poor Bowery was feeling vulnerable. Especially after the state legislature passed a new excise law with strict provisions. Named for the state legislator who sponsored it, the Raines law raised the drinking age from sixteen to eighteen, substantially increased the liquor tax, and forbade the sale of alcohol on Sundays except in hotels, which were required to serve a meal and offer accommodations for at least ten guests. But Senator John W. Raines hadn't thought his bill through very carefully: Saloons got around the law by creating hotel rooms in floors above the bar or in back rooms—where sometimes they built wooden partitions and called them "rooms"— which they used for prostitution. As for the food requirement, "Raines hotels" only had to throw in a few sandwiches for their patrons. So the Raines law de facto encouraged prostitution and resulted in more dives opening along the Bowery. McGurk's Suicide Hall, in fact, opened as a Raines law hotel in 1895.

The Bowery wasn't going to be cleaned up anytime soon. In 1898, the police compiled a list of every place of entertainment on the Bowery. Of the ninety-eight found, they classified only fourteen as "respectable," one of which was the former Bowery Theatre, where Edwin Forrest played Hamlet and Daddy Rice jumped Jim Crow. It had been purchased in 1879 by a German named William Kramer, who owned the adjoining Atlantic Gardens. Kramer renamed it the Thalia, and by 1898, all its productions were in Yiddish.

CHAPTER NINE

THE JEWS

Jews associate Yiddish theater with Second Avenue, but it began on the Bowery. Yes, the Bowery! This, remember, is where all the theaters were, and you could rent them for cheap because the street was so déclassé. If your play was successful, well, then you might move it to Second Avenue. But in the meantime, the Bowery nourished the Jews, and they gave back in the form of their homespun productions in the *mamaloschen* (mother tongue), which, like the street itself, was considered low class and crude. But from its humble beginnings, Yiddish theater evolved into one of the most quintessentially American art forms: the Broadway musical. What a perfect collaboration, the Bowery and Yiddish! Together they helped shape our popular culture, and it all started in the 1880s, when hundreds, sometimes thousands of Eastern European Jews debarked daily from ships onto Ellis Island.

Most were refugees from the pogroms of czarist Russia, and they all spoke Yiddish: a mixture of medieval German and Hebrew but with local variations depending on whether you came from Russia, Poland, Belarus, Ukraine, Hungary, Romania, Lithuania, or Latvia, and spiced up with words from the surrounding lingua franca. The already Americanized Sephardic and German Jews in New York who'd preceded this latest influx—Ashkenazim they were called, after the Hebrew word *ashkenaz* for "German"—were just as appalled by their strange language and customs as were the gentiles.

The new Jewish immigrants squeezed into the Lower East Side. Soon they outnumbered the Germans and the Irish already living there, who then started moving to neighborhoods north. By the turn of the century, the Lower East Side was the most densely populated place on earth: 300,000 Jews were living in the area bounded by East Houston, Canal, and Grand streets, the Bowery, and the East River, which calculated to 500 people per acre. The neighborhood acquired a new moniker: the Ghetto. Extended families and sometimes a boarder or two—perhaps he came from the same shtetl and had no relatives in America to take him in—lived squished together in one or two tenement rooms, where they also made their livings, sewing piece-work for clothing manufacturers fifteen hours a day. Or they employed their knowledge of the needle trades that they'd brought with them from Europe in sweatshops, producing clothing under inhumane conditions. And all over the Lower East Side, in particular along Orchard Street, which once marked the boundary of Stephen Delancey's lush estate, they worked as peddlers, hawking everything you could think of from pushcarts: tin cups and plates, oranges, apples, clocks, hot sweet potatoes, herrings, potted geraniums, rubber boots, cheap fabric, eggs sold individually, pickles, and prayer books.

The Jews were considered the most pernicious aspect of what those well-intended Protestant reformers delicately called the tenement house problem, which also included the Irish and the other new immigrants, the Italians. The latter were settling in the nightmarish slum Mulberry Bend on the opposite side of the Bowery from the Jews. The Italians were as poor as, if not poorer than, the Jews. They had a higher death rate. But neither they nor any of the other ethnic groups who dwelled in the slums of New York lived in such grotesquely crowded conditions as the Jews.

"It is perfectly obvious that the privacy which is essential to decent living are unknown in these Hebrew homes," wrote the snooty Frank Moss, a prominent reformer who served as the Reverend Parkhurst's counsel, in *The American Metropolis,* his 1897 book about New York. "The ignorance and the dirtiness of New Israel are not its only dark features. It is a distinct center of crime. It is infested with petty thieves and house-breakers, many of them desperate; and the criminal instincts that are so often found naturally in the Russian and Polish Jews come to the surface here in such ways as to warrant the opinion that these people are the worst element in the entire make-up of New York life." Moss's freely expressed anti-Semitism was then the social norm. (However, in 1909 he was appointed assistant district attorney, and by then New York's Jews had enough political clout that Moss felt compelled to apologize for the nasty things he'd written about them eight years earlier.) But one thoughtful young reporter, writing in 1900 about the Ghetto, had a different take on the Jews. While he criticized them for spreading the socialist ideas that they brought from Russia ("their influence has been bad rather than good, politically") and found their personalities on the whole offensive, he nevertheless saw them as an asset to America. Once here, he wrote, they stay, because, driven out of their native country by violence and hatred, have nothing to go back to. In this, Jews were unlike other immigrants; many Italians, for example, went back and forth, with the goal of earning money and ultimately returning to their native country.

"The Jew," he wrote in the *Real Estate Record and Builders' Guide* of December 4, 1900, "is the yeast of any slum."

The same reporter also marveled that the Jews, despite their impoverished lives, had their own theaters—four, in fact—along the Bowery. One was the Thalia, previously the Bowery Theatre. Another was the People's Theatre, occupying the space that was once Tony Pastor's Opera House.* So the same Bowery theaters where American

---

* There was also the grungy little Oriental at the corner of the Bowery and Hester Street. This was probably New York's first Yiddish theater, opened in a former dance hall by a few Romanian Jews around 1879. Another was the Windsor, where Lillie Langtry played Lady Macbeth on her New York tour. At one time the Lower East Side had as many as twelve Yiddish theaters.

The Thalia Theatre, Bowery

artists found their voices were now providing space for a whole new dramatic form: Yiddish theater. On the Bowery, Yiddish theater took root, bloomed, and leapt into American culture: to Broadway and then all the way to Hollywood.

Yiddish theater started in the Eastern Europe of the 1870s: from Jassy, Romania, it spread to Bucharest, Kiev, Odessa, Lemberg, and other cities, before being outlawed by the czar in 1883. The ban was lifted in 1904. In the interval, the center of Yiddish theater shifted to New York's Lower East Side, where Jewish actors and playwrights landed along with their coreligionists starting in the 1880s. There, they re-created their art form for hundreds of thousands of displaced and homesick Jews, who couldn't get enough of it. Theaters provided escape for immigrant Jews from their miserable lives. Performances took place even on Friday nights, the Jewish Sabbath, when religious Jews wrapped themselves in their prayer shawls and went to pray in their little hole-in-the-wall shuls. The religious—*frummers,* in Yiddish—were aghast at the actors and theatergoers who were desecrating Shabbos. But who cared what the religious Jews thought? This was America, not the shtetl.

Everybody went to the theater: mothers with babies, peddlers, young girls who slaved in sweatshops, boys who worked for tailors on Orchard Street, Hester Street shopkeepers, anarchists and socialists, scholars, poets, and journalists. The cheapest seats cost only twenty-five cents. After the show, some extended their night out in hot, smoky rooms at one of the nearby cafés or wine cellars to guzzle wine—the Jews' preferred alcoholic beverage—out of earthenware jugs, eat garlicky pickles, and crack walnuts in between their teeth. People shouted at each other, trying to be heard over the sweet, maddening *thump-thump-thumping* of the cymbalon, a gypsy instrument. If you were lucky, an actor you'd just seen onstage might drop in. Everybody would turn around and stare as he made his entrance. And when he got up to leave, a besotted fan would run over to pay the tab.

Oh, how the Jews adored their actors. They went to the theater to see their favorites, not so much a particular play. Jewish actors multitasked: they formed the companies, leased and managed the theaters, and often wrote the plays in which they performed. Jacob Adler and Boris Thomashefsky were the undisputed kings of this tight little world. If you were a fan of one, you were obliged to hate the other. The fans—*patriotn*—obsessively kept track of their respective idols. The two men had a complicated relationship. Sometimes they collaborated on plays, but most of the time they tried to put each other out of business. When Adler played Othello at the People's Theatre in 1897, Thomashefsky retaliated by mounting his own production of Hamlet at the Thalia across the street. For a short time the two formed a company together, but their partnership did not last long; no theater was big enough for two such gigantic egos. Adler and Thomashefsky each led glamorous, tumultuous lives. Adler rode to the theater every day in his own carriage, complete with a footman, as crowds gathered on the sidewalks to watch. "Adler's coming, Adler's coming!" they would shout. Then he would tip his stovepipe hat toward them, revealing his head of beautiful white hair, and everybody would applaud. Adler married several times. He had one child, Celia, with his first wife, Dinah, and six with his second wife, Sara, and several out of wedlock. The Adler acting dynasty included his daughter, Stella Adler, in whose workshop numerous American luminaries trained, including Marlon Brando.

Jacob Adler liked his women young. He cut a striking figure, but Tomashefsky, with his cleft chin and shock of thick curly black hair, was a god. He exuded so much sex appeal that he was accused of corrupting the morals of Jewish women. One woman was overheard describing her fantasy: she would walk out of the theater and be run over by a streetcar. Then Thomashefsky would rush over to her, pick her up, and she would die in his arms. His serial womanizing included trysts on performance nights during intermissions. Thomashefsky had four children (one of them, a girl named Esther, died of diphtheria in 1895) with his wife Bessie. She, an actress in her own right, was a tiny blonde thing who ran off with Thomashefsky when she was sixteen. The Thomashefskys worked together in many Yiddish productions. (In 1901, the couple staged *Uncle Tom's Cabin* with Boris as Uncle Tom and Bessie as Topsy.) Bessie finally left her philandering husband in 1911, but the couple never divorced. After the separation, she continued her career on the Yiddish stage by herself, on her own terms.

Boris Thomashefsky's specialty was *shund*, theater for the masses. (It translates into something like "junk"; as is the case with many Yiddish words, it has no satisfactory equivalent in English.) Thomashefsky often played biblical heroes, which required him to wear short costumes with tights, thereby conveniently exposing his gorgeously shaped

Boris Thomashefsky

calves to the swooning women in the audience. His big hit was *Alexander, the Crown Prince of Jerusalem*. There were melodramas about immigrant families torn apart when their American-born children marry gentiles (goyim), clanky operettas based on Old Testament stories filled with spectacle and speeches (*Bar Kockhba, or the Last Days of Jerusalem*), inane domestic comedies about second wives—*Blimele*, or the *Second Wife*, 1910, in the People's Theatre—and stories about unsophisticated *gruener*, greenhorns. (Boris and Bessie Thomashefsky produced an entire "green series.") Boris Thomashefsky descended from a long line of Russian cantors, and his productions always included music and songs, so as to show off his beautiful baritone voice. (Many of the songs became permanent fixtures in Jewish popular culture, for example the lullaby "Raisins and Almonds.")

There was always a large audience for shund, which was being churned out by Lower East Side theater groups as they went along. Some Jewish actors, among them Jacob Adler, craved serious plays, but as yet there were no Yiddish plays with sophisticated content: Yiddish, the language of the Ashkenazic kitchen and marketplace, was not used to create literature until perhaps the mid-nineteenth century. In late 1891, Adler made the acquaintance of Jacob Gordin, an erudite Russian journalist who had arrived in America just six months earlier.

"Why don't you write something for me?" Adler urged Gordin. The journalist had never written plays, nor even stepped inside a Yiddish theater in Russia. He spoke Yiddish, but could not write it; his langue de plume was Russian. But Adler was offering him money, which he needed, badly. (His wife and nine children were still in Russia waiting for him to send money for the passage over.) So he quickly learned to write in Yiddish, and within a few months he composed his first play: *Siberia*. For this Adler paid him $100. The play flopped, and Gordin then decided to use Shakespeare as the basis for a Yiddish melodrama. This was a revolutionary idea, since most of his audience didn't even know who Shakespeare was. Gordin changed the venue of *The Yiddish King Lear* to Vilna, a city with a large and vibrant Jewish population, and he made the protagonist, played by Adler, not a king, but a wealthy businessman named Dovid Moysheles. Denied even food by his daughters, the blind Reb Dovid is reduced to a beggar. He roams the streets, crying: "Alms for the Yiddish King Lear!" ("*Shenkt a neduve der Yid-dish-er Kenig Leeeee-ar!*")

The Yiddish King Lear was a major success, and soon every Yiddish theater company was doing Shakespeare. Sometimes a translation was pretty faithful to the original. (Boris Thomashefsky advertised a version of *Hamlet* that he was starring in as *fartaytsht un farbesert*, "translated and improved.") But mostly the plays were only loosely based on Shakespeare—and some very loosely, indeed. Thomashefsky wrote his own version of *Hamlet*—*Der Yeshive Bocher* (1899)—which took place in a Hasidic community. Nonetheless, Yiddish Shakespeare connected the newly American Jews to the outside world they'd been deprived of all those centuries in Europe, where they were confined to ghettoes and shtetls. Jewish playwrights, in turn, brought Shakespeare—that is, their version of him—back to the very same Bowery theaters where once Edwin Forrest and Junius Brutus Booth played Hamlet and Macbeth.

One year after *Lear* premiered, Gordin and Adler collaborated on a melodrama called *Der Wilder Mensch* (*The Wild Man*). It told the story of Lemach, a severely disabled young man. His father, a rich Odessan wheat merchant, marries Zelda, a cabaret singer half his age. He brings her into his household to the dismay of his children. Gordin wrote the character of Lemach, played by Adler against type, as the village fool. Lemach's movements are spastic; sometimes he repeats other people's words. (Today he probably would be diagnosed as autistic and also with cerebral palsy.) Everybody, even the maid, beats him and taunts him. *Neboch,* they call him (the word best translates "pathetic"). Zelda destroys the family: her lover, Vladimir, spends all the old man's money, and she throws his daughter out onto the street. Lemach, driven mad by his infatuation with his stepmother, knifes her to death as he screams: "You're my bride!" Gordin's subject matter pushed the limits way beyond what was then considered respectable. At the same time, everybody was blown away by Adler's performance, and his reputation spread north of the Lower East Side all the way to Broadway.

In 1901, after a producer saw Adler play Shylock in a Yiddish production of *The Merchant of Venice* at the People's Theatre, he hired the actor to reprise the role on Broadway.* Adler did not know English, so he spoke his lines in Yiddish, even though this was historically inaccurate: Venetian Jews spoke not Yiddish but Ladino, the Jewish-Spanish dialect, or Italian. Adler again played Shylock in

---

* Adler also played King Lear on Broadway.

1903 and 1905, both times on Broadway. His portrayal received good reviews, but after the engagement was over, Adler returned to the Lower East Side. In 1908, he opened his own theater, right off the Bowery, at the corner of Grand and Chrystie streets. He never went back to Broadway.

After the success of *The Wild Man*, Gordin was besieged by Jewish actors begging him to write for them. Using bits and pieces of European authors—Schiller, Ibsen, Gorky, Goethe—as raw material, he began producing plays at a furious pace. Soon Gordin was making enough money from his writing to bring his family from Russia. He had five more children with his wife and numerous affairs with other women. Gordin was handsome and charming, a big man who sported a bushy black beard. New York's literary establishment became fascinated with the man; they called him the Yiddish Shakespeare.* His plays had suggestive titles: *Di Yiddishe Safo* (*The Jewish Sappho*); *Tares Hamishpokhe* (*The Sanctity of the Family*, a really loaded expression akin to, say, "family values"; originally it refers to the separation of husbands and wives during menstruation as proscribed in the Talmud); and *Got, Mentsch, un Tayvel* (*God, Man, and Devil*, which was based on the Faust legend). They dealt with subjects you weren't supposed to talk about: women's place in the home, extramarital love affairs, family secrets. Abraham Cahan, a writer and socialist who was held in high regard among New York's immigrant Jews, railed against Gordin in the *Forverts*, the Yiddish newspaper he'd help found. Gordin's plays,

---

* When Henry James returned to New York in 1898—he had left some twenty years earlier, during which time his native city had turned into something unrecognizable to him—Gordin escorted the famous writer around the Bowery and the Lower East Side. James had a fascination with Jews; at the same time they revolted him. Gordin took James inside a Yiddish theater, which James described as small and crammed: "an oblong hall, bristling with pipe and glass, at the end of which glowed for a moment, a little dingily, some broad passage of a Yiddish comedy of manners. It hovered there briefly, as if seen through a spy glass reaching, across the world, to some far-off dowdy Jewry." *The American Scene* (London: Chapman & Hall, 1907).

Cahan wrote, were destroying traditional Jewish values. How else to account for all the broken families and prostitution on the Lower East Side? He blamed Gordin's plays for bringing shame upon the Jews.

Gordin, of course, was merely writing about the real lives of this first generation of Jews on New York's mean streets. Most new immigrants were men, many of them married with families whom they'd been forced to leave behind in Europe until they could make enough money to send for them. This might take years; so there were a lot of lonely young Jewish greenhorns on the streets. It all translated into good money to be made in sex trafficking. Pimps imported Jewish girls directly from Europe, whom they housed in tenements—there was a stretch of these "tenement brothels" along Allen Street—right alongside families, who, as they were eking out their livings, stitching together clothing or making wigs from human hair (perhaps to be used as *sheytls,* the wigs that Jewish law mandates women wear after they are married), were subjected to the sounds of a girl next door noisily turning tricks.

Hellish descriptions of these places survive in sworn testimony given in 1900 to the Committee of Fifteen, a citizen-based campaign to combat prostitution. A woman who worked as a cook for several madams along Allen Street described—in Yiddish—how "business" in one of these tenement brothels was conducted:

> The girls give the money that they get from the man to the madam, and the girls get a check for each 50-cent man. Each night these checks that they get from the madam are taken by a keeper. After the money is turned over to the boss, the pimp comes around, once a week, to collect the money. A girl must turn in 32 checks before her board charges are covered. The pimp has absolute control. If a girl wants a pair of stockings she must have the consent of the pimp.
>
> He even tells her where to buy her things. I know of the following pimps: Joe Taljener, who one time struck me in the face; Sholom at 149 Allen Street; and a hunchback who gives out the checks

at 149, and who boasts he is not afraid of anybody, and can be found there every night.

Jewish prostitutes also solicited in the Yiddish concert saloons then popping up all over the Lower East Side. The Eldorado on the Bowery had a sign in Yiddish in the window proclaiming:

Extra! Extra! Tonight we will present "The Unlucky Girl," best Roumanian peppers, Hungarian meat patties, liver; a large glass of beer, five cents, admission free.

To think that Jews had concert saloons, just like the goyim! "A scandal!" wrote journalist Abraham Cahan in the March 17, 1902, *Forverts*. "It has to be stopped! The prostitutes who roam through the streets have turned the music halls into a market for themselves. Every music hall is a house of assignation. And as for the waiters and door-keepers, well, it is the same trade as being a bouncer in an Allen Street brothel."

But dives like the Eldorado also provided work for actors: Al Jolson, Eddie Cantor, and Sophie Tucker started their careers in such places. They functioned as just one piece of the Bowery's economy.

All of this was controlled by a Tammany boss named Big Tim Sullivan.

CHAPTER TEN

THE KING OF THE BOWERY

Big Tim Sullivan

The Bowery called Tim Sullivan the King, loved him madly, and he loved it back. Everybody knew that he took graft, but so what? What New York politician didn't, and Sullivan was so much better than the rest of them. He gave back more than he took by looking out for his supporters. His reign on the Bowery began in the mid-1880s when he was a young man and lasted thirty years. People saw him on the

Bowery every day, sauntering along the sidewalk or schmoozing with the locals in a saloon. But he never drank.

Born in a Greenwich Street tenement during the Civil War to impoverished Irish immigrants, Timothy Daniel Sullivan grew up as one in a gaggle of hungry, ragged children in a Five Points slum. His Dickensian childhood included an alcoholic stepfather who beat his mother, which explains why he was a lifelong teetotaler. His mother tongue was Bowery patois, and he spoke it with pride. His many critics, who included members of the city's Protestant establishment and journalistic muckrakers, reviled him as a "slum politician." Much information about Sullivan exists in the form of newspaper clippings and legislative records that reveal him as a savvy politician and businessman. But alas, he left behind no personal letters. Sullivan was a complicated person and a big, handsome lug, measuring six feet two inches tall. Thick chested and broad shouldered, his heavy black eyebrows emphasized his sparkling blue eyes. He dressed expensively—he wore silk underwear, silk shirts, had his suits made by an uptown tailor, and favored bow ties—but not ostentatiously. He was simultaneously magnetic and withdrawn, and he was obsessively private about his personal life. He had a wife, but they were estranged. He fathered several children with other women, all of whom kept quiet and out of sight. Perhaps Tim Sullivan's only true love was the Bowery itself and the people who lived there. Every year on Election Day eve, when he gave his speech at the annual Tammany rally, he got all choked up and cried.

Early on, Sullivan found his calling: politics, which, in Tim Sullivan's impoverished New York Irish world, meant strictly Democratic and Tammany. Sullivan was fiercely loyal to the organization that cared for the city's immigrant poor like a benevolent father and was despised by New York's high-and-mighty. His attachment to Tammany started the day his teacher, Miss Murphy—he was perhaps six years old—noticed that his worn-out shoes had two big cracks in them that were letting in the snow. She called him aside and gave him a folded piece of paper, inside which she had scribbled a note that she told him to take to the brother of a Tammany leader. In this way Sullivan got his first new pair of shoes. Sullivan never forgot Miss Murphy. He loved to tell that story, especially at election time.

Sullivan was already working his first job when he was just six, shining the boots of cops in the Fourth Precinct station house. By the time he was twelve, he had left school and was heading up a gang of newspaper boys down on Park Row. Along with leadership, Tim was already displaying what would be his legendary generosity: the writer Owen Kildare, another native son—"the bard of the Bowery"—remembered joining Sullivan's pack as a homeless seven-year-old. Sullivan, he wrote, lent him a nickel to buy newspapers to hawk and advised him to invest it in the best-selling one. As a teenager, Sullivan put together his own newspaper distribution business. With the money he earned from it—and some help from Tammany—he bought a saloon on Leonard Street when he was twenty-one. This constituted an important first step in Sullivan's political ascension: saloons functioned as de facto political clubhouses, and any Tammany boss worth his salt owned one. Sullivan then acquired several more. One was located right across the street from the Tombs and was the hangout of court officers and judges with whom Sullivan was whispered to have connections. Another Sullivan saloon served as headquarters to the city's most violent gang, the Whyos.* Danny Driscoll, the Whyos' leader, was Sullivan's friend. (In 1886, Driscoll was convicted of murder and publicly hanged in the courtyard of the Tombs.) Sullivan had a lot of unsavory friends; another was Owney Geoghegan, the former prizefighter who became famous as the owner of an especially notorious Bowery dive. Like them, he didn't hesitate to use his fists when the occasion called for it. One story about Sullivan concerned the time when, as a young man, he came across a young punk beating up a woman near the Tombs. Sullivan yelled at the guy to stop,

---

* The Whyos were the descendants of the Dead Rabbits, the Irish gang from the Five Points who'd engaged the Bowery Boys in the famous 1857 street battle.

upon which the latter turned his fists on Sullivan, who then beat the guy until he was bleeding and unconscious. The Sixth Ward—it encompassed the Five Points, where Sullivan grew up—loved that story and marked that moment as Sullivan's entry into politics.

Sullivan also was said to own stakes in pool halls and gambling joints, and to profit, at least indirectly, from prostitution. But these unsavory connections could never be proven, and he always angrily denied that he made money off exploiting the flesh of these poor women. In any event, by his mid-twenties, Sullivan was wealthy. Later, he invested in legitimate businesses: burlesque and vaudeville houses,* racehorses, and two racing tracks in Jamaica, Queens. He got into the theater business through his friend Henry Miner, a New York pharmacist, politico, and businessman who owned five theaters, the most famous of which was Miner's at Delancey Street and the Bowery, which is where Sullivan always made his annual campaign speeches. (Supposedly the "vaudeville hook" was invented at Miner's.) Sullivan all his life held on to his capital, and died a rich man; his estate was valued at $2 million. But he spent all the dollars that flowed into his pocket with abandon. Much of his cash went into gambling—he loved the horses and the fights—but he was also exceedingly generous with his money when it came to his friends and anybody else who asked him for help. His generosity was one of his greatest gifts—and weaknesses as well.

On the Bowery, people also called Sullivan Big Tim and the Big Feller. Another moniker was Dry Dollar, because, as a young saloon owner, he had the habit of wiping down the counter before putting your change on it. Sullivan's fame spread beyond New York and across the country. Everyone in America knew who Big Tim was. His story was the Bowery version of the American dream.

---

* Sullivan also owned stakes in a string of theaters on the West Coast in partnership with a Seattle businessman named John W. Considine, who later became a big dealmaker in Hollywood.

In 1886, when Sullivan was all of twenty-three, his moxie and charm impressed a much older politico and gambler named Fatty Walsh, whose Bowery saloon doubled as a clubhouse for a small group of Democrats who were trying to go it alone, without Tammany. Walsh wanted Sullivan in his corner and backed him as a Democrat for the Second District's state assembly seat. The young man easily won and debarked for Albany with his wife, Helen. There he quickly learned his way around the assembly. Filled with gratitude toward the voters who'd elected him, he began to write bills to better their miserable lives. One of his first would forbid newsstands from monopolizing El stations because he wanted to protect those poor hawkers of newspapers—most of them little boys and some women—from unfair competition. The bill did not pass, but others that Sullivan introduced did. He also learned how to block bills; it was all a matter of procedure. But in 1889, when he tried to block a bill championed by Chief Inspector Thomas Byrnes of the New York City Police Department—it was from him that the expression the "third degree" was derived—Byrnes, furious, bit back. Sullivan, he told the newspapers, was the friend of thieves, thugs, and criminals. And while it was no shame that Sullivan blacked the boots of policemen in the Fourth Precinct station house when he was six years old, "it's a disgrace to this city to have a scoundrel like him helping make laws for it."

Byrnes's ad hominem attack demanded a response. But Sullivan didn't like to speak in public, even in front of his supporters—here was yet one more contradictory piece of his huge personality—or especially in front of the Albany legislature, filled as it was with all those stiff-assed patrician lawmakers. They made him feel self-conscious of his lowly Irish Catholic origins. But it had to be done, and a few weeks later, Sullivan stood up in the assembly and told his colleagues that in light of Byrnes's attack on him, he owed it to them to give them an honest account of his life. He did not want them to think that they were sitting with a criminal as Byrnes maintained. No siree bob! It was true, Sullivan said, that as a child he worked as a bootblack. But everything else Byrnes said about him was a lie. Sullivan reminded the assembly that he was born and brought up in his district—"a small one, there are 7,900 voters"—so he knew everybody there.

"But if any one of them went bad and turned thief, I could not help that. If he met me on the street, I would not throw a stone at him." His voice welling with emotion, Sullivan told his colleagues that his father died when he was four years old, leaving his poor mother with four children to feed. By the time Sullivan was six, he was selling newspapers. Why, between then and the day he entered the legislature, he never in his life lost two days' work. So how, Sullivan asked the assembly, would he have found the time to associate with thieves?

Tim Sullivan's speech, delivered in coarse Bowery vernacular, made the assembly members—even the Republicans—cry. Really, it was remarkable. And even though Byrnes ultimately got his bill passed, he inadvertently turned Sullivan, the slum politician, into a populist hero. Soon the newspapers were calling Tim Sullivan the most influential Democrat in the assembly. The official publication of the New York State Legislature wrote: "Sullivan has the reputation in Albany of getting almost anything he wants. Consequently important bills are put into his hands."

Tammany all the while was paying close attention to Tim Sullivan up in Albany, and by the time he made that later-famous speech, he'd abandoned Fatty Walsh's independent club and joined the organization at their invitation. What an honor it was for Sullivan to have been asked to join New York's preeminent Democratic boys' club! The fact was the organization needed him badly. For all Parkhurst's ranting from the pulpit about Tammany's choke hold on New York, the 1890s posed a challenge to the organization. Jews were pushing out the Irish from the Bowery, and neither they nor any of the other new immigrants then pouring into New York—Italian, Chinese, Greek, Syrian, Turk, Hungarian, Serb, or any of the other myriad nationalities—felt any allegiance to Tammany. But Tammany could not survive without their votes and Sullivan, they believed, could deliver.

Indeed he did: when Sullivan switched over, the district who'd supported him followed him to Tammany, in the words of the *New*

York Sun (September 14, 1913), "as soon as Sullivan crooked a forefinger." The district from then on voted Tammany in every election, and in 1892, the organization rewarded Sullivan by making him the boss of the entire area—the Sixth Assembly District—that encompassed the Bowery and the entire Lower East Side. By then Sullivan was serving his fourth term in Albany as assemblyman. The following year, he left his seat to run for state senator (from the Ninth Senatorial District) and easily won. Now Tim Sullivan was Tammany's man, and all of Lower Manhattan was de facto his oyster. Life was good; this was when people began referring to Sullivan as Big Tim. The most important part of his new job was to make the Bowery vote Tammany.

Sullivan expressed confidence that he could get the job done. "Hully gee! Ain't I the lucky duck!" Tim told the *New York Times* when a reporter asked him how he liked his new position. "Would you make any changes in the district?" the reporter asked. He replied: "You bet! I'm going to make every duck in the district vote the Democratic ticket. With all the good hustlers in the district now, I think we can fix it so they can't keep up a Republican organization." Fix it he did: a few months later, the Republican presidential candidate Benjamin Harrison won exactly 3 votes, while winning Democratic candidate Grover Cleveland won 938. Sullivan told Tammany boss Richard Croker that was one vote more than he'd expected for Harrison, "but I'll find the guy who did it if it's the last thing I do."

"Never mind, Sullivan," Croker said. "You did good work."

Sullivan never did find the guy, nor do we know exactly how Sullivan worked his magic during the presidential election of 1892. But from that time on, his constituents consistently voted for whoever the Tammany candidate was, especially if it was Sullivan himself. Although just to make sure the district did right by him, Sullivan sometimes hired thugs from Monk Eastman's gang on the Lower East Side or their rivals from the other side of the Bowery, the Five Pointers (successors of the Whyos) to stand menacingly around the polling places on Election Day. Or Sullivan sent his hires to Bowery lodging houses early in the morning, before the bums were kicked out for the day, collected them, brought them to the polls, registered them, and then had them vote. Then the bums—"repeaters"—were brought to another polling place to repeat the process. For their services, each bum received $1, three meals, and a pint of whiskey. When Sullivan ran for state senate in 1893, twenty voters listed his headquarters, 207 Bowery, as their address—"the low, vile, gambling house and dive, the headquarters of Sullivan and his henchmen," an outraged *Tribune* reporter wrote (October 19, 1893). "The countenances of the majority of these men are a plain index to their character. Bullet-headed, short haired, small eyed, smooth shaven, and crafty looking, with heavy, vicious features that speak of dissipation and brutality, ready to fight at a moment's notice."

At the same time as Sullivan turned the Bowery and its adjoining and increasingly polyglot neighborhoods into a solid Tammany stronghold, all the vice businesses there that had gone dark during Parkhurst's hysterical assaults came roaring back to life. You could attribute the comeback of all those saloons and pool halls to the loophole in the Raines law that was supposed to rein in Sunday drinking but instead encouraged saloons to double as cheap brothels. The weakness in the Raines law did not tell the whole story: vice also returned to the Bowery because Sullivan encouraged it for the simple reason that he profited from it. Everybody knew this was true, but it couldn't be proven. Neither the Lexow investigations that were conducted in 1894 as a result of the Reverend Parkhurst's crusade nor another state investigation into municipal corruption five years later—the Mazet Committee—resulted in even one subpoena, let alone an indictment, against Tim Sullivan. His influence ran too deep. Sullivan controlled everything below Fourteenth Street, which people called "the Dead Line," because as soon as you stepped over it, your chances of getting killed increased. Nobody did business below "da line" without kicking back to Big Tim. In return, he watched your ass. Not just he, but the entire Sullivan clan: Tim placed his family members in strategic political positions in every ward below da line. Besides his brother Paddy, he had a truckload of cousins. His favorite was Little Tim, who took over Big Tim's assembly seat when the latter became a state senator in 1893. Like his cousin and mentor, Little Tim was known for his generosity. He was a chip off the old block, all right, but you could say a much more delicate version: he was soft-spoken and polite, and while his Irish good looks—deep violet eyes, fair skin, heavy black eyebrows—recalled Big Tim's, his physique was slight. Also, like his cousin, he neither smoked nor drank. Little Tim, though, distinguished himself from the Big Feller through his lifestyle: his was a model of propriety. He was a devout Catholic who lived with his wife and their son on East Twelfth Street. The Bowery Prince, his constituents called him, to distinguish him from his big cousin, the King. They respected Little Tim, but Big Tim was like God Almighty to them, and he in turn loved them as if they were his flock. He knew every man of importance in his district, and virtually every house there had a picture of him on the wall. Despite his financial success, he lived in modest digs—he occupied the attic floor of a little three-story house that he owned at 38 East Fourth Street—as if to remind his supporters that he came from the same gritty streets as they did. If a mother needed to bail out her no-good son from the Tombs or money to feed her children that night because her alcoholic lout of a husband had drunk it all up or a guy needed an excuse to skip jury duty or help with a building permit or a son had no money to pay for his father's funeral, they only had to go to Big Tim. ("Help your neighbor, but keep your nose out of his affairs," he once said.) He gave generously and without conditions and all year around. At Christmas, Tim treated thousands of destitute men from the nearby flophouses to turkey dinners at his three-story clubhouse at 207 Bowery—the original structure is gone, its site now occupied by a Chinese restaurant—which, besides ample amounts of food included entertainment drawn from Sullivan's many connections in the theater community. The Christmas feast was always hosted by Little Tim. The men returned to the clubhouse in February, where they waited in lines that stretched for blocks along the Bowery to receive free shoes and socks, courtesy of Big Tim. In the months leading up to summer, local businessmen and saloon owners bought thousands of tickets, at $5 each, to Sullivan's annual Fourth of July "chowder," which they distributed to the local tenement dwellers. (Shelling out money for chowder tickets was considered a campaign contribution, although some people said that this was just one more way that Sullivan collected graft.) The chowders started in the morning, when the Big Feller himself led a parade composed of entire families from among his multi-ethnic constituents down to the docks, where they boarded steamboats that ferried them up the East River and over to College Point, Queens. There, thousands of men, women, and children danced, played games, gambled, and gorged on beer, clams, chicken, and pie until nightfall, when they were treated to a firework display before being ferried back to the suffocating streets of the Lower East Side. A singer named Annie Hart—in the 1920s she would star in the groundbreaking musical *Show Boat*—even composed a number called "Tim Sullivan's Chowder Party" that she regularly performed at Tony Pastor's Fourteenth Street Theatre. If in the fall Sullivan was up for reelection, which was the case every other year, he made sure to stop a few times at every saloon in his district—there were 135 in all, according to the *Times* (October 25, 1895)—to schmooze and treat everybody to beer. Since he was a teetotaler, he'd toast to everybody's health with a glass of sarsaparilla. Or sometimes he'd drop into a boardinghouse and ask the landlady if he could stay for dinner. Then he'd praise the woman's cooking and remind her to spread a good word about him to the other ladies, even though they couldn't vote. Still, Sullivan thought, they might influence their husbands, fathers, and brothers to vote for him.

Sullivan, in fact, believed that women deserved the vote. The women's suffrage movement had its beginnings in Upstate New York, and women's organizations there periodically authored bills to give women the vote and delivered them to the state legislature. Tim Sullivan supported every single one of them; in 1891, as a young assemblyman, he even helped author one. Sullivan was devoted to his own long-suffering Irish mother, Catherine Sullivan, and it was because of her that he learned that women deserved respect. When she died in 1893, he arranged for her the largest funeral the Bowery had ever seen: four magnificent black horses pulled the hearse down the Bowery, followed by 145 carriages. Every Democratic politician from the neighborhood sent flowers to the wake. There were so many bouquets, and some were so huge that you couldn't see Mrs. Sullivan's coffin when you walked into the funeral parlor. "Tim stuck to his mother since he was a lad of six," one of his cronies there told a *World* reporter (September 17, 1893). "I never saw a mother more proud of her boy." But this model of filial piety was a complete flop when it came to his personal life. He and his wife, Helen Fitzgerald, who grew up with him in Five Points—they married when she was eighteen and he was twenty-five—were long separated by the time people were calling him King of the Bowery. They had no children, although it was rumored that early in their marriage she had given birth to a baby who died in infancy. He never talked about Helen, and his friends knew better than to ask him. For all his big, sexy, public persona, Big Tim was an enigma.

The eminently pragmatic Big Tim Sullivan saved some political spoils for a few Italian constituents and a lot more Jews. The reason for the disparity is that he merely tolerated Italians, but he had a special affection for Jews. (Legend has it that the famous gambler Arnold Rothstein used to hang out in one of Sullivan's pool halls.) He attended the weddings and bar mitzvahs of all the "smart Jew boys" he did business with, and they were always welcome at Sullivan's Bowery clubhouse. Sullivan made a racketeer named Max, a.k.a. Mochs Hochstim—a big-bellied dandy who'd been brought to New York from Austria as a child—Tammany captain for the Eighth Assembly District ("da Ate") in 1900. This was quite the coup for Hochstim, because while local Tammany clubs as a practical matter embraced Jews, the latter—being not merely not Irish, but not even Christians—remained outsiders. Hochstim repaid Tim's generosity and open-mindedness by making him vice president of the Max Hochstim Association, which served as a front for prostitution and various other rackets on the Lower East Side. Sullivan's ties to Hochstim begged the question of whether he in fact made money off women's flesh, at least indirectly; at any rate, hundreds of local businessmen, legitimate and not, belonged to the "Association." They had to; if somebody balked at joining, Hochstim sent his goons to attack you. Or he might come at you himself. He liked using his fists; once he was arrested for assaulting a German newspaper reporter named Henry Frendenthal in front of Essex court, because he didn't like what Frendenthal had been writing about him in the *Staats-Zeitung*. For this, Hochstim served two months in the Tombs. Jail time only added to his mystique: people began calling him Mochsie the Invincible. Wherever he went, his pet bulldog, Jip, accompanied him. All the Lower East Side merchants lived in fear of him, and they all had to pay him kickback. When a Mrs. Urchittel refused to pay Hochstim the money that the gangster demanded, the police took the poor woman's children away from her on the grounds that she was running a disorderly house. Once a man who had no money to pay for "protection" begged him for leniency. Hochstim's answer: "Why don't you put up your wife as collateral?" But Hochstim treated his own wife, Annie, like a queen. She was only fifteen when he married her, when he was twenty-six. At the elegant apartment at 44 St. Mark's Place, Annie, decked out in the diamonds her husband bought her, regularly presided over a Lower East Side version of Mrs. Astor's Four Hundred—the One Hundred Select Club. "All members of the club are married," the *World* reported in 1899, "and assist their husbands in their political aspirations."

Trafficking in Jewish girls provided one of Hochstim's most lucrative income streams. He found his victims in the dives and the streets of the Lower East Side. Others he imported directly from Europe and set up in tenement brothels along Allen Street. Some of the brothels were owned by his friend Marty Engel, who also served as an alderman on the city council representing the First District. Engel also ran a kosher chicken business at the Essex Street Market, right across the street from the eponymous courthouse where Hochstim had his bail bond racket, in which Engel was a partner. In 1891, the bartender at a Bowery dive smashed Engel's face with a beer keg after Engel said something to him that he didn't like (exactly what has been lost to history), and Engel was rushed to Bellevue Hospital. There, a surgeon reconstructed Engel's *yiddische* face so as to make him unrecognizable. "His nose, formerly aquiline, now presents a flat, Mongolian aspect," wrote the *Pittsburgh Post* (August 19, 1891). Hochstim was proud of how well he treated his girls. He fed them, clothed them, and never, ever fucked them. He also urged them to learn English: because this was America and you were nothing if you couldn't speak English. Hochstim claimed that some girls even approached him from the gutter, rather than the other way around, and asked him to pimp them. He even taught his girls to save their money. He said that because of him, many were able to bring over their poor parents whom they'd left behind in Europe.

Another major source of Hochstim's income was the grungy Essex Street police court, where the dregs of society in New York ended up after they were arrested.* Every day thugs from the Hochstim Association—its headquarters were right across the street, at Alderman "Silver Dollar" Smith's saloon—hung out on the courthouse steps, waiting to post bond for the poor souls passing through who had no other way to obtain bail money. For his services, Hochstim charged a fee that he split with the cops—a lucrative arrangement for both parties. Silver Dollar's real name was Charles Solomon; they called him Silver Dollar because the floor of his saloon was embedded with 1,000 silver dollars, which drunks were always trying to pry out with "cold chisels." (Silver Dollar's son was known as Half Dollar.)†

---

* The Essex courthouse was torn down in 1903.

† Hochstim, Engel, and Smith liked to hang out together at the Russian baths— the *schvitz*—one block from the Bowery, at 403 Lafayette Street, *World*, June 13, 1894. From 1910 until the 1930s the baths were a gay hangout, according to Chauncey, *Gay New York*. Today a parking garage stands on the site.

In 1897, at a public gathering, a prominent Jewish lawyer asked Hochstim if he would consider running for state assembly. "Gents," Hochstim replied, "you couldn't get me to go to Albany for all the money in the world." Four years later, he was sentenced to three years in Sing Sing for violation of election laws. Hochstim served his time and returned to the Lower East Side. By then—1904—some of the Jews in his old neighborhood were doing well enough that they were moving away—up to Harlem or the Bronx or across the river to Brooklyn—and nobody gave a damn about the man they once feared as Mochsie the Invincible. He ended up eking out a living as the manager of the Orpheum Theatre on Second Avenue until he died in 1921, debt-ridden and in obscurity.

As Hochstim was languishing in a Sing Sing cell, Tim Sullivan was at the pinnacle of his power. He was often in the news; yet, for all the enormity of his persona, he was elusive, and in essence a loner. Except for his cousin Little Tim, he trusted nobody. "He will allow a man to see his hand if the man can be of service to him, but he believes in himself more than he does in others, and this faculty gives his followers confidence in him," the *Tribune* wrote about Sullivan on September 29, 1901. There were plenty of rumors about his personal and business affairs, but most could not be substantiated. He led a strange and peripatetic life. While in Albany, he lived in a hotel; when he was in New York, he now stayed in a suite of rooms at the Occidental Hotel at the corner of Bowery and Broome (now the Sohotel), which he also used to host his all-night poker games. (He still owned his Fourth Street house, but rarely stayed there.) His real home was the Bowery. This is where you could usually find him if you could find him at all, holding court in his clubhouse at 207, or drinking his beverage of choice, sarsaparilla, with his constituents in Bowery saloons. In between those manly pastimes, he had plenty of women. He had numerous affairs, but if the press knew about them, they weren't talking. Neither did his friends. Sometimes Big Tim was seen in public with prostitutes. He was also known to like actresses, of whom, because of his connections in the theater world, he had his pick. One of his paramours was the sweet singer Christie MacDonald, a favorite of composer Victor Herbert's. Sullivan was so taken with MacDonald that he introduced a bill in the New York legislature in 1896 to force theaters to enlarge their dressing rooms, but the bill failed. He fathered a child with MacDonald, a daughter, whom the actress gave up to the New York Foundling Hospital in 1903. (Another singer, Elsie Janis, later famous for entertaining the troops during the Great War, was rumored to have had another of Sullivan's illegitimate offspring. She was twenty-six years younger than he was.)

In 1902, Tammany decided it was time to send Tim Sullivan to Washington. By then he had been a state senator for nine years. They ran him for Congress in the heavily Democratic Eighth District, which encompassed the area (the Sixth Assembly District) that he'd controlled like a munificent dictator for the last nine years. During the campaign, Big Tim bragged that he'd do a better job representing his district in Washington than the silver-tongued Daniel Webster ever could. ("I don't look through the colored glasses of some over cultured, educated gentlemen," he declared during a campaign speech in Miner's Theater, next to his Bowery clubhouse.) Sullivan easily clinched the election and headed down to Washington. A few months later, when asked by a reporter how he liked Congress, he answered: "Oh, Congress is all right. The work is better—more dignified—than up in the senate, in Albany. They haven't got any hills to climb down at Washington. There it is as level as a plain. Everything is on the level down there. Why, in Albany, there's nothing but hills, geographical and political."

So there was Big Tim Sullivan, Tammany boss and consummate Albany deal maker, suddenly a freshman Democrat in a Republican-controlled House of Representatives, in a strange city where he knew nobody. How lost he felt—and how utterly miserable. Unless the issue of racing was on the congressional calendar, he skipped sessions. Often he was out of town, either back on the Bowery or in Hot Springs, Arkansas, one of his favorite vacation spots. He was reelected for a second term in 1904, returned to Washington, and complained to the *New York Times* on March 21, 1905, how much he hated it there. ("Great game there. Why, they run along for a few days in the House, talking about something nobody understands, and then they announce they will vote on a bill in ten days. By that time I'm disgusted and come over to New York to forget Congress. Finally I see something in the newspapers to remind me of it, and I go back in time to vote.") One year later, he approached Tammany to work out a return to the state senate, and he resigned his congressional seat. Afterward, Sullivan said that his three years in Washington were the loneliest of his life. ("In the House, it was hard to get acquainted, and impossible to know all the 'boys' as I did in the Senate chambers at Albany.")

Sullivan returned to Albany in 1907. God, how great he felt to be home again. The legislation he introduced included a bill to make Columbus Day, October 12, a legal holiday. This gift to the thousands of Italians who lived in his district took him two tries—the first time, then-governor Charles Evan Hughes vetoed it—before it passed.

But then his world began to crumble.

The nation had a ravenous appetite for muckraking journalism, and Sullivan made for an attractive target. He was attacked by the media, first by Hearst's *Cosmopolitan* in 1907 and then by *McClure's* in 1909, in stories about corruption and vice in New York. But neither of these influential publications had anything new to say about him; both dragged up old stories about Sullivan, the "slum politician" and "the king of the underworld." *McClure's* directly accused Sullivan of profiting from "white slavery," thereby reviving that old bugaboo that his enemies for years had tried to pin on him. Sullivan was devastated. On November 1, 1909, he made his customary preelection speech at Miner's Theater. The place was packed to capacity an hour before Big Tim appeared; some 2,000 people had to be turned away. He had never gotten over his fear of speaking in public, and usually his election speeches lasted only a few minutes. This time, he spoke for half an hour. He spoke about himself and all the nasty things that the *McClure's* reporter, George Kibbe Turner, wrote about him. The "white slavery" accusation particularly stung him. "I am not an angel," he told the crowd. "I don't want anyone to think I am. I don't want you to think

I am even a good-living man. But this man Turner had better keep out of this neighborhood. There is no man who believes more in women or their virtue than I do."

As he spoke, all the women and most of the men were crying. Then, on November 1, 1909, the *New York Times* wrote: "His voice grew almost pathetic, and a tear drop trickled down and off the end of his nose." Big Tim was feeling vulnerable these days, for multiple reasons. Rumor had it that he wasn't feeling well. And, two months earlier, his cousin Florrie, with whom he'd been close, had died of syphilis in an upstate sanatorium. Florrie had been dying, slowly, for the last two years—"gone wrong in the head," the *Washington Post* (June 28, 1909) politely said.

Right after the election, Tim left for another trip to Hot Springs. On the train from New York, he came down with a severe cold, according to one newspaper account, which added that he was coughing so hard that his rib cage became inflamed. Sullivan wired ahead to the resort where he was booked to inform them that he needed medical attention, and when his train pulled into the station, he was carried directly into a waiting car in which two doctors were sitting. The three of them were quickly driven to the hotel, and the physicians examined Big Tim. He was not in any immediate danger, they later told a reporter. Even so, they planned to keep a careful eye on him. The story fueled continued speculation about the Big Feller's health. He was next seen at the funeral of Little Tim Sullivan on Christmas Eve. His beloved cousin and only confidant died on December 23 of Bright's disease. He was only forty. The day before he died, Little Tim told a group of political cronies who were sitting at a vigil around his bedside that the Sullivan reign on the Bowery was finished.

"Big Tim is sick, and Florrie is dead," he told them.

Big Tim Sullivan had syphilis. On Christmas Day, he went to his Bowery clubhouse to host the annual dinner for the needy in place of his just-deceased cousin.

Sullivan took Little Tim's death hard, and he was growing weak from the effects of his own disease. But he wasn't, as Big Tim had put it, finished. Not yet. He was still Timothy D. Sullivan, King of the Bowery. *McClure's* attack on his integrity continued to gnaw at him. He returned to Albany right after New Year's Day 1910 and introduced a bill in the senate to go after all the white slavers, which drew snickers from some of his colleagues. During the next months, Sullivan was in and out of the hospital. On July 4, he somehow managed to travel to Reno, Nevada, for the sensational "fight of the century" between African American Jack Johnson and retired heavyweight champion James Jeffries. Sullivan, in fact, was the stakeholder. The day after the fight, Sullivan, overcome by the scorching desert heat, suffered a seizure. When he returned to New York, he told his friends he would not run again for senate. But they begged him to change his mind. As founder and king of the Sullivan dynasty, he had a sacred duty to keep it going, they told him. Especially so soon after the deaths of both Florrie and Little Tim. Big Tim backed down, accepted the nomination, and, with his mortality staring at him head-on, felt newly energized. On the day before the election, he held his usual preelection rally at Miner's Theater, which was, as always, packed to capacity whenever the Big Feller appeared. In January, he told them, he was going to tackle some controversial issues in the senate.

"One of my first acts after the Legislature convenes will be to introduce a bill to clip the claws of the gun toter and the tough," he announced. His audience, who lived in fear of gun violence every day, cheered and applauded. New York had no restrictions on gun ownership, and on the Bowery, you could buy a .38 in a pawnshop as easily as a glass of beer in one of the saloons. With guns, drunken husbands settled scores in saloons, muggers robbed, and the down-and-out committed suicide. Gangs shot at each other and sometimes caught innocent victims in the crossfire. But other New Yorkers didn't care about gun violence, because they thought of it as something that affected only the city's poor and foreign-born, who lived below the Dead Line. Until one day a Harvard graduate and violinist from an old

Maryland family named Fitzhugh Coyle Goldsborough walked into one of those Bowery pawnshops—January 23, 1911—and purchased a revolver for a few dollars. Goldsborough was mentally ill. For months, he had been sending threatening letters to a young novelist named David Graham Phillips, who had paid no attention to them. Goldsborough lived near Phillips, in posh Gramercy Park. Because he had been stalking the writer for months, he knew Phillips's daily habits, for example that Phillips went every day to the Players Club on East Twenty-first Street for lunch.

Now Goldsborough, his newly purchased gun in his pocket, headed back uptown to the Players Club in Gramercy Park, where he hid in the entranceway and waited. When the writer arrived for his daily lunch, Goldsborough fired five shots into him. Goldsborough then pressed the nozzle of the revolver to his own temple and blew his brains out. Phillips died the following day.

This tragedy particularly incensed a New York politician named George Le Brun. For a while he had been thinking that New York needed a law to restrict gun ownership: as secretary to the city coroner, Le Brun had seen one too many bullet-ridden bodies carried into the city morgue. And now, because it was not some poor slobs on the Lower East Side who had just been shot dead, but two patricians, people realized that gun control was everybody's concern. This was Le Brun's opportunity to act.

The first thing he did was approach Big Tim, who told him that he had his full support.

"I'll do anything to stop those shootings by gangsters," Tim told Le Brun. "It's terrible when an innocent person gets killed. Everyone runs to me and then they want me to have the cops do something. But even when gangsters kill each other I still have troubles. When the police make an arrest, the friends and relatives come knocking on my door for me to get a lawyer or arrange bail. And they're hardly out the door when relatives of the victim come to me for a contribution to pay for his burial."

Le Brun was taken aback by Sullivan's response. ("Big politicians, it seems, also have their problems," he later remarked.) But Le Brun knew Tim was his man. "Go ahead and draft a bill," Big Tim told Le Brun, which the latter promptly did. Le Brun also sent letters to twenty of New York's wealthiest and most important citizens asking for their support. He also reached out to the police brass, the D.A., and judges.

In April 1911—three months after Phillips's murder—Sullivan introduced a bill to the senate that made it a felony for anybody to carry a gun without a permit. Sullivan had never gotten over his fear of public speaking, and the senate's august surroundings made him feel especially self-conscious. Consequently, he rarely spoke on the floor, but now he was going to make an exception. When it was announced that the Big Feller intended to make a speech supporting a gun law, assembly members flocked to the senate to hear him:

> Last Saturday night there was a couple of gangs fighting on the street. A mother with a baby in her arms came along and was shot dead. That alone oughtta pass this bill. No, I ain't alone in wanting to pass this bill. There's a lot of other people in this city. Here's a little list: There's the City Club, and District Attorney Whitman, and Police Commissioner Cropsey, and . . .

Tim continued to name New York's biggest players, among them John D. Rockefeller Jr., "a personal friend of mine," at which point all the legislators broke into laughter. Sullivan resumed reciting his list of supporters of the gun control bill. At the end of the speech, he said:

> If this bill passes, it will do more than carry out the commandment, "Thou shalt not kill," and will save more souls than all the talk of all the ministers and the priests of the state for the next ten years.

Five minutes later, the senate passed the bill with only five dissensions. It then easily passed the assembly, and the governor signed it into law. Gun manufacturers mounted an immediate challenge. The new law was unconstitutional, they insisted. Hadn't Big Tim ever heard of the Second Amendment? But Sullivan was unfazed. If there are any legal issues with the law as passed, he said, then we will amend it. Which is what has happened, several times. To this day, the statute remains on the books, and we still call it the Sullivan law. It was the nation's first law that required guns to be licensed, and it is among the most stringent gun control laws in America.

Just as New York was realizing the urgency of passing a gun law, hundreds of suffragists descended on Albany to present yet one more bill to the legislature. For years they had been doing this: New York was where the suffrage movement started, at the nation's first women's convention in Seneca Falls, in 1848. But most bills never even made it to the floor. Big Tim Sullivan, sick as he was and already busy politicking for a gun law, immediately got behind the suffrage bill. This was a cause dear to his heart.

"Perhaps you didn't know that the famous senator from the Bowery has the intention of supporting the next suffrage bill," wrote *Evening World* columnist Nixola Greeley-Smith, thirty-one, in a full-page story about Sullivan in January 1911. This granddaughter of Horace Greeley, a newspaperwoman since age eighteen, was by then famous. With her fiercely progressive views and well-honed interviewing skills, Greeley-Smith loved throwing tough questions at powerful figures, and she had approached the Sullivan interview with the skepticism of a seasoned reporter. She pictured Big Tim as the embodiment of a corrupt politician—"a large and roseate person, completely surrounded by diamonds."

But when the King of the Bowery actually stood before her, she was utterly charmed.

"I saw a stately person in marvelously fitting black clothes. He was a monument of stable simplicity, from his shoes to his black tie, in which a beautiful white pearl coyly rested," she wrote in her article.

She noted the twinkle in "the very blue Sullivan eyes." Contrary to her usual practice, Greeley-Smith did not ask Big Tim any embarrassing questions. Instead, she let him do all the talking.

"I've been watchin' the folks goin' to their work of a morning, comin' over the Brooklyn Bridge and fillin' the ferryboats and the crowdin' down in the subway. And the tings that hits me right in the eye is the fact that there's nearly as many women as men in these mornin' crowds of workers. If the women have to work like that alongside of men, then they ought to be able to vote alongside them, too," Sullivan told the lady reporter. Greeley-Smith asked Big Tim if he thought women should be able to run for office. Tim said: "If man is the mighty affair he thinks he is, why is he afraid of political competition by women? But if he's not such a mighty affair, then it's time he stepped down and gave the ladies a chance to show what they can do in politics."

Sullivan saw to it that the suffrage bill got onto the floor of the legislature in June, but it did not pass. As women in New York and throughout the country pressed on with their fight for the vote, word that the famous Tim Sullivan was supporting their cause circulated. His support mattered, as Illinois's *Rockford Register-Gazette* wrote on June 29, 1911: "Mr. Tim Sullivan having declared himself in favor of woman suffrage, the question may as well be as good as settled." The following year, he tried to get another suffrage bill through committee, but it was killed. Still, Sullivan was sure that it was only a matter of a few years until women in New York got the vote. He was right: it happened in 1917. New York was one of fifteen states where women's suffrage predated the ratification of the Nineteenth Amendment in 1919.

It was just around this time that another smart young woman in Albany caught Big Tim's attention: Frances Perkins, who some twenty-five years later, as FDR's secretary of Labor, would be instrumental in shaping the New Deal. In 1911, she was thirty-one, and as executive secretary of the New York State Consumers League she was lobbying for a bill to limit the workweek to fifty-four hours. The bill, which had been languishing in the state legislature for two years, had taken on added urgency in March 1911, when 146 workers died in the Triangle Shirtwaist Factory fire.

"In those days, I had no power," Perkins later wrote in a memoir about her time in Albany. "And it just wasn't expected of you to have power or influence. So the approach was 'please help,' not 'we demand.'" The concept of social legislation was something new, and lawmakers were not interested in it. Moreover, it was hard for even a seasoned legislator, let alone an inexperienced young female lobbyist, to get a bill onto the floor of the rough and testosterone-driven New York legislature. Still, Perkins kept at it. One after another, she asked legislators for their help. Politely, like a lady. And one of the politicians who responded to her was Big Tim Sullivan.

These two could not have been more different. She came from an old New England family and had a master's degree from Columbia; her critics called her the patrician reformer. He was a Tammany boss with questionable business interests who grew up impoverished on New York's mean streets. But this highly educated young woman of privilege shared something in common with Sullivan: a passion to improve the lives of the working poor—specifically women. In New York City alone, she told Sullivan, 400,000 women toiled away in factories under miserable conditions.

When Perkins asked him to help get the bill through, he said: "Me sister was a poor girl and she went out to work when she was young. I feel kinda sorry for them poor girls that work the way you say they work. I'd like to do them a good turn. I'd like to do you a good turn. You don't know much about this parliamentary stuff, do you?"

"You know I don't know anything," she answered. Sullivan sprang to action. In June 1912, through a series of complicated political maneuvers—as the ranking member of the senate rules committee, Sullivan knew all the tricks—he got the bill passed, literally seconds before the session closed. The passage of New York's fifty-four-hour workweek law was Frances Perkins's first political victory, and it wouldn't have happened without Big Tim. She knew the Sullivans had a sleazy reputation, but she admired them for their activism. She wished she had gotten to know the Sullivans better.

"If I'd been a man serving in the Senate with them," Perkins later wrote, "I'm sure I would have had a glass of beer with them and gotten them to tell me what times were like on the old Bowery."

As Big Tim was working hard in the state senate to enact some of New York's earliest social legislation, his illness was advancing. As soon as he returned to New York at the end of the senate session in June 1912, the Sullivan clan moved him out of his Occidental Hotel digs on the Bowery. They installed him in a suite of rooms at the St. Denis, a prominent old hotel on Broadway (that Tim's half brother, Larry Mulligan, had just purchased), along with a doctor they'd hired to look after him 24/7. "The Sullivans without a Bowery setting will be hard to imagine, and a blow to the Bowery," the *Times* wrote on June 19, and Tim wasn't having any of it. He kept breaking loose and going over to the Bowery, where he was seen wandering about, seeking out his old haunts. His family then moved him out of sight to a Yonkers sanitarium.

Three months later, he attended the vigil of his estranged wife, Helen Fitzgerald, as she lay dying of consumption. He stayed at her bedside along with her relatives until the end. When he appeared at the funeral, people were shocked at his appearance: Big Tim's once-massive body had shrunk by sixty pounds, and he appeared agitated. Newspapers delicately spoke of his "melancholia" and "nervous exhaustion." The *New York Times* wrote: "He is broken down as a result of complication of diseases." The newspaper speculated that he had suffered crippling financial losses, because during the previous two years, he had signed $70,000 worth of promissory notes, much of them to unscrupulous people who took advantage of the Big Feller's increasingly impaired state. (Even so, Sullivan was so wealthy that even with all that cash flowing out of his bank accounts, his finances remained sound.) By then it was election season, and Tammany nominated Big Tim as the 1912 candidate for state senate.

It was as if they were running a dead man for office. A few weeks later, Tammany suddenly reversed course and nominated another Democrat for the seat. But they ran Sullivan for the congressional seat he'd resigned from four years earlier.

Tim Sullivan won.

Instead of going to Washington—he wasn't well enough, the newspapers said—he went with his family to California, to take "the cure." They swore that Tim was doing much better, and when he returned, they said, he would go to Washington and take office. Instead, when Larry Mulligan and Tim's brother Patrick brought Tim back to New York, they put him back in the sanitarium in Yonkers. He continued to deteriorate. Sometimes he insisted that his food was poisoned or that somebody was injecting gas into his room. At times he became so agitated that he had to be physically restrained. But in between his intervals of insanity, he had moments of lucidity.

In January 1913, Larry Mulligan and Patrick Sullivan petitioned for and won guardianship over Tim. At the hearing, a doctor said for the record that Sullivan was suffering from paresis. Finally, the dreaded word had been uttered out loud and printed in the newspapers. As Mulligan testified that his half brother could no longer take care of himself or his finances, his voice choked up. After he finished speaking, he broke down and sobbed.

Patrick Sullivan took his brother Tim to his country home in the Eastchester section of the Bronx. There, three male nurses took shifts watching over him day and night. One beautiful morning in late August 1913, Tim woke up feeling cheerful. He begged his brother to take him out. Larry drove Tim all the way to Coney Island and then back to the Bronx, where they both enjoyed a hearty dinner. Then one of Tim's nurses helped him change his clothes—he chose a salt-and-pepper suit, black striped silk shirt, and black silk bow tie—and he, together with his three nurses, settled in for a pinochle game. It lasted into the early morning hours, and when everybody finally went to sleep, the nurse on shift sitting next to Tim's bed dozed off. When the nurse woke up, Big Tim was gone. Even with three nurses and the entire Sullivan clan looking after him, he could not be contained.

Imagine the panic. Sullivan's brothers, aided by friends, began looking for him everywhere. They scoured the surrounding farmland, found nothing, and then expanded their search to the city. They inquired in every Bowery saloon, every hospital, and every morgue. Nothing. Where was he? Meanwhile, newspapermen, hungry for a scoop, were scurrying all over the place, scribbling on their pads, and filling up their columns with bizarre theories. BIG TIM VANISHES! the headlines read. Every day, his face projected from the front pages of every paper. Days passed, but he was still missing.

As he did throughout his life, Tim Sullivan eluded everybody. A few hours after he disappeared and before anyone even realized he was missing, a train was barreling toward a Bronx station a short walk from Patrick Sullivan's home. The flagman on duty noticed what looked to him like a bundle lying on the tracks. He frantically signaled the locomotive driver to stop, but the train was going too fast to avoid what was actually a man's body. By the time the engineer stepped on the brakes and stopped the train, the locomotive and the tender had run over the body. It was crushed, but only below the waist. The body ended up at the nearby Fordham morgue, where it lay for eleven days. Somebody attached a tag to the torso: "August 31. Received body of unknown man killed on New York, New Haven and Hartford Railroad near Pelham Parkway." From the Bronx, the body was transferred to the Bellevue morgue, the last stop for unidentified bodies before they were shipped across the East River to be buried in a potter's field, on Hart Island. Just as this particular corpse was to be loaded onto a wagon, a policeman on duty glanced at the face.

He gasped: "It's Big Tim!" Yes, it was he, a hair away from being buried in an anonymous pauper's grave. Instead Timothy Sullivan was given the grand funeral befitting the King of the Bowery. His body, enclosed in a massive mahogany coffin, lay in state for three days on the third floor of his clubhouse at 207 Bowery. Next to the bier, a brass candelabrum held twenty-four lit candles. On the wall behind it hung a silver crucifix. The room was filled with elaborate floral arrangements sent by his many friends and political cronies. During this time, thousands of people waited patiently on the street below to pay their respects to Big Tim. They climbed the stairs a few at a time to view his body: ladies in furs and gentlemen in silk hats stood side by side with bums in rags and women from the tenements holding screaming babies. Finally, at ten thirty in the morning on September 15, the coffin was carried down the stairs, covered with a blanket of roses and chrysanthemums, and placed in a hearse, to be pulled down the Bowery by two black horses. Thousands more people choked the street: estimates of their numbers ran as high as 75,000. "Never in the history of the Bowery was there such a composite gathering of mourners," the *Tribune* wrote. "They included United States Senators and Representatives in Congress, prize fighters, justices of the Supreme Court, clergymen, gangsters, thugs, saloonkeepers, lawyers, business men, merchants and laborers, rich men, poor men, beggar men and thieves, good women and otherwise." The cortege proceeded up the Bowery for a bit, turned the corner at Prince Street, and continued to the Saint Patrick's Old Cathedral on Mott Street. There, a funeral mass was celebrated. No eulogy was performed over the body, which was odd, and added another layer to the many mysteries surrounding Big Tim's life.

For weeks after his death, pictures of the deceased leader were displayed in the windows of the street's saloons, stores, barbershops, lodging houses, and tenements. Every moving picture theater along the Bowery—by then there were many; they'd replaced all those dime museums that were killed in the name of reform—paid tribute to Big Tim by projecting a black-bordered picture of him at the end of each show. Underneath, the caption read: "The Bowery mourns its best friend."

The cause of Sullivan's death was uncertain, and at his family's request, an inquest was held. Some wondered if he had committed

Tim Sullivan's Funeral, Bowery

suicide, but his family refused to believe it. He was, they said, too good a Catholic to kill himself.*

The annual Sullivan Christmas dinner limped along for two more years, but in 1916, Tim's brother Paddy, who'd been trying to carry on the Sullivan legacy, didn't have the heart to do it anymore. Instead he gave fifty cents to hundreds of poor souls who came by the

---

* An inquest was held one week after Big Tim was buried (on September 24, 1913, at Calvary cemetery in Queens) in the Bronx Coroners Court. The flagman testified that he saw the locomotive run over Sullivan's body. Then he went over and felt the liver. "It was cold, not quite cold, but much below the heat of a normal person's body," he told the coroner's jury. "I was satisfied, right away, that we had not killed the man, but that he was dead before we got there." The jury ruled that Sullivan's death was an accident. But many questions remain unanswered. Why did Sullivan go to the train station? Perhaps to hop a freight to New York, as he had done several times before? Or to commit suicide? Or, as the flagman insisted, was he dead before the train ran over him? If so, how did he die? And why did two weeks elapse before Sullivan's body was identified?

old clubhouse at 207 Bowery on Christmas Day, under the gaze of Big Tim, whose picture hung on the wall.

Sullivan's thirty-year reign corresponded to the Bowery's most indecent best. But by the time of his death, the street that all the guidebooks warned people to avoid at night, at all costs, but in the same breath listed all the best places for slumming, had lost its delicious edge. The dime museums, dance halls, concert saloons, Paresis Hall and other gay dives were gone, killed off by the reform movement. Almost all the Yiddish theaters had moved over one block to Second Avenue. People felt so nostalgic about the good old Satan's Highway that in 1902 a replica Bowery was constructed on Coney Island as part of the Dreamland amusement park.

Into the spaces once occupied by these dens of iniquity and fun moved more of the Bowery's dependable staples—pawnshops, secondhand clothing stores, and tattoo parlors. Properties along the Bowery were worth way less than on the other major streets of the city; and for the most part, since the Civil War, its appearance had hardly changed. Once in a while, a new theater got erected on the Bowery, or a three- or four-story brick building. Or a bank: yes, curiously, there were a handful of them, all grand and ornate structures—one of them, the Bowery Savings Bank, was designed by McKim, Mead and White, the snootiest of New York's Gilded Age architects—standing haughtily over the Bowery's old brick buildings.*

There was yet another factor that caused the undervaluation of Bowery land: the addition of two more tracks to the El, which necessitated moving the structure to the middle of the street. Since 1876, when the El was erected, the location of its tracks directly over the sidewalks made the Bowery's denizens miserable. But when this massive civil engineering project was finished in 1915—it involved all of Manhattan, as a third track was added to every elevated line, thereby

---

* Others were the Victorian-cum-Gothic Dry Dock Savings Bank, which was demolished in the mid-1950s for a gas station, the Germania Bank, the Atlantic Savings Bank, and the Citizens Bank.

creating express service—the Bowery was now in perpetual darkness, had twice as many tracks as previously, and double the pollution and noise. (Big Tim had tried unsuccessfully to limit the tracks to three instead of four in the state senate.)

Moreover, thanks to the El, all the bums had a place to hide. Since the Civil War, this catchall term for the homeless or severely alcoholic or anybody who was running away and didn't want to be found became so closely associated with the Bowery that by the 1880s, the two words were fused together into that memorable expression "Bowery bum." After the Great War ended in 1918, their numbers were growing, because all the arms factories had closed, and thousands of veterans needed jobs. The American economy crashed, then got worse, and desperate men flocked to—where else?—the Bowery. Former soldiers pawned their medals and found comfort in the saloons. But Prohibition closed down all the saloons beginning in 1920, and the Bowery went straight to hell.

CHAPTER ELEVEN

THE BUMS ON THE BOWERY

I n 1924, the World League Against Alcoholism issued a glossy sixteen-page pamphlet devoted entirely to the new, dry Bowery.

"The saloon was the hub around which all vice revolved [on the Bowery]. Prohibition blasted it into smithereens," it bragged.

But the ecstatic do-gooders didn't give a thought to what Prohibition meant for the bums. Saloons did not just offer booze: they satisfied many basic needs that were otherwise going unmet. During the day, the saloon was a place where you could sit around and schmooze; on cold, snowy nights, Mrs. Sarah Bird told the *Tribune* in 1895—she was a woman of great wealth who devoted her life to her "boys," as she called the Bowery unfortunates—saloons were "the only lighthouses for these wrecked mariners, so brilliant and so glowing that I did not wonder these homeless men were allured to shelter within." Bums had favorite spots where they hung out with their friends, and an owner looked out for them. They could leave their money with him, and he'd put it in his safe and keep it for them. Or he'd let them use his address like a post office box. If a bum got sick from alcohol poisoning, he headed over to the Alligator, a five-cent-a-shot joint where the British-born "Doc" Shuffield—once a surgeon in a London hospital, whose nose was mapped with the tiny red veins that belie chronic alcoholism—had his "office." Clad in a greasy frock coat and shabby silk hat, the doctor cared for any bum who needed him. Some owners had a "flop room" at the back of their saloon, where they let drunken bums spend the night sprawled out on the sawdust-covered floor or slumped in chairs, the spit dribbling out of their mouths. It wasn't much of a bed, but it beat sleeping in a doorway or on the sidewalk under the El, where you might get robbed or worse.

Without saloons, the bums were lost. During the day, if they had a dime, they could sit and doze in one of the Bowery's cheap moving-picture houses that now occupied some of the old theaters until somebody threw them out. Otherwise, they wandered the streets. "All day, the bums patrol the Bowery. They fill the vacuum in this region of inertia. They walk, as on a tightrope, the razor edge of vacancy between the turbulence of the east side and the racketing traffic of the warehouses," a *New York Times* reporter wrote in the September 19, 1924 story, "The Street that Died Young." "Slowly, in draggled procession, they move from the 'Y' on East Fifth Street to the Salvation Army and down to the drinking fountain at the Branch Y. Not to go in—simply they follow herd-like as the crowd moves, to stand, and spit and watch the movement of the street—and then down for an afternoon on the benches of the Manhattan Bridge."

Concurrent with the shuttering of the saloons in the early 1920s, the American economy roared back, which meant there was now work for the bums who wanted to get off the Bowery. So by the mid-twenties, the street's vagrant population, which had shot way up after the end of the Great War, shrank, making the Bowery feel empty. ("No loungers on the street corners, no sad, dejected figures, shuffling through the gloom, no drunkards sagging homeward from the dirty bars. All that made the color and the terror of this dark and wondrous street gone into forgetfulness!" a reporter from the *St. Louis Post-Dispatch* wrote on August 20, 1922.) All the Bowery missions where drunken sinners found redemption were now half empty. "Prohibition has eliminated a lot of the dirty work of the missions," the World

League Against Alcoholism claimed in its pamphlet. "Now they can focus on their real purpose: saving souls."

Today, with the advantage of hindsight, we know that Prohibition failed spectacularly as a social experiment. Among its countless, unintended effects was to further depress the value of Bowery real estate. All those shuttered saloons resulted in a lot of empty spaces, which owners then frantically leased to whomever could pay the rent: one tenant sold bar fixtures to people who ran speakeasies out of their homes, another rented out crutches, wheelchairs, and blood-tinted bandages to beggars faking physical deformities. A few longtime jewelers remained, and diamond merchants opened an emporium at the intersection with Canal Street. This remained the center of New York's diamond district until after World War II. The Bowery seemed an anomalous choice of location for the diamond business, but rents there were low.

"For two centuries, the Bowery was the place where everything happened," the *New York Times* reporter wrote mournfully in "The Street That Died Young." "And now suddenly, it is the place where nothing happens at all."

The dip in the bum population along the Bowery proved brief: by mid-decade, the missions and flops were filled again. Desperate men ended up on the Bowery, but then might vanish and once more reappear, so it proved impossible to keep count of them. In 1924, the director of the Bowery Mission estimated there were 250,000 men around the country who considered the thoroughfare their home. "But they are never here at the same time," he told the *New York Times*, adding that a recent survey showed 12,000 men living in transient housing on the Bowery. This number didn't include the bums living on the street, so no doubt it was higher. And in 1930, 300 volunteers—social workers, college students, insurance men, police, speakeasy owners, and anybody else who cared to—took New York's first-ever census of the Bowery homeless. The results: "14,000 tragic failures in life," the *Brooklyn Eagle* (November 3, 1930) somberly reported. Yes, there were so many reasons to end up on the Bowery; one of them was to drink. Here people found the company of other alcoholics: even with all the saloons gone, they could find booze on the Bowery as easily as anywhere in New York, the wet capital of dry America. The Bowery, like everywhere in New York, had speakeasies. The term referred to any place liquor was illegally served, from a basement to the 21 Club. The same 1930 census reported that there were seventy-seven speakeasies on the Bowery. Normally a person needed to know somebody to get into a speakeasy but not there. No, on the Bowery, anyone could just walk right in and ask for a drink, which now cost four times as much as it did before Prohibition. At O'Leary's, owned by two brothers, the older a former fighter with a broken nose, a pot of homemade soup was always bubbling on the stove for the bums who frequented it. The place was "not for the squeamish, in stomach and nostril, for the sight and smell of a score of sodden derelicts is none too pleasant," wrote Al Hirschfeld, who included a sketch of it in his 1932 collection of speakeasy cartoons.

If a bum could no longer afford booze, for a nickel he could buy "smoke," a mixture of wood or denatured alcohol—the latter was used in antifreeze—and water. (Water poured into a bottle of alcohol caused a vapor to snake up the neck, hence the name.) It was "one of the deadliest fruits of the Volstead Act," wrote a concerned citizen in a letter to the New York Times in 1929. "It's the drink a man will take to only when he's down and out, desperately cold and hungry, with no prospect of a job." If smoke didn't outright kill you—in 1930, thirty-one men died after ingesting it in just one month—it made you very, very sick. Federal agents made frequent raids of these so-called shock houses, which, along with their poison, offered shelter on cold winter nights. When Prohibition was finally repealed in December 1933, one of the first things New York cops did was to ax the shock joints, which put the thousands of bums who'd been spending their nights on the floors of these places out on the street.

As the Depression dragged on and men couldn't find work, increasing numbers ended up on the Bowery. Dive bars opened in place of the saloons that Prohibition had killed off, and once again the Bowery offered places where a guy could drink himself to death legally, in the company of other alcoholics. Virtually all were male; here and there, a woman found her way into the strange, closed-off world of the bum, which to outsiders simply designated any man who ended up on the Bowery. But to those living there the word had a specific connotation. Bums—"the whiskey-soaked panhandlers and petty sneaks, usually old and life-worn wrecks"*—occupied the lowest rung on the Bowery pecking order, and hobos the highest. Hobos, also called stiffs, were the men who hopped on and off the rails, and in between survived by performing manual labor. They treasured their independence, hated drunks, and considered bums the lowest form of human flotsam. The flops were filled with hobos in the wintertime, but when the weather turned nice these men headed for the road to find work. Hobos laid rails for the tracks; chopped down trees, harvested wheat in the Dakotas, Kansas, and Minnesota; worked in the hops fields, walnut groves, and vineyards in California; picked berries in the South and apples in Upstate New York. When the weather got cold again, they returned to the Bowery, where, during periods of labor unrest in the 1920s, they easily found work as scabs—"finks"—during strikes. Hobos were a proud bunch. They had their own International Brotherhood Welfare Association, a yearly convention in Columbus, Ohio, published the *Hobo News*, which cost ten cents a copy, and operated "hobo colleges," of which there was a branch at 350 Bowery in a loft above a hardware store. Classes were held there every evening, where men discussed Marx, Gorky, and Schopenhauer. The public was welcome at the Hobo College, although a sign hung on the wall, sternly warning: NO MISSION STIFFS, SCABS, DRUNKS, OR SKUNKS WANTED HERE. Hobos, you see, had particular contempt for missions and even more for the stiff who succumbed to them. Missions represented the opposite of the hobo ethos, which was above all else about independence. Missions, along with prayers, offered shelter and food, so their presence along the Bowery was essential,

---

* *St. Louis Post-Dispatch,* "The Bowery Passed Out with Booze," August 20, 1922.

especially after the demise of saloons. Missions also provided something metaphysical—call it religion, for convenience's sake—and not
only for the bums but also for the entire Bowery. The Bowery was
more than just a street: it was, is, a place that transcends time, occupying a fixed point in our memories, through its many and complex associations, and the missions formed part of its fabric. In fact, tours of
New York often included a stop at a Bowery prayer meeting. Missions
on the Bowery filled a big, glaring hole: it was the only main thoroughfare in New York with no churches. It was as if respectable forms of
worship had deliberately sidestepped Satan's Highway, which, by the
way, fell within the parochial borders of eight Roman Catholic churches.
The Bowery's Catholic soul, wrote a priest in a 1907 church publication, is "dormant: the Bowery has always remained a thing apart
from what is considered parish life." A thing apart, indeed. There were
dozens of synagogues on the Lower East Side but none of them were on
the Bowery, either. There were just all those Yiddish theaters, where
some of the playwrights were questioning the existence of God.

Bowery missions ran the gamut from big operations like the
YMCA and Salvation Army to little storefronts started by any crackpot
who wanted to. The Catholic Church, embarrassed by all the good
works the Protestants were doing along Satan's Highway, finally
opened its own mission right off the Bowery at 157 ½, at Broome
Street. ("What our non-Catholic brethren are doing we can do. We
must fight the fire of hell on the Bowery with the fire of the Holy
Spirit. Satan should not and will not have all to say on one of the greatest thoroughfares of the world.") But redemption did not come cheap:
In 1906, the Salvation Army estimated that each sinner who was "raised
from the depths and turned from his evil ways" represented an outlay
of $21. Whereas it cost only $10 in the Tenderloin, and $7 in Harlem.
The discrepancy, according to the Salvation Army, was due to the
fact that the Bowery needed "a larger force and one of peculiar fitness."
The good folks knew what they were talking about: "More than any
other organization, and through the varied character of its work, [the

Salvation Army] knows its New York and the sin to be coped with by the fishers among men. It has sectionalized and studied the metropolis so carefully that the percentage of those to be saved within the radius of any one mission may be reckoned upon almost to a nicety."

Missions began popping up on the Bowery after the Civil War, as the street was attracting growing numbers of lost souls; by the 1920s there were at least ten. The Salvation Army, one of the first, started in England in the 1860s. It was the creation of a renegade Methodist minister—indeed, the Methodists themselves were considered radical—named William Booth. He found he could not abide being chained to a pulpit and instead felt compelled to wander around London's East End, hold outdoor meetings, and convert the wretcheds he encountered right on the street. Booth's movement caught on and spread. In 1880, his daughter, Evangeline, to whom he'd given the rank of captain, accompanied by six lieutenants—five women and one man—boarded a ship in London and crossed the ocean. After a miserable storm-tossed voyage in steerage, they disembarked in New York. Upon which the little group, all wearing dark blue uniforms edged with yellow and hats encircled by wide scarlet bands on which were inscribed the words "Salvation Army" in gilt letters, sang a hymn:

> With sorrow for sin, let repentance begin,
> Then conversion of course will draw nigh.
> But till washed in the blood of a crucified Lord,
> You will never be ready to die.

This marked the Salvation Army's first prayer service on American soil: clearly, there was no time to lose. After going through the requisite immigration paperwork, the little unit marched through the streets of Lower Manhattan as onlookers stared, until they reached the boardinghouse where they were to stay. One of the women carried a red and blue flag—the two colors symbolized the blood and purity of Christ—emblazoned with the words "Salvation Army" inside a large yellow sun. The following day, the city refused to grant Booth a permit for street meetings. Undaunted, she approached Harry Hill, who operated one of New York's biggest, baddest dance halls out of a two-story wooden house on Houston Street off Broadway, and asked him if she might use it for a Sunday prayer meeting. The Salvationists were a pragmatic sort; what more convenient venue for a mission than a saloon, where drunk and dissipated souls were already gathered and ready for saving? Hill, for his part, figured that promoting Christian values in his dance hall could only be good for business, so he obliged. At the missionaries' first evening at Hill's, they prayed, sang, and talked about Jesus to the audience of painted women and scary-looking men between performances by scantily clad women shaking their butts and singing dirty songs. By the end of the evening, the Salvationists had their first American convert: Ash Barrel Jimmy, so-called because a cop found the poor drunk stuck in an ash can one cold winter night, his feet sticking up in the air. Booth and her army then moved a few blocks down from Hill's place to Steve Brodie's, at the latter's invitation. Booth realized that the wicked old Bowery was the perfect place to headquarter the Salvation Army, and they opened their own facility in 1890.

Next door to the Salvation Army headquarters was the Bowery Mission, which opened in 1879 and still exists. It was the largest and most famous of all the missions on the street. All the big names on America's evangelical circuit—Dwight Moody and, later, Amy Semple McPherson—visited it and made sure that the newspapers knew. Victor Benke, a famous organist, was discovered at the Bowery Mission. He was a classically educated musician from a well-to-do family in Austria, but he ended up on the Bowery broke and perennially drunk. One Sunday in 1894, he wandered into the Bowery Mission. His face was streaked with dirt, and his shock of black hair was uncombed. "Relievers," the coarse, baggy suit that pawnbrokers give a man to wear when he hocks his clothes, hung from his skinny body. He took a seat among the other bums and watched the stout, sweet-faced Mrs. Sarah

Bird leading a prayer meeting. When it came time to sing hymns, she said: "Boys, there is nobody to play the piano today. Can anybody help me?" Benke jumped up, rushed to the piano, sat down on the bench, and began to play. Mrs. Bird took Benke under her wing, and he became the Bowery Mission's official organist. He gave frequent recitals. He also played for churches uptown and even at Carnegie Hall. Whenever the famous evangelical preacher Dwight Moody was in New York, Benke played for him.

Every night at one in the morning, the Bowery Mission gave out free bread and coffee to anybody who wanted it. The line, sometimes as many as 1,000 men, began forming at ten o'clock. For some, this was the only meal of the day. Afterward, the bums drifted along the Bowery, looking for somewhere to settle down for the night. For twenty-five cents they could sleep in a flop or they might get lucky and find a bed in one of the missions that offered "accommodations." But even if they did, they'd get thrown out early in the morning. Some missions only let bums in if they went to the prayer meeting. At the Salvation Army, the price of admission included the requirement that they take a bath. Every mission on the Bowery had some sort of requirement or restriction for a bum who might use their services, until 1911 when a thirty-five-year-old man named Dudley Upjohn opened his All Night Mission at 8 Bowery. It was open 24/7, no questions asked. There was just one thing: instead of beds, the All Night Mission offered only wooden chairs.

Upjohn came from the cream of New York society. His grandfather, the British-born architect Richard Upjohn, champion of the Gothic Revival style, designed Trinity Church. His father, Richard Mitchell Upjohn followed in Upjohn *père's* footsteps, designing Gothic-style churches and other structures throughout America. (One of Dudley's brothers, Hobart, was also a church architect.) Dudley had no interest in the family profession, but he was listed in the social registry and honored the Upjohn name by serving as an usher at Trinity Church. He married Mary Morton Pickslay, the daughter

Bread Line on the Bowery

of a wealthy diamond merchant, in 1902 and worked for the Mutual Life Insurance Company. Dudley was a disappointment to his father, Richard, and the latter treated his son badly. ("Try to curb your tongue, and to eradicate the bitterness in your heart. For the Bible says 'out of the bitterness of the heart the mouth speaketh.' And be gentle and loving to your children who would love you if you would let them," wrote Emma Upjohn to her husband in 1895. "And be patient with Dudley. You may not agree with him, but you need not be telling him so all the time. He has chosen his profession and is trying to do good work in it.")

After Richard Upjohn died in 1903, Dudley felt lost: grieving an abusive parent is complicated. He became obsessed with the lives of the downtrodden, and it became his habit to head down to the Bowery after work every night, where, he later wrote, he "walked, talked, and prayed with hundreds of men, some of them thieves, gamblers and drunkards, or addicted to the dreadful habits of morphine, opium, or cocaine, but never once did I forget that under all of these conditions there was a lost soul belonging to Christ whom I felt I must bend every energy to win back to God almighty."

One night, Dudley wandered into a Chinatown mission during a prayer meeting and found a seat in the back row. The room stank from rancid body odors and alcohol-infused breaths. Upjohn watched and listened as a man stood in front of the audience and testified that he used to be just a lousy Bowery crook. "I lost count of how many times I was thrown into prison. But five years ago, I was saved!" he shouted, and some men in the audience responded: "Hallelujah!"

The man—his name was Jack Carroll—captivated Upjohn. When Carroll asked if anybody was ready to repent and let Jesus into his heart, Upjohn knelt down along with a handful of drunks and bums. Upjohn prayed. He asked God to take away, in his words, "my self-righteousness and selfishness." At the end of the prayer service, he introduced himself to Carroll. The two decided to team up and establish their own mission, which would stay open 24/7, unlike the others. Upjohn quit his job at Mutual Life, and he also left his wife. The couple had no children, and two years later, Mary Upjohn travelled to Reno and got a divorce from Dudley, on grounds of desertion. Soon after, she remarried.

Using his own money, and funds he solicited from Trinity parishioners, Upjohn rented the three-story building at 8 Bowery, and this became the All Night Mission. Every Christmas Eve, he escorted a group of bums to Trinity Church for the midnight service, while no doubt mentally pointing his middle finger in the direction of heaven and all those High Church Upjohns.

In 1902, one Johnny Callahan rented half of a squat, two-story building at 291–293 Bowery that John McGurk for the previous twelve years was using as an annex to his adjoining Suicide Hall. McGurk's notorious Bowery dive had recently closed, and Callahan turned the space into Hadley Rescue Hall, a Methodist mission. Talk about creative building reuse! Callahan, like many an evangelical, was a wounded healer. He started drinking when he was nine, when his "dear old grandmother" introduced him to alcohol. He then did some jail time, ended up on the Bowery, and found Jesus. He built up enough credibility to be hired as a chaplain at his alma mater, the Tombs. In his opinion, Prohibition was a wonderful thing. Callahan let bums stay overnight at Hadley Hall, no strings attached. They didn't have to delouse or listen to Callahan's sermons.

The only catch was that he threw the men out every morning at five. He did this because he always began his daily preaching at seven, and he needed those two hours to fumigate the place after "150 soiled persons made his church a community bedroom." Early one morning in 1925, five bums, led by a massively built, handsome man dressed in a corduroy suit and a soft hat, picketed Johnny's mission. They carried placards that read: "This place is Unfair to Organized Ease and Is Opposed to the Eight-Hour Sleep." The police came and chased the demonstrators away. The man leading them was one of the Bowery's best-known eccentrics, whom everybody called Mr. Zero. This mystic and champion of world peace was also a self-appointed champion of the hungry and unemployed, a number one nudnik, and a hell of an organizer. He lived on the Bowery, where he distributed clothing and operated a breadline out of a hole-in-the-wall on the corner of Ninth Street. He also ran a dingy basement restaurant, the Tub, on St. Marks Place, which offered meals for five cents. This was a tiny space, so on days when the overflow was too much to handle, he'd lead the army of hungry souls to a five-cent joint uptown near Pennsylvania Station that could accommodate large crowds. It was called Blake's Hell of a Place. Mr. Zero's real name was Urbain Ledoux. His moniker came about when one day when a man asked him what his name was, and Ledoux answered: "I am nothing to you but bread and water. You were athirst and I gave you to drink; you were hungry and I gave you to eat. That's all!" A *Tribune* reporter was present, and the next day a headline appeared in the newspaper: THE MYSTERIOUS MR. ZERO.

People really didn't know what to make of Mr. Zero. New York's officialdom considered him a dangerous radical. Most of the bums on the Bowery adored him, although sometimes you'd hear grumblings among them that he was a phony and an opportunist. (One told the

Tribune in 1923: "He gets money from the rich and throws the 'bo [hobo] coffee and a doughnut and in this way enriches himself and gets publicity through the newspapers.") The Quebec native had served as American consul in Prague in the early 1900s and then started a successful business that produced denatured alcohol. But during the Great War he'd become a peace activist, and from there he progressed to feeding and sheltering unemployed veterans, many of whom were landing on the Bowery. Mr. Zero felt strongly that America had an obligation to care for its veterans and poor. He often said that the 52,000 men who became millionaires on account of the war—where he got that figure is unknown—should give up half their money for public and social works. Mr. Zero liked drawing attention to his cause by holding demonstrations in large public spaces. Several times he brought an army of unemployed men to Bryant Park, behind the New York Public Library, for what he called a "slave auction." He'd present each prospective laborer stripped to the waist, in a deliberate allusion to the slave markets of old, and call for the highest bidder. Every Easter, he led fifty or so men, all wearing tattered silk hats, down Fifth Avenue. This was his contribution to New York's beloved annual Easter Parade.

In 1927, the *New Yorker* wrote a story about Mr. Zero. How the audiences of New York's most rarified and narcissistic publication did love reading about those Bowery eccentrics! In 1940, it ran a now-famous story about another one. This, by the great urban raconteur Joseph Mitchell, told the story of Mazie Phillips, a bottle blond with a filthy mouth and a heart of gold whom he'd first discovered as a young reporter at the *World* during the 1930s. Mazie and her brother-in-law owned the Venice movie theater down on Park Row under the shadow of the El. She lived with her sister Rosie at Knickerbocker Village, just south of the Venice. Mitchell described a woman who, like some great mother goddess of the Bowery, took care of all the bums. She also kept a supply of lollipops on hand to distribute to all the neighborhood kids. Unfortunately she also scared them with her gravelly voice, clownish makeup, and striking outfits of vivid yellow, red, and green velvet. Every day Mazie sat in the ticket booth of the Venice with her little doggie on her lap and a cigarette hanging from her brightly lipsticked mouth. She let bums use the Venice as an all-day dormitory. Although if a guy was obviously louse infected she'd turn him away, because she didn't "run no scratch house." Every night, Mazie walked up and down the Bowery like a nurse making her rounds in a giant hospital ward, checking on her bums. She handed out dimes and quarters and bars of soap to them. Sometimes she gathered a group of hungry guys and took them to one of the hash houses for a square meal. Or she'd help a man up from the sidewalk and escort him to one of the flophouses—the Gem, the Ritz, the Plaza, the Puritan, the Newport, the Delevan, the Alabama, the Majestic, the Mascot, the Nassau, the Comet, the Uncle Sam House, the Mills, the Union, the Dandy, the Savoy, the Columbus, the Defender, the Niagara, the Owl, the Victoria House, the Grand Windsor Hotel, the Houston, the Palace, the Progress, the Palma House, the Crystal, the Lion, the Sunshine, the Marathon, the Boston, the White House—these were some of them. (David Isay and Stacy Abramson in their 2000 book *Flophouse* state that during the Depression, the Bowery had close to one hundred flop-houses, but they do not source this pretty astonishing assertion.*) Mazie would hand the clerk the thirty-cent fee and then drag the bum to his cot for the night, lie him down, still dressed, cover him with a blanket, and leave. She never took her guys to the missions: Mazie loved to drink, so the missions didn't much like her, and she didn't like them, either. If she came across a bum needing his alcohol fix, she offered him a bottle. This, she believed, was the humane approach. Mazie was Jewish, but she had a special affection for Catholics, because in her experience it was nuns who took the best care of the desperate people in this world. Mazie performed her good works for some sixty-odd years, from the time she first arrived in New York from her native

---

* Only the Boston accepted black clientele. On October 1, 1949, the *New York Age*, a black newspaper, reported that the NAACP was getting complaints that certain flophouses were turning away "Negroes."

Boston in the 1890s. In the late 1950s, she was still walking around the Bowery and surrounding streets, doling out her lollipops and quarters to the children and looking after the bums. When she died in 1964 "after a long illness," the *New York Times* wrote, "Men sat on doorsteps, lamenting her death. Some drank to her memory, as she had often done for others."

In 1934, one year after the repeal of Prohibition went into effect, a federal operation targeted hundreds of places in New York for evasion of the liquor tax. At the Home Tavern, a dive bar at 267 Bowery, agents found a secret compartment—a relic of Prohibition—filled with bottles of "hot" booze, which they confiscated along with all the bar fixtures. The raid put the Home Tavern out of business, and this suddenly empty space caught the eye of one Sammy Fuchs. The thirty-year-old father of two was born and raised in a tenement on the corner of the Bowery and Hester Street, along with a gaggle of brothers and sisters. As a teenager Sammy worked at an uncle's Lower East Side dairy restaurant, but his cousin pushed him out of the business. Sammy, a big, muscular guy (he worked out regularly at a boxing gym) who had a face like a map of Israel, then did whatever he could find to eke out a living. During Prohibition, he worked as a lookout for bootleggers, but that gig naturally dried up with the repeal of the Eighteenth Amendment in 1933. So when the Home Tavern closed, Sammy saw an opportunity. He signed a lease on 267 Bowery, got the place a liquor license, hung up old pictures of boxers on the walls, and reopened it as Sammy's Chop House. It attracted a combination of neighborhood types, and Fuchs seemed a reincarnation of an old-time Bowery saloon-keeper. If a man came into his bar hungry, he fed him. If a bum was sick, Sammy made sure he got proper care. He also watched over bums for their respective families. They might send Sammy money to care for their loved one, which he deposited in a safe he kept behind the counter. The safe also held letters written by bums that Sammy would give to their relatives upon the bums' deaths, so they would know what happened. When a bum without family died on the Bowery, Sammy paid for his funeral, thereby ensuring that he did not end up in a potter's field. Sammy felt protective of bums from the time he was just a boy. In 1923, he and his pal Cookie Kahn—he and Sammy used to pool their pennies to share a greasy potato knish—made a pact. They swore that the first thing they would do when they earned some money was to take care of the Bowery's forgotten men.

One day in 1941, as Sammy was eking out a living from his neighborhood bar, a customer dropped in out of the blue. The man was a British tourist. When Sammy asked him what he was doing down on the Bowery, he replied that when he was growing up in England, he'd heard many stories about New York's bad old Bowery. Now that he was in New York he was curious to see what remained of it. Not much, Sammy told him, but the Brit planted the germ of an idea in the bar owner's head. Soon after their conversation, Sammy got himself a cabaret license. Then he hired a few washed-up old vaudevillians—Norma Devine, a huge woman in tight-fitting satin gowns who shook her booty like nobody else, and Mabel Sidney, "a buxom party who sings not only loud but good," and another woman named Tilly Schneider—to perform at his place. Before long, Sammy's was attracting people from all over. Not just uptown slummers, but tourists, too, and military men on leave. This being wartime, the city was full of sailors who were heading to the Bowery anyway to get a tattoo.

Sammy's little neighborhood bar on the Bowery became a national sensation, as the street, gut-punched first by Prohibition and then the Depression, continued to slowly decay. The postwar boom in the American economy made unskilled jobs plentiful, so the bum population along the Bowery—and skid rows across America—was declining. Its population density was lessening, and the grimy old buildings were getting emptier: all bad omens for an urban neighborhood. The restaurant supply and lighting fixtures stores remained, but the diamond district was starting to shift uptown to Forty-eighth Street. In the 1940s, the Bowery was like an old person with COPD—chronic obstructive pulmonary disorder—and Sammy's was a godsend. On weekend nights, hundreds of people converged on the sidewalk in front of the entrance, waiting for revelers to leave so they, too, could squeeze in and experience the Bowery world that Sammy Fuchs had inadvertently created. He needed more space, so in 1944 he bought the building next door, broke through the wall, and combined the two ground floors. He then renamed his bar Sammy's Bowery Follies. "I gotta have a larger place, or these uptowners are goin' to crowd out the escapists. And if I don't have no escapists I just the same as ain't got no place," Sammy told a reporter who dropped in while the place was in midconstruction. "Escapists" were Sammy's regulars: Tugboat Ethel, the old man with the matted white beard who called himself Jesus Christ, and Coney Island May. They— and what the famous photographer Weegee called "a lulu of a floor show"—were the main draw at Sammy's. Weegee just loved Sammy's. He took hundreds of photos there and along the Bowery as well.

Weegee was born Usher Fellig in 1899 in Lemberg—now Lviv, in Ukraine, but then a center of Yiddish culture—and he came to New York with his family when he was ten. In the 1930s and '40s, Weegee was the premier photojournalist of New York's mean streets for all the tabloids. He did his job with great respect for his subjects and an obvious and passionate love for New York. Weegee's specialty was photographing crime scenes. He had a police radio in his car, so he often got to the scene before the cops did, and he used the trunk of his '38 Chevy as a darkroom. His grimy black-and-white shots came to typify New York noir. The first book-length collection of Weegee's photos, *Naked City*, devoted a lot of space to Sammy's. When the book came out in 1945, Weegee threw a party at—where else?—Sammy's. *Naked City* helped spawn an entire industry of black-and-white crime movies set in New York City. One film, in fact, borrowed the title of Weegee's book—directed by Jules Dassin, *Naked City* opened in 1948 and won several Oscars—and was then turned into a 1950s television series that people were watching all over America, safe and sound in their suburban living rooms. They'd fled the cities after the war, when returning veterans could buy little Levitt houses for $100 down.

Sammy Fuchs Serving Drinks at his Bowery Follies bar

America's cities were getting poorer and uglier, the Bowery was getting seedier, and Sammy's—it became an obligatory stop on the Gray Line bus tour—partied on. Some nights, Jimmy Durante—he grew up on the Bowery—played the piano there, and local politicians regularly stopped by to pay court to Sammy Fuchs. The Bowery Follies was making Fuchs a lot of money. He spent it all gambling and drinking and continued to take loving care of the neighborhood bums.

After the war, as white folks were running away to the suburbs, real estate values in the city plummeted. But New York property, no matter how skanky, never becomes completely worthless. During bad times it may be worth less, but that only translates into opportunity for speculators who then rush in and snap it up. This is what happened in New York during the 1950s and '60s, especially in certain choice areas of the city, one of which was the West Village. Developers were knocking down irreplaceable old structures along lower Fifth Avenue and the blocks around Washington Square and replacing them with awful white-brick high-rises, but the neighborhood's artsy vibe kept humming, which, along with the charming old houses on its twisty little streets, caused real estate values there to rise. So all the beatnik poets, musicians, and artists were getting pushed out of the West Village. They moved east across Sixth Avenue and Broadway in search of cheaper spaces and found them on the Bowery. Artists rented lofts in former flophouses, enfant terrible William S. Burroughs lived in the old YMCA building at 222 Bowery, and writers LeRoi Jones (who later changed his name to Amiri Baraka) and his Jewish wife from Queens, Hettie, hosted poetry readings in their top-floor loft in an 1844 building at 27 Cooper Square. A few doors north of the Joneses, everybody hung out at the Five Spot Café to hear jazz musicians Charles Mingus, John Coltrane, Charlie Parker, and Thelonious Monk. A few blocks down, at 295 Bowery, the activist and writer Kate Millett was living over the space that once housed McGurk's Suicide Hall, and what a fitting address this was for the author of *Sexual Politics*, which, when it was published in 1970, made her an instant feminist superstar. Tony and Sally Amato bought a former cigar factory–turned-mission at 319 Bowery in 1962 and turned it into a doll-size opera house. And the following year, the Bouwerie Lane Theater opened across the street in a former cast-iron-style bank building, one of many little theaters then popping up around the neighborhood. So alongside the Bowery's shrinking but visible population of destitute souls lived a close-knit community of artists and writers, many of whom were raising their kids there. But most people saw the Bowery as the most gangrenous limb of a diseased city; indeed, in postwar America, all cities were viewed as cancerous, in need of drastic surgery.

In 1954, a young man named Lionel Rogosin with a chemical engineering degree from Yale quit his job at his family's lucrative synthetic textile business, got himself a camera, and began making a movie about the Bowery. He envisaged a film in the quasi-documentary style of the Italian neorealists, who were then all the rage. ("No set no actors no dialogue," Rogosin wrote in his notes.) For the next two years, he hung out at the bars with all the bums. One of them, an old, toothless guy named Gorman Hendricks, whose alarmingly swollen belly attested to his years of alcohol abuse, acted as Rogosin's guide through the Bowery, like a dissipated Virgil leading Dante through Hell. But Rogosin couldn't find a coherent narrative, so he enlisted the help of the film writer Mark Sufrin. Together, the two banged out a script that incorporated the lives of the bums whom Rogosin was following around. (Rogosin financed the film with his own money. It cost $60,000, which was a considerable sum in the mid-fifties.) The result was *On the Bowery,* which he shot from July through October 1956. The black-and-white 35-millimeter film takes place over three days. It centers on a relationship between two men: Rogosin's guide, Gorman Hendricks, and a handsome young drifter, Ray Salyer, who has just arrived on the fabled street, suitcase in hand. The two meet for the first time at a dive bar, where Hendricks takes Salyer under his wing. Just as the former did for Rogosin, but in this film-slash-documentary version of Rogosin's journey, Hendricks betrays his charge. (Rogosin was de facto creating *cinéma vérité,* before the term existed.) Hendricks introduces Salyer to a group of bums, and the men bond over a bottle of cheap wine that Salyer provides. That night, Salyer, drunk, passes out on the sidewalk. Hendricks, who has been following him, steals his suitcase, riffles through it, and finds a watch inside. He pawns it the next morning; meanwhile, Salyer, who has woken up to find his suitcase gone, finds work for the day. Later that afternoon, Salyer runs into Hendricks again and confides in him how badly he wants to stop drinking. That night, Salyer, full of resolve, goes to the Bowery Mission, but his addiction overwhelms him: in the middle of the night he bolts and goes on a bender. He ends up sleeping on the sidewalk. The following morning, the two men run into each other again, and Hendricks offers Salyer half of the money from the watch

Ray Salyer and Gorman Hendricks in *On the Bowery*

he has stolen from him. Salyer tells Hendricks that all he wants to do is drink. The latter replies: "You have to get off the Bowery!" The scene then cuts over to Hendricks sitting at the bar with three bums, where he and Salyer first met. The bar is called, of all things, the Confidence Bar and Grill. One of the bums asks Hendricks if he has seen Ray. Hendricks brags that he tried to help Ray, and that he's left the Bowery.

To which one of the men says, "He'll be back!" And there the film ends.

When the film was released in 1957, the *New York Times* turned up its nose. ("Sordid and pitiful," the newspaper's film critic Bosley Crowther wrote.) But many critics praised it, and it made Ray Salyer an instant celebrity. He was invited to the opening, afterward appeared as a guest on *The Tonight Show*, and got offers from Hollywood agents. But it was all too much for him, and one night he hopped a freight train and was never heard from again. Gorman Hendricks died of alcohol-related causes before the film came out—literally in a Bowery bar—and Rogosin dedicated *On the Bowery* to him.

Europeans loved *On the Bowery*. It won the Grand Prize for Documentary at the 1957 Venice Film Festival. But apparently it revolted America's then ambassador to Italy, Clare Boothe Luce, wife of *Time* publisher Henry Luce, who was at the festival: when Rogosin approached her, she literally turned her back on him, and her husband's *Time* magazine ignored the film. Still, it was nominated for Best Documentary at the Oscars. But few theaters in the States showed it, so it did not do well; in Europe, however, the lines of people waiting to see it snaked around blocks. Only twelve years had passed since the war, and the darkness of *On the Bowery* appealed to them. But America wanted happy endings and Doris Day, not the Bowery. Rogosin's film soon vanished from the mainstream, but it had a following among the art house crowd. Today, sixty years after its release, *On the Bowery* has been rediscovered. Now accessible in independent theaters and streaming services, it is considered a masterpiece. John Cassavetes and Martin Scorsese cited the film as a major influence on their respective works.*

In a marvelous confluence of life with art, the Bowery leg of the Third Avenue El was being dismantled as Rogosin was making his film. For the first time in some seventy years, the Bowery, and the bums who'd found hiding places underneath the tracks, lay exposed to the sunlight. So the bums were migrating to the benches in Washington

---

* Interesting fact: In 1960, two film students at NYU, Dan Halas and Alan Raymond, made a ten-minute 16 mm documentary consisting of interviews with Bowery bums. Each was asked: "How do you like the Bowery?" and the answers they got were devastating. One bum, weeping, tells the filmmaker that he ran away to the Bowery after he accidentally killed his wife by running over her in the driveway of their house in Cincinnati.

Neither Halas nor Raymond knew of Rogosin's film when they made *How Do You Like the Bowery?* Raymond told me: "Our filming style was actually influenced by the recent development of *cinéma vérité* documentary shooting, an observational style using minimal portable camera and sync sound equipment." For their efforts, Halas and Raymond received a D in the course. (Alan Raymond and his wife, Susan, produced the groundbreaking documentary *The American Family* for PBS in 1973.)

Square Park and outside St. Mark's Church in-the-Bowery, where they'd razz the parishioners on Sundays. During the week, they'd come inside the church and defecate in the pews. Or they'd sleep beneath the bust of Peter Stuyvesant just inside the entrance to the cemetery. The pastor, Father Allen, told the *New York Times* (November 20, 1961): "I don't know what we can do about the Bowery. I am a Christian and I say that the Bowery is a judgment upon our society. There is something sick about our society. Knowing that, we can't let loose our hostility against the derelicts."

People wrung their hands and asked, What to do about the bums? Where can we unload them? Meanwhile, Robert Moses's massive-scale urban renewal was knocking down and reconfiguring entire neighborhoods, and one of the areas to be bulldozed was the Bowery's entire eastern flank: a total of twenty-nine acres from Delancey to East Ninth Street, bounded by Second Avenue, Chrystie Street, the Bowery, and Third Avenue. All the flops and the dive bars and the Bowery Mission and the Salvation Army hotel next door and even McSorley's saloon—immortalized in a *New Yorker* story by Joseph Mitchell—would disappear and, Moses insisted, so would the bums. But to where? There were no provisions to rehouse them. Officials made vague suggestions about opening a facility on Ellis Island or shipping the bums to Camp LaGuardia, a former women's prison in Upstate New York. The truth was few gave a damn about what happened to the bums on the Bowery—even as, ironically, their numbers were diminishing.

But in the end, the bums stayed put, because urban renewal completely bypassed the Bowery. The snail's pace of the city's bureaucracy was initially the reason why; but then the recession of the 1970s and President Reagan's simultaneous halting of all federal housing aid and, finally, New York's near bankruptcy in 1975 killed off urban renewal for good. The terrible economy of the 1970s combined with new laws in New York State that dumped the mentally ill into the streets turned the city into a place associated mostly with a constant and justified fear of crime, the sight of abandoned property, and the ubiquitous homeless, among whom a new type that came to exemplify those ugly, dark days: the bag lady. On the Bowery, the numbers of homeless men, declining for years, now increased and the flophouses, which had been losing business, were once again full, used by the city to house the overflow from the Men's Shelter—the "Muni"—around the corner on Third Street. But these were a different kind of homeless: drug addicted and young, some black or Hispanic; formerly, the Bowery's population had been overwhelmingly white. Sometimes the newcomers preyed on the bums. The old-timers made for easy targets and felt so unsafe on the Bowery that most left for other areas of the city where the homeless were then congregating. There was nobody left on the Bowery to protect them. Even Sammy Fuchs was gone—he died in 1969—and his wife closed the nightclub a year later.

These were bleak and dangerous years on the Bowery. But then in 1973 a music entrepreneur named Hilly Kristal rented an old dive bar under the Palace (one of the hotels the city was using to house the homeless) for $600 a month. In his words, the place "stunk of dirty old men, vomit and urine. I had to fumigate it." Hilly's plan was to turn the place into a club that featured live music, and in a way he was picking up the thread of Sammy's Bowery Follies.

CHAPTER TWELVE

PUNK

Hilly Kristal was a big, scruffy, hairy, Jewish ex-marine who grew up on a New Jersey farm in the 1930s. He had a big personality that combined warmth, chutzpah, and sex appeal. Women adored him. (His ex-wife, Karen, said he slept around, even when they were still married.) Hilly loved music of all sorts—folk, jazz, and, especially, country and bluegrass—and he had talent, in the form of a beautiful voice. During the 1950s he sang professionally; for a time he was a member of the Radio City Music Hall chorus. But he never really broke through as performer, so Kristal segued into music's business side. For a few years (1959–1961) he managed the Village Vanguard—one of the hot spots where singers like Joan Baez and Bob Dylan kicked off the folk music revival—and by the mid-sixties Kristal was operating his own club, Hilly's, on West Ninth Street. Then he closed that club and started another on West Thirteenth Street, which was a mostly residential block. The people living there were paying a lot of money to live in Greenwich Village and didn't appreciate having Hilly's on Thirteenth as a neighbor, with all the noise and drunken patrons. Among regulars were Hells Angels, whose New York headquarters were close by, at 77 East Third Street.

In or around 1969 Hilly grew tired of all the complaints he was getting from neighbors on Thirteenth Street, closed his club there, and leased the space at 317 Bowery, below the Palace flophouse. Since most of his new neighbors were bums and junkies, he assumed they weren't going to give him any problems over the noise. He called his new place Hilly's on the Bowery, and it occupied a long, dark, narrow room illuminated only by the neon beer signs that hung above the bar. He fitted out the space with a seventy-five-foot bar and a pool table. At the end of the space was a small stage. The bums living upstairs in the Palace Hotel and the five other nearby flophouses provided Hilly Kristal with built-in clientele. Every morning, the men lined up along the sidewalk outside, waiting for him to open so they could get their first drink of the day. Hilly's also became a hangout for Hells Angels and their girlfriends; they already knew Hilly, and his new place was only five minutes away from their headquarters.* Hilly considered the Angels to be great customers. ("I tell you, if I had any real trouble I wouldn't hesitate to call them, if there was any emergency.") Since he couldn't afford to rent an apartment, he moved his king-size bed into the back and slept there. For company, he kept a dog named Jonathan, who never got house-trained. So Hilly's always stank of dog feces.

Hilly's goal was to make his bar into a mecca for country music, so he changed its name to Country Bluegrass Blues and Other Music for Uplifting Gormandizers. He hung a white awning adorned with big red letters that spelled out CBGB OMFUG over his entranceway and advertised in the *Village Voice*. While he waited for bluegrass bands to find his club, he opened it to any band that needed a place to play. The idea was to attract clientele who would come in and drink, because this is how music clubs turn a profit. The only condition he set for a band was that their music had to be original—which also meant that he didn't have to pay anybody royalties.

By the early seventies, rock 'n' roll, which had attained such glorious heights during the previous decade, was aging out and disco was com-

---

* The Hells Angels bought 77 East Third Street in 1969, and have been there ever since.

ing in. "To stay alive, it was going to have to keep on moving," *Village Voice* reporter Lorraine O'Grady wrote in October 1973. And what was holding it back? Then *Voice* music critic James Wolcott had an interesting thought: "No longer is the impulse for creating rock revolutionary—i.e. the transformation of oneself and society—but conservative: to carry on the rock tradition." The great rock artists— the Stones, for example—were continually recycling their old material in concerts. "Rock is getting as arthritic, or, at least, as phlegmatic, as a rich old whore," Wolcott wrote in the August 18, 1975, issue. The music companies that grew fat and rich off rock during the previous decade were now producing music so inconsequential, so insipid—the Bee Gees, disco, Olivia Newton-John, Donny and Marie Osmond, the Carpenters—that it seemed to evaporate as you listened to it. Meanwhile, record producers were prowling the New York club scene, on the lookout for the next big hit. Scraggly kids played guitar in their parents' suburban garages and tried to emulate the peculiar sounds of the Velvet Underground. This band, an early expression of the punk movement, was then performing regularly at Max's Kansas City, the hypercool and druggy hangout on Park Avenue South where Andy Warhol held court in the back room with his Factory crowd. Max's was one of the few venues in New York that booked rock groups, which were perceived, with much justification, as bad for your business: along with their music, they always brought drugs. The only other possible venue for a baby rock band to play was the Mercer, a funky arts complex housed inside the University Hotel, one of New York's worst welfare palaces. Otherwise, you were reduced to playing at rent parties and gay bathhouses. The New York Dolls, who debuted on the Bowery in 1971 at a Christmas show for the city's homeless, had a regular gig in the Oscar Wilde Room at the Mercer. The Dolls were all about spectacle: sequined tops, hip-high patent leather red boots, faces plastered with makeup, and hair. As for their sound, the less said, the better.

Besides rock groups, the Mercer housed six off-Broadway theater companies, each named for an author or a playwright. *One Flew Over* the Cuckoo's Nest and The Effect of Gamma Rays on Man-in-the-Moon Marigolds both debuted at the Mercer, and a production of Macbeth starred Sam Shepard, Rip Torn, and Geraldine Page. But in 1972 the production of Marigolds was forced to relocate uptown because the theater leaked so badly. The University Hotel, besides being, in the words of the New York Times on August 4, 1973, "a cesspool of squalor and crime" was also a structural wreck. For the previous few years, cracks were spreading through the walls, and in January 1973, worried tenants warned that the front façade was bulging. Finally, the entire building collapsed the night of August 9, 1973. Four people died. The Mercer was no more,* which meant there was one less place to go hear rock music in New York.

A few months later—December 1973—Hilly Kristal opened his new club on the Bowery.

The following spring, three rattily dressed young men approached Hilly one day as he was standing on a stepladder outside his club, adjusting the white awning that festooned the entrance. Two of them, who went by the names Richard Hell and Tom Verlaine, were old boarding school buddies; the third guy was named Richard Lloyd. These three, along with a fourth player, had recently formed a band they called Television. (Richard Hell, who wrote poetry, borrowed his nom de plume from Paul Verlaine's Une saison en enfer, which is why Tom took the name Verlaine.)

The guys asked Hilly what he was doing, and he invited them into his bar. They were looking for gigs they told him, so he asked them if they played country and bluegrass. Yeah, sure, they said. Hilly added them to his list of bands that were going to perform the following Sunday afternoon. On March 31, 1974, Television played their set to a mostly empty room that included three Hells Angels and a drag artist who went by the name Wayne—later Jayne—County, a member

---

* An NYU dorm now stands on the site.

of Warhol's Factory. For a time, County performed with a band called Queen Elizabeth; he'd strap on a vagina and fuck himself with a dildo. Television's playing was simply awful, but Hilly gave them a second chance a few Sundays later, when he featured them with another garage band, four kids from Queens who sported spiky haircuts and black leather jackets. They lived around the corner from the Bowery, and they called themselves the Ramones. Hilly later recalled: "They were even worse than Television. Their equipment kept breaking down and they kept yelling at each other." But he continued letting both groups play at his club, and in the spring of 1974, every little rock band in New York was showing up at CBGB's door, begging for a slot. Among those who made it into the lineup were the Stilettos, who fronted for Television one night. They were three women aiming for a 1970s version of a girl group, and one of the singers was a former Playboy bunny with a perfect body and a face like a beautiful doll's, with cupid-bow lips. Her name was Debbie Harry, a daughter of working-class New Jersey, as was another woman then performing at CBGB's: the artist and poet Patti Smith, who by then was well known in the downtown scene. She'd appeared often at the Mercer Arts Center, and now she was at CBGB's, performing with the band Television. (People said she was in love with Tom Verlaine.) Smith arrived in the East Village in the late sixties when she was twenty years old, after dropping out of college and working in various factory jobs. There she met a very young Robert Mapplethorpe—who would later make the world gasp with his explicit S&M-themed photography—and became his muse and lover. The couple lived together on and off until the early 1970s, poor as church mice and creating art that pushed through all boundaries. Smith's breakthrough came in February 1971, when she did a poetry reading to the twang of Lenny Kaye's electric guitar at the St. Mark's Poetry Project, at St. Mark's Church in-the-Bowery. Two months later, she performed in *Cowboy Mouth*, a play with Sam Shepard, which she also cowrote with him.

Patti Smith's gig with Television at CB's lasted five weeks, and her pals—among them Andy Warhol and Allen Ginsberg—came to see her. "It was the greatest atmosphere to perform in. It was conspiratorial. It was physical, and that's what rock 'n' roll's all about—sexual tension and being drunk and disorderly," Smith later said of CB's, which was still essentially a neighborhood bar. On a good night, there were perhaps fifty paying customers. Most of them were the musicians who played there in their black leather jackets and grungy T-shirts, along with their girlfriends. But some were filmmakers: among them was Jim Jarmusch, who was busy creating a "cinema of transgression." All these artists, along with the musicians, were then living along the Bowery or on the adjoining streets of the East Village. Drugs were everywhere and the streets were dangerous, but it was a thrilling time to be living there if you were young and an artist. The neighborhood had a bombed-out feel, with its blocks of nasty, graffitied tenement buildings, occasional garbage-strewn lots where scrawny ailanthus trees grew, and real estate values that were so depressed some landlords were literally walking away from their properties. So a starving artist could find a place to live and work there for practically nothing, if you didn't mind living next to the squatters and drug dealers: the urban despair inspired dark, nihilistic art. Like the Dadas in the Paris of the twenties, you were against everyone and everything.

In the summer of 1975, as the economic recession tripped by, the 1973 oil embargo dug in deeper, and it felt like New York was going to hell, Hilly put ads in the *Voice* announcing that CBGB's was going to host a rock festival, and he was looking for bands. What a great idea this was, not least because it was such a healthy antidote to the awful reality of life then in the Big Apple, as banks refused to refinance municipal loans, in response to which Mayor Abe Beame desperately slashed budgets and fired cops and sanitation workers. To express their displeasure over layoffs, the latter staged a wildcat strike over the July Fourth weekend, resulting in piles of garbage baking in the sun. Every morning, New Yorkers woke up and wondered if this was the day that their city was going to declare bankruptcy. What would it mean if New York, for all its griminess and crime, yet still the financial capital of the world, crashed? People were afraid, but when New York asked Washington for help, President Gerald Ford's reply—that he would veto any bailout bill Congress might pass—inspired perhaps the most famous newspaper headline ever: FORD TO CITY: DROP DEAD.

But never mind: at CBGB's, life was good. For three weeks, from the end of July to mid-August, forty-plus underground bands—Day Old Bread, Dead Boys, Television, the Planets, City Lights, the Marbles, Tuff Darts, Bananas, Talking Heads, the Shirts, the Demons, White Lightning, Jelly Rolls, Mink DeVille, Pretty Poison, Johnny's Dance Band, the Ramones—were screaming angry lyrics to the three-chord compositions that are standard in rock music. Debbie Harry performed that summer, too, as lead singer in a mostly sugar-pop-inspired band—although delivered with a sneer—that she and her boyfriend, Chris Stein, had recently formed with three other guys. They called their group Blondie, because when Harry walked down the street, construction workers wolf whistled and hooted and yelled: "Hey blondie!" Gorgeous as she was, Harry was way more than her looks: as a performer, she was magnetic.

Hilly didn't particularly like the music he was supporting, but people were coming to listen to it and buying drinks. So at least he was paying the rent. As many as six bands a night were playing at CBGB's during those three midsummer weeks, when New York is at its hottest and muggiest. The air-conditioning, completely inadequate for the space, finally broke down. To be crammed into this suffocating, smoke-filled hole of a bar along with all those sweat-dripping young bodies was not for the faint of heart. The noise level reached predictably earsplitting levels, and some groups—notably the Ramones—multiplied the auditory discomfort by using a technique known as "distortion," in which they turned up the amps and multiplied the signal many times over (this produces a "sonic sound," which takes you away from the actual sound). Still, the media was checking out

Blondie, CBGB's, 1977

CBGB's, because they sensed that something important was happening there. "Rock poses problems of image and amplitude that seem to daunt all but the most intrepid of club owners," wrote *New York Times* critic John Rockwell, who attended the festival. "Thus CBGB, an otherwise unprepossessing bar at 315 Bowery, is to be congratulated for presenting many of the younger bands in recent months." He noted that most of the players were in their teens or early twenties. Critic James Wolcott covered the CBGB festival for the *Voice*. "What the place itself is doing is truly extraordinary: putting on bands as if the stage were cable television [which in 1975 was in its infancy]," he wrote on August 18, 1975. "Of course not every band that auditions gets to play, but the proprietor, Hilly, must have a wide range of taste, because the quality of talent runs from the great to the God-condemned. As with cable TV, what you get is not high gloss professionalism, but talent still working on the basics."

Said Rockwell: "One suspects that several of CBGB's 40 bands will become butterflies in the airy realm of rock success. Because this festival reaffirms beyond anything else that New York, which has sometimes been accused of being more a market place than a producer of homegrown talent, is full of musically active people. In these days of municipal self-doubt, it's a cause for consolation."

In the fall, John Holmstrom, a graphic artist, and Holmstrom's friend Legs McNeil, who were hanging out at CBGB's, got together and started working on a fanzine dedicated to what was happening there. ("I wanted to make the visual equivalent of rock and roll," Holmstrom said in a 2012 interview with *Politico*.) They decided to call the new publication *Punk*, a vague term then being bandied about that implied the dark, negative, outlawish, scatological, and nauseating. Like New York in 1975, and like the Bowery. The first issue of *Punk* appeared in January 1976. It was printed on newsprint, and its contents included an interview with bad boy Lou Reed ("An exclusive interview with the original street punk turned fine artist!"), a gross-out cartoon about a piece of shit going down a sewage pipe, and an interview with the Ramones, flanked with a photo spread. There was also an editorial explaining *Punk*'s mission:

> Death to Disco Shit! Long Live the Rock! Kill Yourself. Jump Off a fuckin' cliff . . . Anything. Just don't listen to that disco shit . . . The epitome of all that's wrong with western civilization is disco. Eddu-cate [sic] yourself. Read *Punk*.

Soon the word "punk" entered the popular lexicon. People were talking about "punk music" and the "punk look"—it originated with Richard Hell and consisted of a dirty, torn T-shirt and spikey hair— and CBGB's was the acknowledged center of this new punk universe. No longer just a neighborhood hangout, people were coming to CB's from all parts, so it lost the intimacy of its early days. Still, it continued to embrace young rock musicians like a nurturing mother. By no means did the music being played there fall solely under the "punk" category.

There were so many kinds of bands: bluegrass, r&b, like the Rice Miller Band and Blue Sky, psychedelic bands, and leftover glitter bands. One day you'd go down there and hear rockabilly with Robert Gordon, or punk with the Tuff Darts, or punk-posing bands, or real devastating punk bands like the Ramones, the Heart-breakers, or Richard Hell. And on another night you would have Willy DeVille doing Otis Redding. Then the Talking Heads were real artsy rock, and the Laughing Dogs, real pop lunatic rock. And then you'd come on another night and there would be these people from a commune in LI dressed all in white and putting these little incense sticks all around. They would be playing this esoteric psychedelic spiritual rock. And you would say, "oh God, only at CBGB."*

So many people were coming to CB's every night that Hilly had to get rid of the pool table. He also built a new, larger stage and invested in a sound system. By 1977, some of the bands—Patti Smith's, then the Ramones, and Blondie—had record deals. (Smith's *Horses* came out in 1975.) But they didn't forget that Hilly Kristal had given them their first break, and they continued to play at CB's, which by then was a tourist destination. Every night, the crowd reached the legal occupancy limit—350 people—and beyond, at which point the heat and the smoke and the noise became so unbearable you felt like you were going to die. So you'd go outside and join the rest of the overflow crowd who were hanging out in front smoking pot.

Sometimes bums from the Palace Hotel came down to join in the

---

* Actress Annie Golden, who performed at CB's in the seventies and now is in the cast of the series *Orange Is the New Black,* in Roman Kozak, *This Ain't No Disco: The Story of CBGB* (Boston: Faber and Faber, 1988), 63.

CBGB's, the Bowery, 1977

fun. If you needed to relieve yourself, you had to squeeze through a tiny space past the stage and go downstairs to the graffiti-covered, urine-scented bathroom, where you'd sometimes find people fucking or getting high. (The bathroom was reproduced, sans the urine smell, at the Metropolitan Museum of Art's retrospective on punk in 2013.) Patrons marked up every available surface of CB's with Sharpies: the walls, chairs, stairs, and bar, along the walls leading downstairs and into the bathroom. It was as if New York's then-ubiquitous graffiti were crawling into CB's from outside, like a contagious disease: in fact, the city was then living its darkest days. During the summer of 1977, a citywide blackout that started on a hot July evening turned into a looting rampage that overwhelmed the police; less than a month later, serial killer David Berkowitz, who for the better part of the year had terrorized all five boroughs with his shootings while taunting the police with letters daring them to catch the Son of Sam, was arrested. Could there have been a better background for the rise of punk music? At CBGB's, the party kept going. The latter half of the seventies was its golden age, and *Punk* photographer David Godlis documented in hundreds of Brassaï-reminiscent images what was happening inside its walls and outside, too, on the Bowery.

CB's was inseparable from its location; when kids heard "the Bowery," they had no other associations with it except for CB's. The Bowery supplied a frisson of real danger to the CB's experience: you risked getting mugged or even knifed on your way there. (The *Times* suggested it was best to go to CB's by cab.) But once you made it inside, you felt safe. Hilly was always there behind the bar. He had a six-foot-four bouncer named Merv, who always wore a yellow construction helmet over his blond pageboy haircut. The two of them watched over you as if they were your parents.

The CBGB phenomenon happened by accident; Hilly's original intention for his club—to showcase bluegrass music—did not pan out. But this is how art often comes about: when time and place ratchet up human anxieties to such a degree that they beg for expression. Hilly created punk during a terrible time in New York, and his club happened to be on the Bowery, from earliest times the incubator of new, raw art forms.

Punk rock, it turned out, had limited appeal in the States. Radio stations did not play it, and in the late 1970s, the punk scene shifted to England, when British clothing designer Malcolm McClaren—it was he who'd dressed the New York Dolls—created a band he called the Sex Pistols. But first McClaren had asked Richard Hell, whom he greatly admired, especially for his original sense of style, to start a band in New York. When Hell said no, McClaren returned to London with all of Hell's ideas, which he then took to outlandish extremes. He added safety pins in cheeks, black leather, and dog collars with spikes to the punk look that Hell had invented. British punk—much more violent and spectacular than the original New York version—then invaded New York and CBGB's.

Then one autumn morning in 1978, Sid Vicious, the heroin-addicted bass guitarist of the Sex Pistols, was found unconscious in a room at the Chelsea Hotel, next to the dead body of his girlfriend, Nancy Spungen: she'd been stabbed in the stomach and bled to death. Vicious was suspected of having killed her, but the possible motive was unclear: perhaps the couple, for whom drugs played a major part in their relationship, had made a suicide pact. He was arrested, bailed out, but never charged. Vicious died of a drug overdose in February 1979. The violent deaths of Spungen and Vicious tainted the punk movement. Record companies rebranded the music as "new wave," "hard core," or "heavy metal." *Punk* magazine folded in 1979, and with it the golden age of CBGB. But Hilly Kristal kept the club going as a labor of love. It remained a venue for young, unknown rock bands, who played there all through the eighties, when New York was drowning in crack and ravaged by AIDS but Reagan was talking about morning in America, and through the nineties as the city's fiscal recovery morphed into a real estate grab. It was during the 1990s when the first signs of gentrification appeared along the Bowery, caused in part by a spillover from Chinatown, to where capital was flowing from Hong Kong in anticipation of the British departure in 1997. When Hong Kong Chinese investors in the mid-nineties bought up old guard Italian and Jewish restaurant supply businesses at inflated prices, other Bowery property owners smelled money. The landlord at Moisha's Luncheonette at Grand and Bowery, where the street's artists and small business owners had been schmoozing over eggs and potato latkes for thirty-plus years, quadrupled the rent, forcing the luncheonette to close. The same scenario forced out Al's, at 108, the Bowery's last dive bar, in 1993. By 2000, glass towers were rising along the street that once symbolized urban despair, and neighborhood residents became alarmed. If the street lost all its gritty old buildings that rented for cheap, not only would longtime denizens lose their homes, but, they feared, the Bowery would inevitably also lose its soul. And yet Hilly, perhaps the most visionary of all the generations of artists who'd made a home there and found a voice—why, he'd incorporated *the street itself* into the strange, daring musical genre that started in his hole-in-the-wall club—had an open mind about Bowery gentrification.

"The whole Lower East Side is changing," Hilly told the *Village Voice* in 2005 (March 2). "That new building across the street from me"—he was referring to a slick six-story loft building at the corner of Bond Street, on the site of a former gas station—"people say it's so ugly but I think it's a nice modern place. A lot of this neighborhood could be nicer and cleaner. So things are gone, places are gone. You want old stuff? Go to Europe. This is New York."

Prophetic words, indeed: one year later, CB's—the birthplace of the punk movement—shut down, just another casualty of skyrocketing property values along the Bowery. But the story of CBGB's demise had a twist worthy of an O. Henry story: Hilly's landlord was not a developer, but a homeless advocacy group, the Bowery Residents Committee. The BRC, today New York's largest nonprofit organization serving the homeless, acquired 315 Bowery in 1993. (BRC doesn't outright own 315 Bowery; rather, it has what is known as a land lease, which means that the owner of record leases it to another party, who then acts as the landlord. This is a common arrangement in New York.) Until 2005, the organization left CB's alone. But that year, BRC acquired a new director, Lawrence "Muzzy" Rosenblatt, a genius at organization and a real son of a bitch. Rosenblatt decided that he wanted Hilly Kristal out, and he had his reasons: CB's was a pigsty, and it owed a lot of back rent. But in addition, these men were, to quote the photographer David Godlis, who documented the heyday of CBGB's, "two Jews who hated each other." Rosenblatt maintained that it was his job to get the maximum rent out of the property in order to benefit the homeless, and his argument was not without merit. He offered Hilly a lease that doubled CB's rent to $40,000 a month, but Hilly balked. On the Bowery, the Muzzy-Hilly feud was being framed as a David versus Goliath story. A "Save CBGB's" movement started, and some of the heavyweights who'd gotten their first break there—among them Debbie Harry and Patti Smith—threw their weight behind it. But at the same time, a lot of people were saying that the time had come for CB's to close. Hilly, perhaps, felt the same. A year after the club's demise, he died of cancer.

Nothing, after all, is forever. Especially in New York, the city that never stops demolishing structures and rebuilding and where new people arrive daily in pursuit of their dreams. After CB's cleared out, Muzzy Rosenblatt rented 315 Bowery to menswear designer John Varvatos, who incorporated the space's history into his brand by preserving the graffiti on the walls and selling vinyl records alongside his $2,500 leather jackets. A few years later, the superstar chef Daniel Boulud solidified the Bowery's new level of chic by opening a new venture a few doors down from Varvatos: an upscale burger joint that, in a nod to punk, he called DBGB. (The restaurant closed in the summer of 2017 after an eight-year run, which is a respectable life span for a New York restaurant venture.) Up and down the Bowery shiny new bars and hotels with their Edison bulbs and craft beer selection display a kind of nostalgia chic. They are Disneyfied versions of the old Bowery saloons, refashioned and glammed up for the young, moneyed class that crowd into these places to party and decompress from Manhattan's ferocious work environment. This is the demographic that now drives the Bowery's economy. They know little of the street's rich and complicated history—and yet they feel nostalgic for it.

Nostalgia is a fuzzy concept. People have nostalgia not only for a past they actually experienced but also for one they can only imagine; it makes them feel good. So the Bowery uses nostalgia as a marketing tool: the Sohotel, for example, at the corner of Bond, makes much of the fact that it was once the Occidental Hotel where Big Tim Sullivan hosted his card games. In New York, even the past is a commodity; and every story begins, and ends, with real estate.

BONES AND GHOSTS

For years, Adam Woodward, a longtime resident of the Bowery neighborhood and owner of two area properties, has been painstakingly piecing together the history of his surroundings. A photo researcher by profession, Woodward's curiosity about the Bowery was first piqued in the late 1990s, after he read Herbert Asbury's 1928 *The Gangs of New York* and realized that many of the stories happened right at his doorstep. (This was a full five years before the release of the Martin Scorsese film that the Asbury book inspired, which caught the public's imagination with its Scorsese-esque—and sometimes inaccurate—depictions of these dark, Bowery-infused, and long-forgotten chapters of New York history.) He began gumshoeing around the Bowery with his copy of Asbury, identifying places mentioned in the book. At the same time, he was tracking down and examining other written sources: newspapers, photos, books, city records, maps, old directories, letters.

Then, in the early 2000s, construction activity along the Bowery was heating up, and long-buried material remains were being unearthed, which workers were then routinely tossing into Dumpsters. Woodward was understandably dismayed. So he began gently persuading whoever was overseeing Bowery construction sites to let him inside to take photos and search amid the rubble. He has been doing this ever since, very carefully. He has rescued hundreds of antique objects that would otherwise have ended up in landfills: bottles, shards, eating implements, newspapers, posters. Once he pulled an old derby and hobo's pack from behind a wall of a half-demolished flophouse. In 2005, he was arrested for trespassing on the lot of a demolished church at First Street and Bowery, and spent forty-eight hours in the Tombs (which is what they still call New York's downtown prison). The property owner came to his rescue and the arrest was expunged from the record, but from then on, Woodward has been careful about having everything in order, including insurance requirements, before exploring and documenting building sites.

"At this point I know so many people involved with the Bowery in various respects that I often know someone who knows someone involved with a project and can get a reference or introduction if all else fails. But in my experience people are usually pretty interested if I can get their ear for a few minutes," he tells me. "Almost every building or lot has a good story somewhere in its history, and if I can pitch that and convince them that there's probably something related to that story behind a wall or buried below the basement floor, we end up walking through the site before the conversation is over."

He is judicious about observing the difference between what he does and the practice of archaeology. "I just salvage as much material culture as I can, which would otherwise be destroyed. If there's potential for archaeologists to get access to a site, I would never disturb it."

In 2004, when an old parking lot between Stanton and Rivington streets was getting torn up for the erection of the New Museum, Woodward paid close attention. He had friends living in a building abutting the site, on Chrystie Street, which afforded him an unobstructed view of the excavation. What he saw astounded him: human bones, a lot of them. Woodward then talked to the backhoe operator, who was clearly freaked out that in doing his job he was disturbing the dead.

Woodward immediately contacted the city about what he had seen at the building site. Officials told him that as there were once slaughterhouses in the area—which was true—he, because he had no training as an archaeologist, was probably mistaking animal bones for human ones.

Undeterred, Woodward went back to the site, collected some bones and part of a tombstone—"only enough evidence to convince the archaeologists who were skeptical when I informed them of what was there"—and took photos. All of this he then sent to the city to be examined. He then received a call from Amanda Sutphin, the city's chief archaeologist.

"She was curt and not friendly to me," Woodward told me. The next day, the entire site was covered with tarping. Soon an archaeological team was called in to conduct a study. They concluded that the remains came from an adjoining property behind the parking lot—in fact, right under the building from where Woodward first observed the bones being bulldozed out of the ground—which was once a burial ground belonging to St. Philips, New York's first black Episcopal church. The city should have known this before it issued the excavation permit, because a survey performed just one year earlier in connection with a proposed Second Avenue subway line specifically dealt with the presence of St. Philips along the proposed route and the probability of finding human remains there.

The land for St. Philips was donated in 1795 by Samuel Delaplaine, whose descendants some thirty years later would publish anti-slavery literature out of their Bowery homes—which are still standing. Delaplaine was one of a group of "diverse well-disposed individuals," as described by the Common Council, who were well-disposed to the "African society" ("free People of color") for a "Negroes' cemetery." Abolitionism was an unusual position in late eighteenth-century New York. Perhaps Delaplaine harbored anti-slavery sentiments because he was a Quaker. Moreover, he had African blood in his family: his maternal uncle, Cyrus Bustill, was the child of his maternal grandfather and his slave Parthena, and the two of them—Cyrus and Samuel—had a relationship. The Delaplaines were descendants of a Huguenot refugee who landed in New Amsterdam after fleeing France. Nicholas Delaplaine, like his contemporary, Stephen Delancey, made a fortune as a merchant, and he passed down immense wealth to his numerous descendants.

St. Philips was one of several cemeteries that once occupied chunks of ground along the Bowery; there were three more along Stanton Street. But after 1809, underground burial was no longer permitted in the city; as New York's population grew, and the city extended northward, the cemeteries' land grew valuable. So one by one, they were closed and their land sold. The bodies buried there were dug up and reinterred elsewhere or, sometimes, simply left behind. The graveyards around the Bowery have long been forgotten. But over the last two centuries, reminders of them surface every so often. In the March 28, 1890, edition of the *New York Times*, a reporter described coming across "leaning, dingy, crumbling tombstones" amid the street's "lively gaslight scene." On March 1, 1901, the *Tribune* reported: "Skull and bones dug up in Bowery." Included was the tantalizing detail that one skull had a hole in it "as if made by a bullet or a sharp instrument."

St. Philips was closed in 1852, its property sold to a liquor dealer—today, an apartment house stands on the exact footprint—and the graves were moved to a plot at Cypress Hills Cemetery in Queens. Well, most of them were. The bones that got left behind and turned up more than 150 years later were reburied in that same plot in Queens, also by the church; it is an active congregation, now located in Harlem. The city, embarrassed and no doubt afraid the story would make it into the press—it didn't—made sure that Woodward was not invited to the reinterment ceremony.

Professional archaeologists resent people like Adam Woodward. Looters, they call them. But in his neighborhood, Woodward has become something of a legend and an elusive one. He slips quietly in and out of building ruins like a graceful ghost in his quest to document the past. Think of Woodward as one who collects long-forgotten stories and hands them to us, like a gift. Ironically, the redevelopment of the Bowery—and the inevitable loss of a lot of its buildings—has given him a precious opportunity to see beneath the pavement of New York's fabled and quirky street. But while he mourns the disappearance of old buildings, he does not begrudge Bowery property owners who cash out on properties that they held on to through the bad times and are now worth millions of dollars.

"It's like a refrain," he says philosophically. "Every fifty years, the city tears down, and rebuilds." And we grieve, because the old buildings that we lose existed before we were born and connected us to the past in a visceral way. Jane Jacobs devoted an entire chapter to the subject in *The Death and Life of Great American Cities,* her cri de coeur against unfettered urban development. But our existential need to remember and honor what came before us clashes directly with New York's culture of tearing down, building high, and getting rich. This conflict has been playing out in New York for nearly 150 years, ever since the first skyscrapers were going up. In recent years, the Greenwich Village Society for Historic Preservation (GVSHP) has repeatedly begged the city to rezone the Bowery—currently, the street has no zoning restrictions, except for the western flank along the Chinatown and Little Italy Historic District—to prevent the construction of tall buildings that are out of scale with the surrounding structures and the character of the street. GVHSP is one of several organizations fighting rampant development along the Bowery. (One developer told the *New York Observer* in 2013 that his dream was to turn the Bowery into "one golden strip.") Others include grassroots groups such as the Bowery Alliance of Neighbors, Three Bridges, and the Historic Districts Council. All have asked the city to designate the entire Bowery as a special historical district, which de facto would limit the height of new buildings. But to date, the city has refused all requests on the grounds that the Bowery is a wide street, next to transportation, and therefore an appropriate location for tall structures.*

Why don't officials care about preserving the Bowery's special character? Do they not know how precious the street is to New

---

* This is what Andrew Berman, executive director of the Greenwich Village Historical Society, told me. When I asked the Department of City Planning to comment, their response was: "The Bowery is an exciting center of commercial and cultural activity that contributes to the economic wellbeing of the area. We remain open to engaging with local stakeholders regarding the Bowery."

York's history? Or do they not care? Or are they too deeply in the pockets of real estate interests to defy them?

One unseasonably warm fall evening—it is, in fact, the day before Halloween—I'm prowling up and down the Bowery, and everywhere I feel the ghosts. On the street, Bowery b'hoys with their soap locks are hanging out, and little ragamuffin girls are hawking corn. Inside the Bowery Theatre, the actor Edwin Forrest is bringing down the house, and sitting in the audience is a young Walt Whitman, who later mourns the passing of the "old Bowery." The theater burned down for the fourth and final time in 1929; the building that now occupies the footprint houses several Asian restaurants. I'm sitting next door, at the rooftop bar of the sleek new twenty-two-story Hotel 50 Bowery, which sits on the spot where once the humongous Atlantic Gardens beer hall overflowed every night with revelers. The owners of 50 Bowery are Chinese Americans, whose immigrant grandfather, Joseph Chu, acquired the property in 1974. Starting in the mid-1960s, immigration laws relaxed, and Chinatown began to expand, first north and then across the Bowery into the Lower East Side. Many of the old properties that Italians and Jews acquired in the early part of the twentieth century were snatched up by the Chinese, then the newest wave in the Bowery's never-ending accumulation of immigrants. Their numbers swelled through the eighties to the present. South of Grand Street, the Bowery is now completely Asian, and this population adds another layer to Bowery history.

It's late morning on a weekday, so the rooftop of 50 Bowery is empty, save for the tourists who occasionally come up to take in the lovely view of the city on this fine day. I ask them, "Why did you choose this hotel?" Most say, "The neighborhood." I ask them if they know that the Bowery was once the avenue of despair. They do not. Across the street is McKim, Mead and White's Beaux-Arts-style entrance to the Manhattan Bridge. Its construction required the destruction of a swath of the Bowery that had one of New York's first

Yiddish theaters, the Windsor. There, the great Joseph Adler, who started a dynasty of Jewish actors, played in Jacob Gordin's—the Yiddish Shakespeare—version of *King Lear*. Two additional Yiddish theaters graced this block of the Bowery—the People's and the Bowery Theatre (renamed the Thalia by the Jews) right next door to where I am now. As I gaze down at the street, I'm imagining Jewish actors strolling around after the Friday night performances are finished, the streets crowded with theatergoers. Besides Adler, there's Boris and Bessie Thomashefsky, David Kessler, and the glamorous, now-forgotten Bertha Kalisch, who starred in a lot of racy plays. "Acting was all impulse," Kalisch told the *New York Times* in 1905 (May 14).

Next, I wander up the Bowery to the New Museum. On the way I pass former flophouses and I remind myself that once this street belonged to the bums. I wonder how many of the desperate souls who ended up on the Bowery died there, inside a fleabag hotel or on the sidewalk. Then I come to the two old federal-style houses, 134 and 136 (their dormers still intact), that once belonged to the Delaplaine family.* A few years ago, I discovered the diary of Phila Delaplaine Reed, daughter of Samuel, who donated the land for the African American cemetery, at the New York Historical Society. Phila lived in one of those houses. Her diary is a sad little document, mostly containing descriptions of the various illnesses she and her husband suffered, along with some minutiae of her life: "Breakfasted on one of five quails, which my husband sent home in a cage, alive, last Monday." She mentions a child, a daughter, who died at age twelve: "Husband showed me some hair today clipt from the dear little head of Charlotte Collin, by Mrs. Allen. The sight of it affected me much—didn't know before that any memento of them had been preserved." Here and there she gives a few hints of the family's abolitionist connections: "Rose at

---

* Artist Sally Young, a longtime East Village denizen and activist, has spent untold hours researching the Delaplaines and anything else about the Bowery that has seized her interest. She led me to the stories about the Delaplaines, and I am indebted to her.

six arranged my room and assorted the *Evangelist Emancipator*"—an abolitionist publication—"according to their date." She also mentions attending the Broadway Tabernacle, then known for its anti-slavery preaching. These few tantalizing hints about the life of a woman and member of a prominent family on the mid-nineteenth-century Bowery make me long for more. If only we knew more of her story. But chances are, this is the most we will ever know. In fact, the Delaplaine houses, which are now owned by a developer, are in danger of being demolished. The Bowery Alliance of Neighbors has fought hard to get them landmarked, but the city's landmarks commission has refused.

I cross the street and enter the sleek lobby of the New Museum. I drink a coffee and think about Phila Delaplaine and the cemeteries and the remains of New Yorkers of African descent that nearly ended up in a landfill. I think about all the ghosts that haunt the Bowery. The furious pace of development along this road cannot erase its past, because that past is always present, even if it is invisible to the naked eye. And those who look for it will always find it.

ACKNOWLEDGMENTS

I wish to thank the following people: Karen Wolny, Laura Apperson, Alan Bradshaw, and all of St. Martin's Press; Peter Joseph; my wonderful agent, Wendy Schmalz; my friends at the Bowery Alliance of Neighbors—Gilda Pervin, David Mulkins, Jean Standish, Michele Campo, Debi Kops, Mitchell Gruber, and Sally Young; Joan Malin; Nancy Wackstein; Andrew Berman and Sarah Bean Apmann; Simeon Bankoff; Vincent Papa; David Beer; James Machlin; Jack Eichenbaum; Kerri Culhane; Eric Sanderson; Dale Cockrell; Sandee Brawarsky; David Godlis; Charlie Katz; Dan Mammano; Robert Wagner; Howard Scher; and Bree Benton.

A very special thank you to Adam Woodward.

To Roberta Israeloff, my friend and colleague.

And to my family, I express my gratitude and love: Alara, Alex, Ayse, Joseph, and Nick, my husband, lover of words and stories.

NOTES

PROLOGUE

While writing this book, I repeatedly consulted a detailed study of the Bowery's structures authored by the architectural historian Kerri Culhane in 2011 for the National Park Service. Culhane's report resulted in the Bowery's listing on the National Register of Historic Places in 2013.

I owe the description of the former parking lot where Whole Foods stands now to Don Mammano, whose family once owned flophouses along the Bowery.

CHAPTER ONE: THE DUTCH

5   *"the island . . . Mannahatta"*: Nicolaes van Wassanaer, in J. F. Jameson, *Narratives of New Netherland, 1609–1664* (New York: Charles Scribner's Sons, 1909); A. J. F. van Laer, trans., Documents Relating to New Netherland, 1624–1626 (Van Rappard Documents, A–F), A. J. F. Van Laer Papers, 1909–1952, New York State Library, Albany, Doc D.

5   *"they numbered perhaps 1,500"*: Eric Sanderson, *Mannahatta: A Natural History of New York City* (New York: Abrams, 2009). There is a beautiful description of the Collect on p. 154ff.

Notes

5   *"a gunshot away"*: Isaack de Rasieres to Samuel Blommaert, letter, ca. 1628, in Jameson, *Narratives of New Netherland*.

6   *"they were to draw straws"*: Cornelis van Tienhoven, quoted in I. F. Phelps Stokes, *The Iconography of Manhattan Island, 1498–1909*, vol. 5 (New York: Dodd, 1915), xvii.

6   *"The rest of the lots would go to the Company directors"*: Stokes, *Iconography of Manhattan Island*, vol. 6, 71; Van Laer, Van Rappard Documents.

7   *"it measured almost 110 feet high"*: Sanderson, *Mannahatta*, 78.

7   *On the Werpoes*: According to the 1651 land grant from the Dutch government to Augustine Hermann, "the land called Werpoes" contained 50 acres on the north side of Kalch Hoek and "adjoining ponds." In 1730, Anthony Rutgers and others said that in spring or at high tide, the area was flooded from both rivers.

7   *"the 'three sisters'"*: Herbert C. Kraft, *The Lenape* (Newark: New Jersey Historical Society, 1986), 115; Sanderson, *Mannahatta*, 120.

9   *On the bouweries*: Stokes, *Iconography of Manhattan Island*, vol. 2, 188; vol. 6, 73.

9   *On the animals eating the crops*: A. J. F. van Laer, April 12, 1640, and May 9, 1640, in *New York Historical Manuscripts (NYHM): Dutch*, 4 vols. (New York Historical Society), 71, 73.

10   *Dutch West India Company instructions for acquiring land*: Van Laer, Van Rappard Documents, Doc D.

11   *On the Indians spreading smallpox*: Kraft, *The Lenape*, 210–12; David Pietersz de Vries, in Jameson, *Narratives of New Netherland*.

12   *"But they feared invasion by whites"*: Wassanaer, November 1626, in Jameson, *Narratives of New Netherland*.

12   *"The Manhates at Werpoes were soon gone"*: Kraft, *The Lenape*, 210, 212; De Vries, in Jameson, *Narratives of New Netherland*.

12   *On religion and the Dutch (they "did not even mention it in the charter")*: Oliver A. Rink, "Private Interest and Godly Gain: The West India Company and the Dutch Reformed Church in New Netherland," *New York History* 75 (July 1994), 3.

12 *"thirty rude shacks . . . on Nut Island"*: Wassanaer, in Jameson, *Narratives of New Netherland*, says twenty-seven; Russell Shorto, *The Island in the Center of the World* (New York: Vintage, 2004), 61, 83.

12 *"One of them was located on the Bowery"*: E. B. O'Callaghan, *The Remonstrance of New Netherlands* (Albany, 1856); Jonas Michaelius, in Jameson, *Narratives of New Netherland*. The actual lists of the farmers' names, complete with which animals they'd been given, are extant. Bouwerie seven, for example, which brushed up against the Indian settlement at Werpoes, was leased to one Evert Focken, who was given four mares, four cows, and fifteen sheep, and so on. The Dutch West India Company's report is cited in Thomas A. Janvier, "The Dutch Founding of New York," *Harper's*, March 1903, 186.

14 *On immigrants to New Netherland*: Oliver Rink, "The People of New Netherlands: Notes on Non-English Immigration to New York in the Seventeenth Century," *New York History* 62 (1981), 21.

14 *"New Amsterdam was falling apart physically"*: O'Callaghan, *Remonstrance*, 1650; Van Laer, *NYHM: Dutch*, vol. 4, 1. It also states that the only cattle that remained in Manhattan were on the director's farm. The director did not actually live there; it was too far away from town. Perhaps he used it as a rustic retreat. His official residence was within the fort.

14 *On the farms*: Stokes, *Iconography of Manhattan Island*, vol. 2, 188, which cites a deposition in 1639 in which three men declare that when Kieft arrived in 1638, he found five farms "without tenants thrown in commons without one single creature remaining in property to the Company, all having been disposed of in other lands": New York Historical Society Collections, 1841, 279.

14 *On Kieft*: Vertoogh Van Nieu Neth, *Anthology of New Netherland, or, Translations from the Early Dutch Poets of New York, with Memoirs of Their Lives*, trans. Henry C. Murphy (1865), 139; Stokes, *Iconography of Manhattan Island*, passim; Van Laer, *NYHM: Dutch*; O'Callaghan, *Remonstrance*. *On Kieft taxing the Lenape*: Van Laer, September 8,

1839, in *NYHM: Dutch*, 60: "Whereas the Company is put to great expense both in building fortifications and in supporting soldiers and sailors, we have therefore resolved to demand from the Indians who dwell around here and whom heretofore we have protected against their enemies, some contributions in the form of skins, maize and seawan, and if there be any nation which is not in a friendly way disposed to make such contribution it shall be urged to do so in the most suitable manner." *On Kieft's attack on the Raritans*: De Vries, in Jameson, *Narratives of New Netherland*.

19 *"The area under attack, which stretched ten miles east"*: Van Laer, *NYHM: Dutch*, vol. 3, 188.

19 *"By then, slaves made up nearly one-quarter"*: Ira Berlin and Leslie M. Harris, eds., *Slavery in New York* (New York: New Press, 2005), 8, 36.

19 *"the Dutch church in Amsterdam sent over a schoolmaster to 'teach and train the youth of both Dutch and blacks, in the knowledge of Jesus Christ'"*: Stokes, *Iconography of Manhattan Island*, vol. 4, 86; *Ecclesiastical Records, State of New York*, 7 vols. (Albany: 1901–16), 1:19.122.

19 *"Occasionally, blacks and whites married each other"*: Charles Gehring, trans., *Curacao Papers* (New Netherland Institute, 1987), 5, says black or Indian women must be baptized before they can marry Christian, i.e., white, men. *"and even on occasion sued them—sometimes successfully"*: Van Laer, *NYHM: Dutch*, passim. In 1639, the court awarded Pedro Negretto back wages for tending the hogs of an Englishman named John Seales. This farmer shows up again in the records in 1643, when he was ordered to pay damages to another man's slave, Little Manuel, after another slave testified that Seales had slashed Little Manuel's cow with a knife.

20 *"The tract came to be called the Negros land, and it consisted of 130 acres of swampy land along the Bowery"*: Berlin and Harris, *Slavery in New York*, 43, 45.

20 *"The Company had already received plenty of complaints about him"*: Shorto, *Island in the Center of the World*, 139–44.

CHAPTER TWO: **THE GOVERNOR WITH THE SILVER LEG**

21   *"the Dutch West India Company's relaxed policy about religion and race"*:
Oliver A. Rink, "Private Interest and Godly Gain: The West India
Company and the Dutch Reformed Church in New Netherland,"
New York History 75 (July 1994), 3.

21   *On the Jews*: The Dutch West India Company to Peter Stuyvesant,
letter, April 26, 1655, in Charles Gehring, trans. and ed., *Correspondence, 1654–1658*, New Netherland Documents 49 (Syracuse: Syracuse University Press, 2000), 93.

22   *On the Lutherans*: Dutch West India Company, in I. F. Phelps Stokes,
The Iconography of Manhattan Island, 1498–1909, vol. 4 (New York:
Dodd, 1915), 141–42, 184, 198.

22   *"He behaved 'like a peacock, with great state and pomp'"*: Van der Donck,
in Jameson, *Narratives of New Netherland*, 342.

23   *"The beer shops never closed"*: Stokes, *Iconography of Manhattan Island*,
vol. 4, 114.

24   *"the first known use of the term"*: Russell Shorto, *The Island in the Center
of the World* (New York: Vintage, 2004), 143n.

24   *"finally forced the Company to act"*: Van Laer, Van Rappard Documents, vol. 1, 211; Shorto, *Island in the Center of the World*, 143.

25   *"'the foam hung from his beard' . . . 'It is treason to petition against one's
magistrates, whether there be cause or not'"*: E. B. O'Callaghan, "Breeden
Raedt," in *Documentary History of the State of New York*, vol. 4 (1851).

25   *"'We notice also that it has been very expensive; the Colony cannot yet
bear' . . . 'mildness'"*: Gehring, *Correspondence, 1647–1653*, 54–56.

27   *"The* Remonstrance *then proposed a bold remedy for this mess: the States
General should take over the colony from the Company and install there a
'suitable municipal government'"*: E. B. O'Callahagn, *Documents Rela-
tive to the Colonial History of the State of New York*, 15 vols. (Albany:
Weed, Parsons, 1853–1887), vol. 1, 266. Afterwards referred to as *New
York Colonial Documents*.

27   *The Dutch West India Company's response*: Gehring, *Correspondence,
1647–1653*, 54–56.

27 *"'Formerly New Netherland was never spoken of and now heaven and earth seem to be stirred up by it and every one tries to be first in selecting the best pieces there'"*: Dutch West India Company to Peter Stuyvesant, letter, February 16, 1650, in Gehring, *Correspondence, 1647–1653*, 84.

28 *On Stuyvesant's purchase of his estate*: Stokes, *Iconography of Manhattan Island*, vol. 4, 122; vol. 6, 142; Gehring, *Correspondence, 1647–1653*, 59, 81, 84, 113.

29 *"all for 6,400 guilders (the equivalent of $2,560), which represented quite a bargain"*: According to Hopper Striker Mott, "Road to the Bouwerij," *Americana*, vol. 8 (1913).

29 *"when the Company ordered him to begin preparing for an invasion by the English from their colonies to the north"*: This was a result of England's Navigation Act of 1651, which mandated that all trade with the English be conducted via English ships. It was a direct assault on the Dutch.

30 *"'For to lie in the fort night and day with the citizens has its difficulties as they cannot be commanded like soldiers'"*: Stokes, *Iconography of Manhattan Island*, vol. 4, 158–60.

31 *"you could cross the East River on foot over the ice from what is now Whitestone, in Queens, to Manhattan"*: New York Colonial Documents, vol. 14, 311, 312.

31 *"'by the friendliest means, even if it were by giving them some contraband articles as presents'"*: New York Colonial Documents, vol. 13, 52–54; Stokes, *Iconography of Manhattan Island*, vol. 4, 161–62.

31 *"Those who didn't comply would remain isolated on their farms at their peril and be fined annually 25 guilders a year"*: Charles Gehring, trans. and ed., *Council Minutes, 1655–1656*, New Netherland Documents (Syracuse, NY: Syracuse University Press, 1995), 185.

32 *On the Plow and Harrow, Werpoes, and Augustine Hermann*: Stokes, *Iconography of Manhattan Island*, vol. 2, 123; vol. 4, 123; vol. 6, 72, 88.

33 *"'Let the free and the Company's negroes keep good watch on my bouwery,' he wrote to the Board while sailing up the Hudson on one of his trips to Esopus"*: Stokes, *Iconography of Manhattan Island*, vol. 4, 204.

33   *On Reverend Henricus Selyns:* "*It was 'a place of relaxation and pleasure,*
      whither people go from the Manhattans for the evening service,' he wrote to
      the classis *in Amsterdam. 'There are there forty negroes, from the region*
      of the Negro Coast, beside the household families'": Reverend Henricus
      Selyns to the *classis*, letter, January 29, Stokes, *Iconography of Manhat-*
      tan Island, vol. 4, 275. *On Selyns's marrying black couples:* Mott, "Road
      to the Bouwerij," 664. *On Selyns's refusal to baptize black children:* Re-
      verend Henricus Selyns to Amsterdam, letter, June 9, 1664, quoted in
      Henry C. Murphy, *Anthology of New Netherland, or, Translations from*
      the Early Dutch Poets of New York, with Memoirs of Their Lives (1865), 88.
      Judith Stuyvesant, however, undertook baptisms.

34   *On the slave trade in New Netherland:* Edgar J. McManus, *A History of Negro*
      Slavery in New York (Syracuse: Syracuse University Press, 1966); Ira Ber-
      lin and Leslie M. Harris, eds., *Slavery in New York* (New York: New Press,
      2005), 49; Stokes, *Iconography of Manhattan Island*, vol. 4, 158. There was
      a perennial slave shortage in New Netherland, and this hindered its
      economy (Gehring, *Correspondence*, 5, 160). At first the Company mo-
      nopolized the slave trade. But it opened up the nefarious business to
      everybody in 1652, and New Amsterdam merchants jumped right in.

34   "*the landowners Wolfert Webber and Thomas Hall petitioned for and were*
      granted permission to also create their own village": Stokes, *Iconography*
      of Manhattan Island, vol. 4, 205.

35   "'*a quantity of beef and pork, payment therefor to be made in negroes'*":
      Stokes, *Iconography of Manhattan Island*, vol. 5, 236, May 31; *New York*
      Colonial Documents, vol. 2, 243; Stokes, *Iconography of Manhattan*
      Island, vol. 4, 237.

36   *On the slaves grieving upon Selyns's departure and* "*You have heard of*
      the sad state of New Netherland": *New York Colonial Documents*, vol. 13, 384;
      vol. 14, 530–33; *Ecclesiastical Records, State of New York*, 7 vols. (Albany:
      1901–16), I: 607–8.

36   *On the arrangements along the river:* Stokes, *Iconography of Manhattan*
      Island, vol. 4, 232. *The description of the arrival of English ships:* Rever-
      end Samuel Drisius to the *classis* of Amsterdam, letter, in Jameson,
      Narratives of New Netherland.

36   "'It is not our least anxiety, that we have so little powder and . . . You can easily judge that this supply will not last long'": Peter Stuyvesant to Dutch West India Company, letter, August 4, *New York Colonial Documents*, vol. 14, 533.

37   *Nicolls on the King*: Stokes, *Iconography of Manhattan Island*, vol. 4, 240, August 29; 241, September 1.

37   *On Stuyvesant's refusal to capitulate*: Stokes, *Iconography of Manhattan Island*, vol. 4, 232ff.

37   *"the Gouvernor with a silver leg"*: John Josselyn, *An Account of Two Voyages to New-England* (Boston : William Veazie, 1674).

37   *On the surrender of New Amsterdam*: Van Laer, Van Rappard Documents, vol. 1, 243, 438; *New York Colonial Documents*, vol. 2, 415; vol. 3, 167; Van Laer, *New York Historical Manuscripts (NYHM): Dutch*, 4 vols. (New York Historical Society); Adriaen van der Donck, in Jameson, *Narratives of New Netherland*.

37   *"One of the stipulations read that from then on, 'this place is not to be called otherwise than New-York, on the island of Manhattans, in America'"*: *New York Colonial Documents*, vol. 2, 415.

38   *"they questioned Stuyvesant whether these freed slaves legally held title to their properties. Stuyvesant assured the new overlords that they did"*: Berlin and Harris, *Slavery in New York*, 53.

38   *"After two miserable, lonely years in the Hague, the Company finally permitted Stuyvesant to leave"*: *New York Colonial Documents*, vol. 3, 167.

39   *On the growth of Bowery Village*: Valentine's Corporation Manual (1866), 579, 799.

39   *"After his death, Stuyvesant's heirs remained on the family property for generations and enlarged it by buying up adjoining lots. (Two descendants built mansions on the estate)"*: Mott, "Road to the Bouwerij."

CHAPTER THREE: BOWERY LANE

42   "'like the cedars on Lebanon'": I. F. Phelps Stokes, *The Iconography of Manhattan Island, 1498–1909*, vol. 4 (New York: Dodd, 1915), 323.

42   *"Nicolls immediately reestablished a municipal government"*: June 12, 1665, in Stokes, *Iconography of Manhattan Island*, vol. 255; Mike Wallace, *Gotham: A History of New York City to 1898* (New York: Oxford University Press, 1998), 78. I.e., he created the offices of mayor, aldermen, and sheriff, the equivalents of the Dutch *schout, burgomasters,* and *schepens.*

42   *"'Its sixteen members—ten Dutch, six English—gathered at one another's houses to discuss matters of common concern and drink punch from silver tankards'"*: Wallace, *Gotham*, 79.

43   *On the King's Highway*: Eric Jaffee, *The King's Best Highway: The Lost History of the Boston Post Road* (New York: Scribner, 2010).

43   *"and the area around the Collect, where a handful of families—black, white, and mixed race—were cultivating small farms"*: Bartlet James and J. Franklin Jameson, eds., *Jounal of Jasper Danckaerts* (New York: Scribners, 1913). Stokes, *Iconography of Manhattan Island*, vol. 6, 70. In 1673, there were twenty-four blacks living between the Collect and Harlem. By 1696, most free blacks along the Bowery had sold out to white neighbors. And by 1696, Wolfert Webber had "accumulated" five of the eight small plots north of Smith's Hill originally given to freed blacks. Webber called them "the Negroe's farm" in his will. See Peter R. Christoph, "The Freedom of New Amsterdam," *Journal of the Afro-American and Genealogical Society* (Fall and Winter 1984).

45   *"virtually all households in New York then had slaves"*: Stokes, *Iconography of Manhattan Island*, vol. 6, 144–45.

45   *On John Clapp*: *"In 1694, Solomon had made Clapp one of the executors of his will, so the two must have enjoyed a friendship together"*: Clapp Papers, New York Public Library, New York; *Abstracts of Wills on File in the Surrogate's Office*, vol. 2 (City of New York, 1893), 293; Stokes, *Iconography of Manhattan Island*, vol. 6, 144–45. The 1696 deed in the Clapp Papers was conveyed to him by Daniel Bastiense, the son of a freed slave. *On Clapp's almanac*: D. T. Valentine, *Manual of the Common Council of the City of New York* (New York: John F. Trow, 1866), 577–78; Stokes, *Iconography of Manhattan Island*, vol. 4, 399.

46   *On the Delanceys*: *"Delancey limited his slave trading (mostly) to Madagascar"*: Edgar J. McManus, *A History of Negro Slavery in New York*

(dissertation, Syracuse University, 1966), 92. *"one Giles Shelley, who parked his wife and son on his farm somewhere along the Bowery"*: Delancey Papers, Museum of the City of New York, New York Historical Society; Wallace, *Gotham*, 106; Kevin P. McDonald, *Pirates Merchants, Settlers, and Slaves* (dissertation, University of California, 2015), 76ff., 92ff. *The description of the oysters*: Peter Kalm's description of New York in 1748, in Valentine, *Manual of the Common Council of the City of New York*, 1869. *On Delancey's religious life*: Kenneth Jackson, *Encyclopedia of the City of New York* (New Haven, CT: Yale University Press, 1995). *History of New York in the Revolution*: Stokes, *Iconography of Manhattan Island*, vol. 4, 344; Delancey Papers, Museum of the City of New York, New York Historical Society, 40/190.108. *On Delancey's property*: *"Originally this piece of property consisted of three plots that Kieft had granted in 1643 to freed slaves; since then, it had changed hands several times"*: Stokes, *Iconography of Manhattan Island*, vol. 6, 87. The three freed slave in question are Anthony Congo, Bastiaem d'Angola, and Francisco. The house was built by May Bickley, attorney general and recorder of the city, "a busy, waspish man," said Governor Robert Hunter (*New York Colonial Documents*, vol. 5, 357). Bickley erected it between December 16, 1718, and April 1724 (W. Harrison Bayles, *Old Taverns of New York* [New York: Frank Allaben Genealogical Company, 1915]; Thomas Jones, *History of New York During the Revolutionary War*, Edward Delancey, ed., vol. 2 [New York: New York Historical Society, 1879], 543ff.). *"he remained a passionate loyalist, and he made sure the King knew it"*: Richard M. Ketchum, *Divided Loyalties: How the American Revolution Came to New York* (New York: Macmillan, 2002), 162ff. *On Delancey's brigade*: Delancey Papers, Museum of the City of New York, Folder 42. *On use of Delancey's estate by Washington during the Revolution*: Henry P. Johnston, *The Campaign of 1776 around New York and Brooklyn* (Long Island Historical Society, 1878), 63. *"sickly, filthy, divided, and unruly"*: "Extract from a Letter from New York," April 12, 1776, in Johnston, *The Campaign of 1776*, 132.

48   *Hall's property*: Stokes, *Iconography of Manhattan Island*, vol. 6, 89.

50   *On Nicholas Bayard*: *On the Half-Way House*: Thomas Farrington DeVoe, *Abattoirs* (Van Benthuysen & Sons Steam Printing House, 1866), 9ff.; Bayle, *Old Taverns of New York*, 157; Stokes, *Iconography of Manhattan Island*, vol. 3, 977; vol. 4, 736; *New York Gazette*, March 24, 1763. *On Bayard's abattoir*: Stokes, *Iconography of Manhattan Island*, vol. 1, 225, 279; DeVoe, *Abattoirs*. *"Bayard died a wealthy man"*: *Abstract of Wills*, 1760–1766, vol. 6, 192–95. *Details about Bayard's estate during the American Revolution*: Johnston, *The Campaign of 1776*, 88. *On the Bull's Head during the Revolution*: Stokes, *Iconography of Manhattan Island*, vol. 5, 1076. Stokes quotes an advertisement in the *New York Mercury*, October 19, 1778: "All Gentlemen Volunteers, That are able and willing to serve his Majesty King George, III. For two Years, or during the Rebellion, In the Honourable Corps of Pioneers, now lying at New-York, under his Excellency Sir William Erskine, And Commanded by Major Simon Fraier, Let them repair to the Bull's Head, in the Bowery; or at the Tryon's Arms, in the Broad-way; or at the Queen's Head, Brooklyn Ferry; or at the SuHling House, Kings-Bridge."

53   *On Richard Varian*: DeVoe, *Abattoirs*, 11–13.

56   *On the British evacuation of New York*: Joint Committee on the Centennial Celebration of the Evacuation of New York by the British, New York Common Council, New York Historical Society, New York Chamber of Commerce, with historical introduction by John Austin Stevens, *Report of the Joint Committee on the Centennial Celebration of the Evacuation of New York by the British* (1883); Stokes, *Iconography of Manhattan Island*, vol. 5; Bayle, *Old Taverns of New York*, 314–45; Wallace, *Gotham*, 259ff.

57   *"A few of the purchasers were Jews"*: Delancey Papers, Museum of the City of New York, New York Historical Society.

CHAPTER FOUR: THE ASTORS

59   *On the Astors*: Astor papers, New York Historical Society and the New York Public Library; Minthorne, *Minutes of the Common*

Council of the City of New York, 1784–1831; "The Bowery," in D.T. Valentine's *Manual of the Common Council of the City of NY* (New York: John F. Trow, 1866); Thomas Farrington DeVoe, *A History of the Public Markets of the City of New York* (New York: 1862); Alvin Harlow, *Old Bowery Days: The Chronicles of a Famous Street* (New York: D. Appleton, 1931); Walter Barrett (pseudonym for Joseph A. Scoville), *The Old Merchants of New York* (New York: Carlton Publishers, 1864); Ira Rosenwaike, *Population History of New York City* (Syracuse, NY: Syracuse University Press, 1972); Thomas Allibone Janvier, *In Old New York* (New York: Harper & Brothers, 1894).

60 *Cattle being paraded up and down the Bowery before slaughter:* Theodore Shank, *The Bowery Theatre: 1826–1836* (dissertation, Stanford University, 1956), 12.

61 *On New York's economy after the Revolution: "'Cash! Cash! O Cash! Why hast thou deserted the Standard of Liberty? And made poverty and dissipation our distinguishing characteristic?'":* Henry P. Johnston, "New York after the Revolution," *Magazine of American History* 29, no.4 (April 1893), 316. *"Not only were land prices low, but rents were high, indeed twice as high as before the war":* Johnston, "New York after the Revolution," 316. *New York's population figures:* Ira Rosenwaike, *Population History of New York City* (Syracuse, NY: Syracuse University Press, 1972), 15–16.

64 *The list of Astor tenants:* based on New York City directories (*Trow's*), which were published annually beginning in 1787.

64 *On Vauxhall Gardens:* Valentine, *Manual of the Common Council of the City of New York,* 586; Thomas Allibone Janvier, *In Old New York* (New York: Harper, 1922), 261ff. *Detail about latticework:* newspaper clip, August 18, 1880, in scrapbook from New York Public Library Theater Division. In 1841, the Vauxhall property was acquired by Henry Jones, who also owned a piece of the Bull's Head Tavern (Astor Papers, New York Historical Society, Box 2, Folder 11). Later P. T. Barnum acquired the Vauxhall property and it degenerated. It was

the scene of the 1850 Astor Place Shakespeare Riots (see 1855 *New York Times* story in Astor Papers).

65   *On the Minthornes' farm*: I. F. Phelps Stokes, *The Iconography of Manhattan Island, 1498–1909*, vol. 6 (New York: Dodd, 1915), 131; "The Minthorne Farms, 1776" (map). *On Dutch grants map*: "Bowery Number 3," Manhattan Past, blog, 2013.

65   *On women on the farm*: Thomas Farrington DeVoe, *Abattoirs* (Van Benthuysen & Sons Steam Printing House, 1866), 333.

66   *On the rapid development of the Bowery*: Sean Wilentz, "The Republic of the Bowery," *Chants Democratic: New York City and the Rise of the American Working Class, 1788–1850* (New York: Oxford University Press, 1984); *Historical Design Report* 58 cites Richard B. Stott, *Workers in the Metropolis: Class, Ethnicity and Youth in Antebellum New York* (Ithaca, NY: Cornell University Press, 1990), 205–9; Edward K. Spann, *The New Metropolis: New York City, 1840–1857* (New York: Columbia University Press, 1981), 343. *On the paving of the Bowery*: Minthorne, *Minutes of the Common Council*, vol. 1, 279. *"fixed and graded"*: Minthorne, *Minutes of the Common Council*, 663–64; In Stokes, *Iconography of Manhattan Island*, vol. 5, 1393, 1805; cf. Minthorne, *Minutes of the Common Council*, vol. 3.

66   *On the filling in of the Collect*: Minthorne, *Minutes of the Common Council*, June 20, June 27, and December 12, 1808, and passim to 1811. Stokes, *Iconography of Manhattan Island*, vol. 5, 1405; Valentine, *Manual of the Common Council*, 1860, 560ff., 645ff.; James Grant Wilson, *The Memorial History of the City of New York* (New York: New York History Company, 1893), vol. 3 203ff.

67   *Canal Street*: *New York Evening Post*, January 2, 1811, quoted in Stokes, *Iconography of Manhattan Island*, vol. 5, 1529; Wilson, *Memorial History of the City of New York*, vol. 3, 204.

69   *"In 1826, he asked the city to cut Lafayette Place—now Lafayette Street—right through his Vauxhall property"*: Alvin Harlow, *Old Bowery Days: The Chronicles of a Famous Street* (New York: D. Appleton, 1931), 316–17.

69   *On the Park Theatre*: Rosemarie Bank, *Theater Culture in America, 1825–1860* (Cambridge: Cambridge University Press: 1997).

70   *On the African Grove Theatre*: Frances Trollope, *Domestic Manners of the Americans* (London: Whittaker, Treacher & Co, 1832).

CHAPTER FIVE: SHAKESPEARE AND JIM CROW COME TO THE BOWERY THEATRE

72   *"Hone made a short speech"*: New York Mirror, June 24, 1826.

73   *On the Bowery Theatre*: Harvard Theater Collection; *The Mirror; New York Post*, November 13, 1826; *New York American*, October 24, 1826; Alvin Harlow, *Old Bowery Days: The Chronicles of a Famous Street* (New York: D. Appleton, 1931); Theodore Shank, *The Bowery Theatre: 1826–1836* (dissertation, Stanford University, 1956).

74   *On Edwin Forrest*: Richard Moody, *Edwin Forrest* (New York: Knopf, 1960); Shank, *The Bowery Theatre*; Dale Cockrell, *Demons of Disorder: Early Blackface Minstrels and Their World* (New York: Cambridge University Press, 1997); *"In the tent scene, so solemn and so impressive"*: Spirit of the Times, quoted in Cockrell, *Demons of Disorder*, 31–32.

78   *The "Bowery B'hoy"*: George Foster, *New York by Gas-Light and Other Urban Sketches* (1850); Tyler Anbinder, *The Five Points* (New York: Penguin, 2002); Ned Buntline, *Mysteries and Miseries of New York: A Story of Real Life* (Dublin: James M'Glashan); Harlow, *Old Bowery Days*; Mike Wallace, *Gotham: A History of New York City to 1898* (New York: Oxford University Press, 1998), 753. *"a stout clerk in a jobbing house"*: Foster, *New York by Gas-Light*.

79   *On fire brigades*: Nigel Cliff, *The Shakespeare Riots* (New York: Random House, 2007), 194ff.; George G. Foster, *New York in Slices* (New York: W. F. Burgess, 1849).

79   *"When he returned to England he kept a portrait of George Washington in his drawing room, and no one was allowed to stand beneath it without taking off his hat"*: William Morange to Edwin Forrest, letter, Collection of

Correspondence, Signatures, and Other Materials from Notable Theater, Art, and Literary Personalities, 1718–1892, Harvard Theater Collection.

80   *On the fires: New York American,* May 27, 1828; Robert Amell, "In and Around the Bowery Theater," Manhattan Unlocked, blog, March 12, 2011.

81   *On Thomas Hamblin:* "Thomas Hamblin," Wikipedia; separation papers, June 25, 1832, Harvard Theater Collection; Mary Clarke, quoted in Susan Branson, *Dangerous to Know: Women, Crime and Notoriety in the Early Republic* (Philadelphia: University of Pennsylvania Press, 2004); Joseph Norton Ireland, *Records of the New York Stage* (1866), vol. 1, 461–62; vol. 2, 244–45; Rosemarie Bank, "Arbiters of National Culture: Newspapers, Thomas S. Hamblin, the Bowery Theatre, and the Miss Missouri Affair," *New England Theatre Journal* 24 (2013), 1–11. *"'the Bowery slaughterhouse'":* Ireland, *Records of the New York Stage,* vol. 1, 461–62; vol. 2, 244–45. *On melodramas* ("The Murder on the Cliff," subtitled "Love Me, Love My Dog"): Shank, *The Bowery Theatre,* 340.

81   *"'sacerdotal agents'":* Ohio Observer.

84   *On Daddy Rice: The figures on his performances of "Jump Jim Crow" at the Bowery Theatre:* Shank, *The Bowery Theatre,* 371–72; Cockrell, *Demons of Disorder;* Carl Wittke, *Tambo and Bones: A History of the American Minstrel Stage* (Westport: Greenwood Press, 1971; reprint of 1930 edition, Duke University Press), 24ff.; William D. Morange to Edwin Forrest and William Duffy, letters, Harvard Theater Collection. *"Jump Jim Crow" lyrics:* "Jump Jim Crow," Wikipedia.

86   *On slavery and abolitionism in New York:* Eric Foner, *Gateway to Freedom: The Hidden History of the Underground Railroad* (New York: Norton, 2015). I am indebted to the community activist, preservationist, and artist Sally Young, who has been researching abolitionist activity along the Bowery for years and generously shared her findings with me. New York was one of several places—others were Massachusetts, upstate New York, and Pennsylvania—where abolitionist societies were then starting to take shape. Most were fueled

by the activism of Quakers and evangelicals, who belonged to the burst of religious fervor following the Revolutionary War, which historians refer to as the Second Great Awakening.

86 *On segregation in New York*: Wallace, *Gotham*, 554; Charles Haswell, *Reminiscences of an Octogenarian of the City of New York, 1816–1860* (New York: Harper, 1890), 181.

86 *"African Americans in the 1830s comprised 18 percent of New York's population"*: Ira Rosenwaike, *Population History of New York City* (Syracuse: Syracuse University Press, 1972).

87 *On George Washington Dixon*: Cockrell, *Demons of Disorder*.

89 *On Charles Finney*: Hambrick-Stowe, *Charles G. Finney and the Beginnings of American Evangelism* (Grand Rapids, MI: William B. Eerdmans, 1996).

90 *On the 1834 race riot*: Cockrell, *Demons of Disorder*; *New York Sun*, July 11, 1834; *New York Post*, July 11, 1834; Linda Kerber, "Abolitionists and Amalgamators: The New York City Race Riots of 1834," *New York History* 48, no. 1 (January 1967), 28. *"and I would gull them if I could"*: George Farren, quoted in *Long Island Star*, July 10, 1834.

92 *On the Virginia Minstrels*: *New York Herald*, March 24, 1895; Cockrell, *Demons of Disorder*, 151–53; Eric Lott, *Love & Theft: Blackface Minstrelsy and the American Working Class* (New York: Oxford University Press, 1993), 139–40.

CHAPTER SIX: THE MOB TAKES THE STAGE

93 *On Minstrelsy*: Mark Twain, *Autobiography*.

94 *On Edwin Forrest*: "Reminiscences of Isaac Odell: A Christy Minstrel," *New York Times*, May 19, 1907.

95 *On Five Points*: Tyler Anbinder, *The Five Points* (New York: Penguin, 2002); Herbert Asbury, *The Gangs of New York* (Vintage: New York, 2008; reprint of 1927 original, Knopf).

96 *On Master Juba (William Henry Lane)*: Eric Lott, *Love & Theft: Blackface Minstrelsy and the American Working Class* (New York: Oxford University Press, 1993), 115; Anbinder, *The Five Points*, 175; Marian Hannah

Winter, "Juba and American Minstrelsy," in Paul Magriel, ed., *Chronicles of the American Dance* (1947).

96   *On Mose (Frank Chaufrau)*: *"Den why de hell dontcha go?'"*: *World Review*, September 7, 1901.

99   *On the Bowery gangs*: Anbinder, *The Five Points*; Asbury, *Gangs of New York*; Peter Adams, *Bowery Boys: Street Corner Radicals and the Politics of Rebellion* (Westport, CT: Praeger, 2005).

100   *"Music now is all de rage"*: "Pompey's Rambles," *White's New Book of Plantation Melodies* (H. Long and Brother, 1849), 15–16.

101   *On the Shakespeare riots*: Richard Moody, *Edwin Forrest* (New York: Alfred Knopf, 1960). Nigel Cliff, *The Shakespeare Riots* (New York: Random House, 2007); Mike Wallace, *Gotham: A History of New York City to 1898* (New York: Oxford University Press, 1998); *Diary of Philip Hone, 1828-1851*, vol.2, edited by Bayard Tuckerman (New York : Dodd Mead, 1889), 360ff.; Macready's diary; see also Karl M. Kippola, *Out of the Forrest and into the Booth: Performance of Masculinity on the American Stage, 1828–1865* (dissertation, University of Maryland, 2003).

103   *On Ned Buntline (E. Z. D. Judson)*: Fred E. Pond, *The Life and Adventures of Ned Buntline* (New York: Cadmus Book Shop, 1919).

CHAPTER SEVEN: THE CIVIL WAR ON THE BOWERY

109   *On Uncle Tom's Cabin*: Eric Lott, *Love & Theft: Blackface Minstrelsy and the American Working Class* (New York: Oxford University Press, 1993). Lott devotes an entire chapter, "Uncle Tomitudes," to the subject. See also George C. Odell, *Annals of the New York Stage* vol. 6. (New York: Columbia University Press, 1927). The descriptions of audiences in 1853 are from the *New York Times*, July 27, and October 25, 1853. *"By some estimates, millions of people"*: Lott, *Love & Theft*. *"it soon fragmented into multiple and often crude stage adaptations"*: the most famous and widely performed was George L. Aiken's version.

111   *On Stephen Foster*: Ken Emerson, *Doo-dah!: Stephen Foster and the Rise of American Popular Culture* (New York: Simon & Schuster, 1997). *"Way down upon de Swanee Ribber"*: "Swanee River," Wikipedia.

112   *On John Brown*: I am indebted to historian Louis DeCaro Jr. for his help in piecing together an accurate picture of John Brown. *On Brown's hanging*: newspapers and description by eyewitness John T. Preston, in the archives of the Virginia Military Institute. *"I never had such illustrious guests"*: Louisa Williamson, letter, archived in the West Virginia Division of Culture and History. *John Brown's remains*: newspaper accounts, among them the *New York Herald*, December 5, 1859. *About the play*: *New York Herald*, December 19, 1859; Mike Wallace, *Gotham: A History of New York City to 1898* (New York: Oxford University Press, 1998), 863.

114   *George Templeton Strong*: all quotations from Allan Nevins and Milton Halsey Thomas, eds., *The Diary of George Templeton Strong*, 4 vols. (New York: Macmillan, 1952).

117   *"Lincoln in New York"*: Edward K. Spann, *Gotham at War* (Lanham, MD: Rowman & Littlefield, 2002); newspapers.

118   *On Wilson's Sixth Regiment, the Sixty-Ninth, and the Fire Zouaves*: Alvin Harlow, *Old Bowery Days: The Chronicles of a Famous Street* (New York: D. Appleton, 1931), 345–46; Charles Ingraham, *Elmer Ellsworth and the Zouaves of '61* (Chicago: University of Chicago Press, 1925).

121   *On population and immigration figures*: Richard B. Stott, *Workers in the Metropolis: Class, Ethnicity and Youth in Antebellum New York* (Ithaca: Cornell University Press, 1990), 1; Richard Plunz, *A History of Housing in New York City* (New York: Columbia University Press, 1990), 67.

121   *On tenements*: Plunz, *A History of Housing in New York City*; Robert W. DeForest and Lawrence Vieller, eds., *The Tenement House Problem* (London: Macmillan Company, 1903). See *New York Times*, October 10 and June 12, 1865.

122   *On the cholera epidemic*: Plunz, *History of Housing in New York City*, 14–20; DeForest and Vieller, *The Tenement House Problem*. There was a major epidemic in 1849, and another in 1854.

122   *Descriptions of the Bowery*: E. Porter Belden, *New-York, Past, Present and Future* (New York: Prall, Lewis & Co., 1850) (from whom we

learn that most New York streets in the mid-1800s were paved with "common round paving stone," or "Belgian blocks," so-called because they were brought over in ships as ballast); "Bowery, Saturday Night," *Harper's*, 1871, 301: "small, narrow-fronted shops, none of them deep, were squeezed in uncomfortably."

123   *On* Kleindeutschland: Kerri Culhane, "The Bowery Historic District," National Registry of Historic Places Nomination Form, 201, passim.

124   *On concert saloons:* Brooks McNamara, *The New York Concert Saloon* (New York: Cambridge University Press, 2002); Odell, *Records of the New York Stage*, 7, 352–438. *The grand jury's report on concert saloons:* New York Times, December 21, 1861; James McCabe, *Lights and Shadows of New York Life* (Pennsylvania: National Publishing Company, 1872); Harlow, *Old Bowery Days*, 373; see also *New York Daily News*, November 1, 1864; Michael Hale Smith, *Sunshine and Shadows of New York* (Hartford, CT: J. B. Burr, 1868), 37. *Police census:* cited in Harlow, *Old Bowery Days*.

126   *"the 'Great Draft Riots'"*: Wallace, *Gotham*; newspaper accounts. *"some 5,000 troops"*: David Quigley, *Second Founding* (New York: Hill and Wang, 2004), 3; *"The thugs hung Franklin's body up again and mutilated it"*: The Draft Riots in New York, report by the Metropolitan Police, 1863; *"Among the buildings the rioters destroyed was an army recruitment office on Grand Street, just off the Bowery"*: Wallace, *Gotham*.

127   *On Lincoln's funeral cortege: Tribune*, April 26, 1865.

128   *On the term "bum":* John D. Farmer, *Slang and its Analogues, Past and Present*, vol. 1 (London: 1890).

128   *On Tony Pastor:* I am indebted to performer Bree Benton, who shared her research on Bowery music with me; Tony Pastor Collection, New York Public Library; Emerson, *Doo-dah!*; New York Times, August 14, 1908.

131   *On the disappearance of the Bowery b'hoy:* Charles Haswell, *Reminiscences of an Octogenarian of the City of New York (1816–1860)* (New York: Harper, 1890), 354–55. Haswell said that 1840 represented the apex of "this peculiar native product."

131 *"After textiles, prostitution was the city's second largest industry"*: Dale Cochran, lecture on concert saloons, Columbia University, May 2, 2014.

CHAPTER EIGHT: **THE DEVIL'S WORK**

133 *On Immigrants: "in the 1870s, New York's population reached, and then topped, 1 million"*: Tribune, May 4, 1919. *On the first Chinese immigrants*: Scott Seligman, *The Tong Wars* (New York: Viking, 2016); *Times*, March 20, 1870, and May 25, 1896. *On Opium dens*: *Times*, May 25, 1896. *On the displacement of the Germans*: *Real Estate Record and Builders Guide (RERABG)*, March 9, 1912, 1.

135 *On tenements*: Richard Plunz, *A History of Housing in New York City* (New York: Columbia University Press, 1990).

136 *On the Bowery and electric light*: RERABG, October 16, 1886 and December 31, 1910.

137 *On Mike Lyons'*: Ephemeral New York, blog, "New Years Day dinner on the Bowery," December 27, 2009; *Times*, 1907. Lyons', at 259–261 Bowery, opened in 1872 and closed in 1907.

138 *On P.T. Barnum's American Museum*: *Times*, July 14, 1865. Barnum's burned down twice: First in 1865, in a spectacular fire. Barnum then rebuilt it at a different location—567 Broadway—where it again burned in 1868. After which, Barnum, rather than rebuilding, decided to take it on the road.

139 *On freaks*: *Times*, October 23, 1881; *The Sun*, March 22, 1888. *On Charles Eisenmann and Francis Frank Wendt*: Robert Bogdan, "Freak Show Images from the Ron Becker Collection," *Syracuse University, Library Associates Courier* 22, no. 1 (Spring 1987). The Ron Becker Collection is an archive devoted to the Eisenmann images. Information about hundreds of these cards still exist; you can find them on e-Bay.

140 *On anatomical museums*: Michael Sappol, *A Traffic of Dead Bodies* (Princeton, NJ: Princeton University Press, 2002); Andrea Stulman Dennet, *Weird and Wonderful: The Dime Museum in America* (New York: New York University Press, 1997); newspaper articles. Ana-

tomical museums had respectable origins, when anatomy became a basic subject in the curricula of America's first medical schools in the 1830s and 1840s. Interest in the subject surged after the Civil War—during which doctors learned to perform surgery literally in the field—so much so that some medical schools organized their jars of specimens in museums that they opened to the public. Soon this idea caught on with some entrepreneurs (amid the booming capitalism of mid-nineteenth-century America, no idea for making money seemed too outlandish), who opened their own anatomical museums. But these establishments proved not to be profitable. So their owners lowered the bar to attract a wider audience, and anatomical museums devolved into a form of queasy entertainment for the masses that found a welcome home along the Bowery.

141 *On Owney Geoghegan: Cincinnati Enquirer,* October 23, 1881; *Pittsburgh Post,* April 10, 1904; also the *Police Gazette* and other newspapers.

142 *On John McGurk and Suicide Hall: Baltimore Sun,* March 8, 1899; D. T. Valentine, *Manual of the Common Council of the City of New York* (New York: John F. Trow, 1916–1917); *World,* March 9, 1899.

143 *On Gay Resorts:* George Chauncey, *Gay New York* (New York: Basic Books, 1994) (*Gay New York* is the definitive book on this subject); "The Slide and the Excise: NYC's Most Notorious 19th Century Gay Bars," The Bowery Boys, blog, June 23, 2015 (this article originally appeared in the 2015 NYC Pride Guide); Cornelius Willemse, *Behind the Green Lights* (Garden City Publishing Co., 1931).

144 *"'As I walked the Bowery on the first spree'":* Ralph Werther, *The Female Impersonators* (New York: Alfred W. Herzog, 1922), p. 205ff.

145 *"'There are plenty of them and they are good customers of ours'":* from the memoir of Charles Nesbitt, a medical student from North Carolina who visited the Bowery's gay scene in the 1890s; quoted in Chauncey, *Gay New York,* p. 384n20.

146 *On renaming the Bowery: South Third Avenue: Times,* September 21, 1892. *Cooper Avenue (after Peter Cooper): RERABG,* May 14, 1898. *Central Broadway: RERABG,* March 18, 1916.

147 *On Chuck Connors*: Hutchins Hapsgood, *Types from City Streets* (New York: Funk & Wagnalls, 1910); Chuck Connors, *Bowery Life* (New York: Richard K. Fox Publishing Company, 1904); Owen Kildare, *My Mamie Rose* (New York: The Baker & Taylor Company, 1903); newspaper articles. *Description of the fake opium den*: *The Sun*, May 24, 1903.

148 *On Steve Brodie*: David McCullum, *The Great Bridge* (New York: Simon & Schuster, 1983); newspaper accounts.

150 *On Anthony Comstock*: New York Society for the Suppression of Vice Papers, Library of Congress; newspaper accounts; Anna Bates, *Weeder in the Garden of the Lord: Anthony Comstock's Life and Career* (Washington, DC: UPA, 1995); H. L. Mencken, "Puritanism: A Literary Force," *A Book of Prefaces* (New York: Alfred A. Knoff, 1917); Kat Long, *The Forbidden Apple* (Brooklyn: Ig Publishing, 2009); Timothy J. Guilfoyle, *City of Eros* (New York: Norton, 1992).

156 *On Reverend Parkhurst*: newspapers; Guilfoyle, *City of Eros*; Charles W. Gardner, *The Doctor and the Devil: The Midnight Adventures of Doctor Parkhurst* (New York: Gardner and Co., 1894); Richard Zacks, *Island of Vice* (New York: Anchor, 2012); Warren Sloat, *The Battle for the Soul of New York: Tammany Hall, Police Corruption, Vice, and Reverend Charles Parkhurst's Crusade Against Them, 1892–1895* (New York: Cooper Square Press, 2002); Reverend Charles Parkhurst, *Our Fight with Tammany* (New York: Scribner's, 1895). *"He once remarked"*: Sloat, *Battle for the Soul of New York*, 109. *Parkhurst's sermon*: Parkhurst, *Our Fight with Tammany*; *World*, February 23, 1892. *On his "research trip"*: Parkhurst, *Our Fight with Tammany*, 55; Zacks, *Island of Vice*; Gardner, *The Doctor and the Devil*.

158 *"In 1898, the police compiled"*: Alvin Harlow, *Old Bowery Days: The Chronicles of a Famous Street* (New York: D. Appleton, 1931), 454.

CHAPTER NINE: THE JEWS

159 *On the Jewish population in the Lower East Side*: *Real Estate Record and Builders' Guide*, December 15, 1900. For a brutally frank depiction of

Jewish life on the Lower East Side, see Michael Gold, *Jews Without Money* (New York: PublicAffairs, 2009), an autobiographical novel by the radical writer Michael Gold. It was originally published in 1930.

161   *On Yiddish theater and individual actors*: Nahma Sandrow, *Vagabond Stars* (Syracuse, NY: Syracuse University Press, 1996); Joel Berkowitz, *Shakespeare on the American Yiddish Stage* (Iowa: University of Iowa Press, 2002). *On Jacob and Celia Adler*: Lulla Rosenfeld, *Bright Star of Exile: Jacob Adler and the Yiddish Theatre* (New York: Thomas Crowell, 1974); Jacob Adler, *A Life on the Stage*, trans. Lulla Rosenfeld (New York: Applause, 2001); Interview with Celia Adler, Nahma Sandrow, 1974, in Dorot Division, New York Public Library. The anecdote about the woman dying in Thomashefsky's arms is also from the Adler interview. *On the Tomachefskys*: YIVO, Yiddish Theater Collection, box 14, folder 1; The Thomachefsky project, Thomachefsky .org (a foundation started by the conductor Michael Tilson-Thomas, grandson of Bessie and Boris). *On Jacob Gordin*: Beth Kaplan, *Finding the Jewish Shakespeare: The Life and Legacy of Jacob Gordin* (Syracuse, NY: Syracuse University Press, 2012). *Description of café*: Gold, *Jews Without Money*.

166   *"He roams the streets, crying: 'Alms for the Yiddish King Lear!'* ('Shenkt a neduve der Yid-dish-er Kenig Leeeee-ar!')"*: Original Yiddish quoted in Rosenfeld, *Bright Star of Exile*. The Yiddish King Lear eschews the tragic ending of Shakespeare's play, in which Lear, along with his third and only loyal daughter, dies. Instead, Reb Dovid is saved by his saintly third daughter, who is not only a *gute neshuma*, but also a doctor, who is able to restore his vision. In America, anything was possible.

169   *Description of the Allen Street brothels*: Committee of Fifteen Archives, New York Public Library, reels 4 and 5.

170   *On Yiddish concert saloons*: Nina Warnke, "Immigrant Popular Culture as Contested Sphere: Yiddish Music Halls, the Yiddish Press, and the Processes of Americanization, 1900–1910," *Theatre Journal* 48, no. 3 (October 1996), 321–335. *Advertisement for the Eldorado*: *Teatur zhurnal* (YIVO).

CHAPTER TEN: **THE KING OF THE BOWERY**

173 *"One story about Sullivan concerned the time when, as a young man, he came across a young punk beating up a woman near the Tombs. Sullivan yelled at the guy to stop, upon which the latter turned his fists on Sullivan, who then beat the guy until he was bleeding and unconscious"*: "Big Tim Sullivan, the Rain Maker," *Current Literature* 47 (December 1909).

174 *"Another moniker was Dry Dollar"*: Gustavus Myers, *History of Tammany Hall* (1901), 344.

175 *"Tim Sullivan's speech, delivered in coarse Bowery vernacular, made the assembly members—even the Republicans—cry"* and the material about Byrnes, including the quote: George Kibbe Turner, "Tammany's Control of New York," *McClure's*, June 1909.

176 *"Soon the newspapers were calling Tim Sullivan the most influential Democrat in the assembly"*: *Brooklyn Eagle*, March 25, 1891.

177 *"'but I'll find the guy who did it if it's the last thing I do'"*: *The Sun*, September 14, 1913.

178 *"For their services, each bum received $1, three meals, and a pint of whiskey"*: *Carolina Israelite*, October 1, 1956.

179 *"'Help your neighbor, but keep your nose out of his affairs,' he once said"*: Daniel Czitrom, "Underworlds and Underdogs: Big Tim Sullivan and Metropolitan Politics in New York, 1889–1913," *Journal of American History* 78 (September 1991), 536–58.

180 *On Sullivan's chowders: "Shelling out money for chowder tickets was considered a campaign contribution, although some people said that this was just one more way that Sullivan collected graft"*: Alvin Harlow, *Old Bowery Days: The Chronicles of a Famous Street* (New York: D. Appleton, 1931); *World*, June 9, 1894.

181 *On Max Hochstim*: US Census, 1900; *World*, August 12, 1897; *Philadelphia Times*, October 4, 1894; *New York Times*, November 2, 1900, and September 9, 1894; Frank Moss, *The American Metropolis* (New York: P. F. Collier, 1897); Mario Maffi, *Gateway to the Promised Land: Ethnicity and Culture in New York's Lower East Side* (New York: New York Univer-

sity Press, 1995); Richard Zacks, *Island of Vice* (New York: Anchor, 2012); Timothy Guilfoyle, *City of Eros* (New York: Norton, 1992); Timoth Guilfoyle, *A Pickpocket's Tale: The Underworld of Nineteenth-Century New York* (New York: Norton, 2007). *On his conviction: Brooklyn Eagle*, December 6, 1901. *On his death: Tribune*, November 22, 1910; The character "Harry the Pimp" in Michael Gold, *Jews Without Money* (New York: PublicAffairs, 2009; reprint of 1930 edition) is based on Hochstim.

180 *"Then he'd praise the woman's cooking and remind her to spread a good word about him to the other ladies": World*, October 30, 1893.

180 *Sullivan and women's suffrage: Springfield Republican*, June 1, 1911.

184 *"Sometimes Big Tim was seen in public with prostitutes"*: Guilfoyle, *City of Eros*, 257, 405n19.

185 *On Sullivan's bill to enlarge dressing rooms: Herald*, February 15, 1896.

185 *On Sullivan's stint in Washington: New York Times*, November 1902; *Boston Globe*, June 26, 1906. *"'In the House, it was hard to get acquainted, and impossible to know all the 'boys' as I did in the Senate chambers at Albany'": Washington Evening Star*, July 4, 1906.

187 *"'Big Tim is sick, and Florrie is dead,' he told them": New York Sun*, December 24, 1909.

188 *On the Sullivan Law: New York Times*, December 4, 1910; *Brooklyn Daily Eagle*, September 17, 1911. *Quotes about George Le Brun*: George Le Brun, *It's Time to Tell* (New York: W. Morrow, 1960).

192 *"The following year, he tried to get another suffrage bill through committee, but it was killed": The Sun*, March 30, 1912.

192 *On Frances Perkins*: Frances Perkins, *Oral History Memoirs*, Columbia University Oral History Collection; George Martin, *Madam Secretary: Frances Perkins, A Biography of America's First Woman Cabinet Member* (Boston: Houghton Mifflin, 1976); *Metropolitan Magazine*, July 1912; Harriot Stanton Blatch, *Challenging Years: The Memoirs of Harriot Stanton Blatch* (New York: Putnam, 1940); Czitrom, "Underworlds and Underdogs."

194 *On Tim Sullivan's decline and death: New York Times*, September 15, 1913; *Brooklyn Eagle*, January 19 and September 29, 1913; *Olean Times*,

September 15, 1913. *"he broke down and sobbed"*: The Tribune, January 23, 1913. *"He was, they said, too good a Catholic to kill himself"*: The Sun, September 14, 1914.

199   On the Bowery's appearance and property values in the early twentieth century: *Century Magazine*, December 1891; *Real Estate Record and Builder's guide*, passim. The *croix de guerre* in the Bowery pawnshop in *Pawtucket Times*, July 16, 1919.

CHAPTER ELEVEN: THE BUMS ON THE BOWERY

201   *On saloons: Tribune,* February 23, 1895; Oliver Odd McIntyre, New York Day by Day, syndicated column, October 19, 1921, and July 14, 1925; Nels Anderson, "The Bowery Project," 1967, Bureau of Applied Social Research, Columbia University, Rare Book Division.

201   *Prohibition along the Bowery*: Daniel Okrent, *Last Call* (New York: Scribner, 2010), 333ff.; *Charleston Daily Mail*, December 11, 1932; *New Yorker*, August 31, 1929; Seen and Heard in New York, syndicated column, February 14, 1931; "The Bowery Passed out with Booze," *St. Louis Post Dispatch*, August 20, 1922.

204   *"wrote Al Hirschfeld"*: Al Hirschfeld, *The Speakeasies of 1932* (Milwaukee: Glen Young Books, 2003).

205   *On hobos: Herald,* April 3, 1924. *"it was the only main thoroughfare in New York with no churches"*: Times, December 5, 1920.

205   *On missions: Catholic Missions* (Society for the Propagation of the Faith, 1907); *Times*, December 5, 1920, lists all the missions along the Bowery; *Times*, April 3, 1910.

207   *On the Salvation Army: Louisville Courier-Journal,* July 29, 1906; "Arrival of the Pioneer Band in This Country," *Times*, March 11, 1880; "Salvation Lass Won't Quit at 80," *Times*, August 5, 1923; "When the Salvation Army Discovered America," *Tribune*, April 27 and May 4, 1919; Michael Hale Smith, *Sunshine and Shadows of New York* (Hartford, CT: J. B. Burr, 1868).

208   *On the Bowery Mission: Atlanta Constitution,* March 25, 1900; *Chicago Tribune*, July 16, 1904.

209 *On the All Night Mission and Dudley Upjohn*: *Times*, 1948 (obituary); *Evening Mail*, January 18, 1912; *Temperance Magazine*, 1911; other newspapers; Richard Upjohn and Richard Mitchell Upjohn Papers, New York Public Library, box 13, file 15.

211 *On Johnny Callahan and the Hadley Rescue Hall*: *Baltimore Sun*, December 21, 1925.

212 *On Mr. Zero (Urbain Ledoux)*: *Times*, April 10, 1941 (obituary); "Urbain Ledoux—Prophet," *New Republic*, October 5, 1921; *New York Tribune*, May 14, 1919; *Brooklyn Eagle*, April 10, 1919; "Snow Man," *New Yorker*, February 5, 1927; Urbain Ledoux, *Mr. Zero?* (1931, a self-published memoir-manifesto).

214 *On Mazie Phillips*: *Times*, June 11, 1964 (obituary). I am indebted to Victor Papa, who shared his memories of Mazie Phillips with me.

215 *On Sammy's Bowery Follies*: *Times*, February 12, 1935. *"a federal operation targeted hundreds of places in New York for evasion of the liquor tax"*: *Life Magazine*, 1944; other newspaper articles; Weegee, *Naked City* (Cambridge: Da Capo Press, 1975). Charlie Katz, the grandson of Sammy Fuchs, kindly shared his memories with me.

219 *On Lionel Rogosin*: Meyer Berger, *Times*, April 16, 1956; "He shot from last July into October, before el-wreckers climbed the trestles," Ontheboweryfilm.com; Interview with Michael Rogosin, *All Things Considered*, NPR, February 24, 2011; Michael Rogosin, dir., *The Perfect Team* (2009).

222 *On the dismantling of the El*: Meyer Berger, "Bowery Blinks in the Sunlight," *Times*, 1956. By the 1930s, elevated trains, long considered a menace to the quality of life in New York, were on the way out.

223 *On the Bowery during the 1960s*: *"Officials made vague suggestions about opening a facility on Ellis Island, or shipping the bums to Camp LaGuardia, a former women's prison in Upstate New York"*: *Times*, February 2, 1960; "Bowery and Its Derelicts Complicate Renewal," *Times*, November 20, 1961. In 1961—an election year—Mayor Robert Wagner, as part of his promise to clean up the Bowery, set up "Operation Bowery," with Hortense Gabler as director. "We will chip away at the problem," he told the *Times*. On *"Operation Bowery"*: "Poverty-

Bowery," 1962, La Guardia and Wagner Archives, LaGuardia Community College, box 060302, file 14.

223 *On the Bowery in the 1970s*: Ella Howard, *Homeless: Poverty and Place in Urban America* (Philadelphia: University of Pennsylvania Press, 2013); Marci Reaven, *Citizen Participation in City Planning* (dissertation, New York University, 2009); newspaper articles.

224 *"stunk of dirty old men, vomit and urine. I had to fumigate it'"*: Hilly Kristal, quoted in Mark Blake, ed., *Punk: The Whole Story* (London: DK Publishing, 2006), 110.

CHAPTER TWELVE: PUNK

225 *On CBGB's*: newspaper articles (*Village Voice, New York Times*); conversations with photographer David Godlis ("Godlis"); David Godlis, *History Is Made at Night* (New York: MATTE Editions, 2016); conversation with Howard Scher; Brian Waterman, *Marquee Moon* (New York: Bloomsbury, 2011); Roman Kozak, *This Ain't No Disco* (Boston: Faber and Faber, 1988); Legs McNeil and Gillian McCain, *Please Kill Me: The Uncensored Oral History of Punk* (New York: Grove Press, 1996); "History by Hilly," CBGB.com; Patti Smith, *Just Kids* (New York: HarperCollins, 2010); "Patti Smith," Wikipedia; John Holmstrom (founder of *Punk* magazine) interview, *Politico*, December 19, 2012; John Holmstrom, ed., *Punk: The Best of Punk Magazine* (New York: Dey Street, 2012); Celine Danhier, dir., *Blank City*, (2011). Christopher D. Salyers, introduction by Richard Hell, *CBGB: Decades of Graffiti* (New York: Mark Batty, 2006); Mark Blake, ed., introduction by Debbie Harry, *Punk: The Whole Story* (London: DK Publishing, 2006).

227 *On the New York Dolls*: Blake, *Punk*, 79; *Village Voice*, October 4, 1973. The Dolls' first album came out in the summer of 1973, when the Mercer collapsed. About them one rock critic said, "The New York Dolls are trash, they play rock 'n' roll like sluts, and they've just released a record that can stand beside Iggy & The Stooges' stupendous *Raw Power* as the only album so far to fully define just

exactly where the 1970s rock should be coming from" (Nick Kent, quoted in Blake, *Punk*, 81). The Dolls' second—and final—album came out in the spring of 1974, a mere nine months later, which they called, presciently, *Too Much Too Soon*. Soon after, the group dissolved in a paroxysm of drugs, alcohol, and rancor.

229　*On Patti Smith*: *New Yorker*, March 11, 2002; "Patti Smith and Lenny Kaye Celebrate the 40th Anniversary of Their First Poetry Project Reading," February 15, 2011, Poetryproject.org.; Lara Elmayan, "Tracing the Patti Smith Trail in NYC from Tomkins Square Park to CBGB," Untapped Cities, blog, May 23, 2016. Kozak, *This Ain't No Disco*; Victor Bokris and Roberta Bayley, *Patti Smith: An Unauthorized Biography* (New York: Simon & Schuster, 1999); Smith, *Just Kids*; Steven Sebring, dir., *Patti Smith: Dream of Life* (Celluloid Dreams, 2008). "'It was the greatest atmosphere to perform in. It was conspiratorial. It was physical, and that's what rock 'n' roll's all about—sexual tension and being drunk and disorderly'": Blake, *Punk*, 111.

230　*On the East Village in the 1970s*: Dahnier, dir., *Blank City*.

231　*"FORD TO CITY: DROP DEAD"*: *Daily News*, October 30, 1975.

231　*On Debbie Harry and Blondie*: Rick Moody, *Interview*, March 17, 2014; Transcript of Harry and Stein interview, 2013; Red Bull Music Academy, New York, Interview with Debbie Harry on *The Blondie Channel*, YouTube.

233　*On the beginnings of "punk"*: conversations with David Godlis; Godlis, *History Is Made at Night*; Kozak, *This Ain't No Disco*.

237　*On the beginnings of gentrification along the Bowery*: *New York Times*, December 25, 1993; "New Generation on Restaurant Suppliers Row," *New York Times*, May 7, 1995.

EPILOGUE: **BONES AND GHOSTS**

243　*St. Philips Cemetery*: Nancy Dickenson and Faline Schneiderman-Fox, "St. Philip's Episcopal Cemetery," *Second Avenue Subway Report*, Historical Perspectives Inc. (June 2003); Phase 1B/2 Archaelogical Investigations, Block 456, Lot 1 (Bowery and East First Street), Patrick J. Heaton for John Milner Associates, 2005.

INDEX

Index

Index

Index

Index

**EMPIRE
STATE
EDITIONS**

SELECT TITLES FROM EMPIRE STATE EDITIONS

William Seraile, *Angels of Mercy: White Women and the History of New York's Colored Orphan Asylum*

Andrew J. Sparberg, *From a Nickel to a Token: The Journey from Board of Transportation to MTA*

Daniel Campo, *The Accidental Playground: Brooklyn Waterfront Narratives of the Undesigned and Unplanned*

John Waldman, *Heartbeats in the Muck: The History, Sea Life, and Environment of New York Harbor, Revised Edition*

John Waldman (ed.), *Still the Same Hawk: Reflections on Nature and New York*

Gerard R. Wolfe, *The Synagogues of New York's Lower East Side: A Retrospective and Contemporary View, Second Edition*. Photographs by Jo Renée Fine and Norman Borden, Foreword by Joseph Berger

Joseph B. Raskin, *The Routes Not Taken: A Trip Through New York City's Unbuilt Subway System*

Phillip Deery, *Red Apple: Communism and McCarthyism in Cold War New York*

Stephen Miller, *Walking New York: Reflections of American Writers from Walt Whitman to Teju Cole*

Tom Glynn, *Reading Publics: New York City's Public Libraries, 1754–1911*

R. Scott Hanson, *City of Gods: Religious Freedom, Immigration, and Pluralism in Flushing, Queens*. Foreword by Martin E. Marty

Mark Naison and Bob Gumbs, *Before the Fires: An Oral History of African American Life in the Bronx from the 1930s to the 1960s*

Robert Weldon Whalen, *Murder, Inc., and the Moral Life: Gangsters and Gangbusters in La Guardia's New York*

Sharon Egretta Sutton, *When Ivory Towers Were Black: A Story about Race in America's Cities and Universities*

Britt Haas, *Fighting Authoritarianism: American Youth Activism in the 1930s*

David J. Goodwin, *Left Bank of the Hudson: Jersey City and the Artists of 111 1st Street*. Foreword by DW Gibson

Nandini Bagchee, *Counter Institution: Activist Estates of the Lower East Side*

Susan Celia Greenfield (ed.), *Sacred Shelter: Thirteen Journeys of Homelessness and Healing*

Elizabeth Macaulay-Lewis and Matthew M. McGowan (eds.), *Classical New York: Discovering Greece and Rome in Gotham*

Susan Opotow and Zachary Baron Shemtob (eds.), *New York after 9/11*

Andrew Feffer, *Bad Faith: Teachers, Liberalism, and the Origins of McCarthyism*

Colin Davey with Thomas A. Lesser, *The American Museum of Natural History and How It Got That Way*. Forewords by Neil deGrasse Tyson and Kermit Roosevelt III

Mike Jaccarino, *America's Last Great Newspaper War: The Death of Print in a Two-Tabloid Town*

Angel Garcia, *The Kingdom Began in Puerto Rico: Neil Connolly's Priesthood in the South Bronx*

Jim Mackin, *Notable New Yorkers of Manhattan's Upper West Side: Bloomingdale–Morningside Heights*

Matthew Spady, *The Neighborhood Manhattan Forgot: Audubon Park and the Families Who Shaped It*

Marilyn S. Greenwald and Yun Li, *Eunice Hunton Carter: A Lifelong Fight for Social Justice*

Elizabeth Macaulay-Lewis, *Antiquity in Gotham: The Ancient Architecture of New York City*

Jean Arrington with Cynthia S. LaValle, *From Factories to Palaces: Architect Charles B. J. Snyder and the New York City Public Schools*. Foreword by Peg Breen

Boukary Sawadogo, *Africans in Harlem: An Untold New York Story*

Alvin Eng, *Our Laundry, Our Town: My Chinese American Life from Flushing to the Downtown Stage and Beyond*

Stephanie Azzarone, *Heaven on the Hudson: Mansions, Monuments, and Marvels of Riverside Park*

Peter Quinn, *Cross Bronx: A Writing Life*

Mark Bulik, *Ambush at Central Park: When the IRA Came to New York*

Matt Dallos, *In the Adirondacks: Dispatches from the Largest Park in the Lower 48*

Brandon Dean Lamson, *Caged: A Teacher's Journey Through Rikers, or How I Beheaded the Minotaur*

Raj Tawney, *Colorful Palate: Savored Stories from a Mixed Life*

Edward Cahill, *Disorderly Men*

Joseph Heathcott, *Global Queens: An Urban Mosaic*

Francis R. Kowsky with Lucille Gordon, *Hell on Color, Sweet on Song: Jacob Wrey Mould and the Artful Beauty of Central Park*

Jill Jonnes, *South Bronx Rising: The Rise, Fall, and Resurrection of an American City, Third Edition*

Barbara G. Mensch, *A Falling-Off Place: The Transformation of Lower Manhattan*

David J. Goodwin, *Midnight Rambles: H. P. Lovecraft in Gotham*

Felipe Luciano, *Flesh and Spirit: Confessions of a Young Lord*

Maximo G. Martinez, *Sojourners in the Capital of the World: Garifuna Immigrants*

Jennifer Baum, *Just City: Growing Up on the Upper West Side When Housing Was a Human Right*

Davida Siwisa James, *Hamilton Heights and Sugar Hill: Alexander Hamilton's Old Harlem Neighborhood Through the Centuries*

Annik LaFarge, *On the High Line: The Definitive Guide, Third Edition*. Foreword by Rick Dark

Marie Carter, *Mortimer and the Witches: A History of Nineteenth-Century Fortune Tellers*

Carey Kasten and Brenna Moore, *Mutuality in El Barrio: Stories of the Little Sisters of the Assumption Family Health Service*. Foreword by Norma Benítez Sánchez

Kimberly A. Orcutt, *The American Art-Union: Utopia and Skepticism in the Antebellum Era*

For a complete list, visit www.fordhampress.com/empire-state-editions.